SECOND EDITION

TEACHING PSYCHOLOGY

A GUIDE FOR THE NEW INSTRUCTOR

FRED W. WHITFORD

Montana State University

PRENTICE HALL, *Upper Saddle River, New Jersey 07458*

© 1996 by PRENTICE-HALL, INC.
Simon & Schuster / A Viacom Company
Upper Saddle River, New Jersey 07458

10 9 8 7 6 5 4 3 2 1

ISBN 0-13-443193-6
Printed in the United States of America

To my parents, Fred and Hazel

Contents

Appendices

Preface

In its first edition, this book was originally conceived as a guide that would allow the new instructor in introductory courses to manage the myriad complex tasks required to teach an effective course. Additionally, the book was not intended to be a heavily referenced work, but rather to contain extensive appendices on teaching and research. I have used my own teaching experiences for the last sixteen years to help illustrate some of the types of problems that you, as a new instructor, can expect to face. I have attempted to write a lighthearted book that will be fun to read and help you through your journey into academia. I, on occasion, stereotyped students, faculty and staff; this was, of course, done with the intent of giving you, the instructor, an idea of what to expect in your new environment. I did not intend to be overly critical of these individuals, but rather, honest about the interactions I have had in the many departments that I have been associated with during my career. Knowing what to expect in a new environment can be an indispensable tool.

The second edition has been revised and updated throughout. I have made substantial changes to the appendices in this second edition. A major change was to eliminate specific journal articles. These can be seen instead in the original journals as elaborated in Appendix D.

Teaching a course in psychology can and probably will be one of the most frustrating and rewarding tasks that you will be asked to perform in your academic career. I hope this book will help you through the rough spots and give you a preview of what to expect in this maze called academia.

Acknowledgments

During the preparation of this book, I have had the pleasure of working with several individuals. Of these people, the ones who stand out the most are Dr. Wesley Lynch, Chair, Psychology Department, Montana State University, for his unceasing support; Peter Janzow, Psychology Editor, Prentice Hall Publishers for his encouragement in all phases of this book; Sandy Romero, head secretary in the Psychology Department at Montana State University, for her proofing of this book; Shelley Ellis for her final proofing of this book; without their help, this project could not have been completed; and finally, Pat, Jessica, Sara, Ruby, and Buck for their support during the preparation of this book.

Fred Whitford
e-mail: upyfw@gemini.oscs.montana.edu
http://www.montana.edu:80/wwwpy/fwpage.html

1

Introduction

Finally I made it! I cannot believe that I was hired to teach Introductory Psychology; this is the best day of my life.

Every New Instructor

After the initial euphoria dissipates, then what? How do you attempt to teach an introductory course at your school? What are the techniques that you should and should not use? How do instructors ever find enough time to prepare lectures? Will I be good enough to be a college instructor? Will my students respect and like me? These and other thoughts go through every new instructor's mind.

This book is intended for the new instructor or the teaching assistant who has little or no experience teaching. I will share some of the time-worn secrets of how you can become a very good instructor. Throughout this book, I will use the experiences that I have gained in my sixteen years of teaching, as well as the many years of teaching experience of my colleagues in the Psychology department. I will help you develop a general plan that you can use to start the formidable task of becoming the best instructor in your department and maybe even your school.

This book is intended to be a starting place with suggestions on how to proceed. My suggestions are just that--suggestions; I would not presume to have the best teaching style but offer these suggestions as a point of beginning for your teaching career. One of the most important aspects of becoming a great instructor is to develop your own personal style; this component of your overall presentation is extremely important and will be discussed later.

The Goal

The goal of this book is to make your journey from new instructor to the best in your department a little easier. Many times when you are new to your department, finding someone willing to help answer the simplest questions will be difficult. I hope to offer answers to many of these questions. Teaching this class can, for many of you, be the best experience you will have in your teaching career; getting a good start can be very important. A few tricks and some of my experiences will surely help you through your first psychology course.

The Task

Teaching introductory psychology is both a rewarding and tiresome assignment. Knowing that you are the first instructor to teach these new students in your department, several of whom may become renowned individuals, is exciting. The new eager freshman, wanting to understand everything about psychology, is refreshing. I look forward to the fall semester and the chance to see these excited new students. Additionally, I teach an evening class at least once a year in order to be exposed to the non-traditional age student who can only take an evening course. These non-traditional students bring a perspective from the *real* world that is often lost in the academic environment. The chance to really make a difference in the way students view the discipline is always exciting. On the other hand, the sheer volume of students in these large introductory level courses can be a tremendous drain of your energy. Depending on your school, your class size may range from 25 to 350 students. You may or may not have additional support from teaching assistants, graduate/undergraduate students or other faculty to deal with the mass of students. As compensation for these large classes, some schools grant release time from other teaching, committee or service responsibilities.

I often spend a great deal of my time handling the mechanics of the registration for the course: determining times and rooms, assigning assistants duties, writing examinations, writing make-up examinations, grading examinations, making exceptions for due dates for papers and examinations for special students (handicapped, learning disabled and athletic students), signing add/drop slips and just attempting to survive the mass of paper work associated with these large sections. Typically, just when you think the extra workload of a class of 250 students is too much, a student will say you are the best teacher he has had in college (but what does he know--this is his first class). This type of interaction with students and encouragement from your peers can help you bear up under the relentless pressure to develop your teaching, conduct your research, and conduct the best course possible.

Arriving on Campus

Becoming Familiar with the Campus

When you first arrive on campus, what should you do to prepare for your teaching assignment? First, I would recommend becoming familiar with the campus. Even before you report to your department, spend a day walking around campus and through all the buildings. After sixteen years I still have not seen all the interiors of the buildings on my campus. I would suggest finding a location where you can have some solitude away from the department and students. This could be in the faculty reading room in the library, the empty football practice stadium or simply an empty bench in an isolated area of campus. Acquaint yourself with the campus layout and define solutions to simple tasks such as finding a parking place (does your school have a faculty parking lot?) or having lunch (which are the best restaurants, or does your school have a faculty club?). Assuming you are arriving during a break in classes, this task can be much easier now than when the students are on campus. An additional consideration is what types of services might you want to take advantage of? Your campus may offer advantages to the faculty, which can include (often at a cost) faculty parking lots, athletic facilities, faculty clubs, special seating at sporting events, or a great museum or library. Find out what is at your school and what you think you will have time to enjoy.

Arrival at the Department

Mid-morning is the best time to arrive at your department and Monday is *not* the best day. You may have been interviewed on campus for your position so the department could be familiar to you. But if you were not interviewed and this is your first day on campus, arrive early in order to find parking and your department's building. Ask to see the chairman in an informal department or call ahead in a formal department for an appointment. Upon your arrival, you will probably have been assigned an office and will have to obtain keys for the building and your office (the campus police often perform this function.) Now that you have arrived in your office, sit and enjoy the quiet of your new surroundings and read the rest of this book.

"The" Book

If there is not a copy of the faculty handbook waiting for you in your office when you arrive, ask that a copy be sent to you as soon as possible. This is "the" book; it contains everything that you will need to know to survive in your new position, i.e., everything from tenure and promotion to how to deal with student grievances. Read "the" book after you finish this one. If you have any questions on the materials in the faculty handbook, ask for clarification from your department chair.

Meeting the Faculty

Walk around the building and see who is in their offices or laboratories. A rule of thumb is that if your arrival occurs during mid-summer, the most productive members will be working and the rest will be on vacation. Introduce yourself to each faculty or staff member that you encounter, most of whom will be interested to meet the newest faculty member. During these interactions remember that first impressions are lasting impressions. Turn to Chapter 9 to see if any of the faculty or staff fit the stereotypes described in the chapter.

Getting a Feel

Hang out for the rest of the day in the department and explore your new environment. Find out how things work. Where is the bathroom? How do you dial off campus? Where is the water fountain? How about the exits? What is your view like? Determine whether the sun shines into your office in the morning or afternoon, which will determine where you will put your computer. These types of questions can be answered by simply spending time in the department. This is your new place of employment and you will spend a large number of your days in this environment. Do you like it? If not, what do you control that you can change for the better? These suggestions will not only acquaint you with your new environment but will also allow you some time to relax.

The Rest of Your Life

Become acquainted with the community. This is an ongoing process and can take years, but the following are suggestions about how to begin: Where is a good place to grocery shop? Where will you buy a beverage of your choice after a hard day at work? Where will you do your laundry? What are the recreational opportunities in the community? Some questions are more obvious than others; however, depending on your personal preferences, most college communities can satisfy most of these needs. Where will you live? What neighborhood is best for your needs? I would ask two sources. The first is obvious, as faculty and staff will be very helpful in describing different options and could know of some vacancies available. The second suggestion is to ask students; there may only be graduate students available when you arrive but these individuals will many times know the best *deals*, especially in the housing market. Where do faculty go to relax? This depends on the faculty members. Many will go straight home after work to a family environment, while others will prefer to stop by a local establishment for happy hour. Some of your first impressions of the different faculty may be formed during these informal get-togethers during the social hour. A point to remember is that you are being evaluated just as you are evaluating other faculty members, so act appropriately. Where do students go to relax? Are you going to want to be in the same social environment as the students or would you prefer to socialize only with faculty and staff? How do you get from campus to your home? What are the safest and fastest routes? Getting to know your new environment can begin by subscribing to the local newspaper as a first step to help answer some of the questions you might have about the local environment. I would also find the latest copy of the student newspaper; this will help define the interests, attitudes, and expectations of the students at your school. Try to get a feel for the town and the campus by either walking or driving around. Take the time to see what the area has to offer. I would schedule at least a Saturday or Sunday exclusively for this activity. The campus and local community are often two distinct communities with only minimal overlap. Try to define both of the communities in terms of your needs and goals.

2

Preparing to Teach

What are the steps necessary in preparing to teach an introductory course? It is best if you have several months to prepare and have a specific plan. I suggest the following outline as the basis of a plan to prepare your course. This plan assumes a three-month window.

Three Months Prior to Class

Deciding What to Teach

I would first turn my attention to what the course objectives are to be. Is this class a broad overview of psychology covering virtually all of the sub-fields or will it be a concentrated in-depth survey of only a few of the specific sub-fields that you or your department teaches? In most academic systems, quarters or semesters, there is not enough time to cover all the material you would like to cover. Academic quarters have about 40 instructional days, and academic semesters about 45 instructional days to cover in some cases an entire text. The question now becomes one of what to delete from the overall coverage in the course. If you have no departmental restraints, you can delete the areas you believe to be least important in the overview of psychology. Check with your introductory course supervisor or department chair to see if such restrictions exist; be careful not to violate a department guideline because you decided that it was not very important. Throughout your preparation and teaching of this course, you can consult your department head or introductory course supervisor for guidance about departmental policies and procedures. A little common sense requires you to consider the biases of the other more established members of the department when considering what is important in an introductory course. This can be accomplished in several ways. The first is simply to ask them either formally or informally. A second method is to ask the students, both graduate (a great source of both real information and gossip) or undergraduates. Finally, review the other faculty members' books and publications for a hint of what the emphasis in the field is as defined by your department.

Departmental Focus

When first deciding on your teaching objectives, it is very important to examine the role of your department. Is this department an undergraduate service department teaching classes for many other disciplines, or a scientific training department with both undergraduate and graduate students, or a department requiring both teaching and research? What level of preparation do other instructors expect from your students when they enter upper division courses in your and other departments? Do other instructors expect specific tools (e.g., research methods, statistics or a specific theoretical view-point) from your students? Who are your students and what are their expectations of the course? Of course this question of students' expectations is very difficult to answer because many students, particularly undergraduates, do not know what they expect. What are the students' academic goals and how does your course meet these goals? Again this is a difficult question, but by asking advanced undergraduates and graduate students, you should be able to answer this question for your specific school. Is the department skewed toward a specific end of the academic vs. applied spectrum? If so, skew your course in that direction. These are the types of questions you must answer in order to define your course objectives. If your course objectives are poorly defined then the rest of the course preparation will be more difficult than necessary.

School Requirements

Many schools provide Introductory Psychology as a core curriculum course and, thus, will have school requirements on the content of this course. These requirements may limit your choices of how and what you teach or add requirements to your course content. At my school, Introductory Psychology is a university core class and there is a writing component requirement, which requires students to use communications skills, both oral and written. In very large classes, this can be a difficult requirement to fulfill, particularly if you have little or no additional support from teaching assistants. Check to see if there are any school restrictions prior to planning your course. Often someone in the administration will check that these requirements are actually fulfilled.

Preliminary Course Objectives

After determining the restrictions on your course, it is time to write down your preliminary course objectives. These objectives should include the maximum amount of coverage that you will try to cover in your course. This list should encompass more material than can be taught in your school term. As the course takes shape, you will have to limit coverage, but if you have a diagram of the course, it should be easier to see where to cut. The use of computer flow charting can be helpful in this stage of planning. At this point, your list is a rough reminder of the overall plan for your course. It is important to develop your set of objectives because other planning components of the course will depend on those objectives. Several other components, such as the text (how long and how difficult), ancillary readings (how many and what sources), and types of tests (essay, multiple choice, true/false or a combination), will be dependent on the course objectives.

A major consideration when detailing your objectives is to consider what level of knowledge you will expect the students to master in this course. The following are examples of six levels of mastery. These can be a starting point for determining the level and objectives of your course.

Recall

The student should be able to recognize the correct answer to a problem from a group of answers. This is the simplest level and can use multiple choice examinations in very large courses.

Comprehension

The student should be able to define a principle in his or her own words at a level that fellow students can understand. This level can be used in small group discussions and oral presentations.

Application

The student should be able to take a principle and use it in an applied situation and give several examples of applied situations. Often, this level is examined with essay type questions or short papers.

Analysis

The student will be able to identify the pattern and principles of a given topic. Additionally, the student will also be able to summarize the main points and comment on the pattern. Usually, examinations are in the form of very long essays or long term papers.

Evaluation

The student will be able to compare and contrast methods and principles and make evaluative judgments about the effectiveness of both. Examination is in the form of term papers.

Synthesis
The student will be able to take divergent principles and master the concepts of these principles and then generate original principles or concepts from these earlier principles. This level is usually only required of graduate students and requires very long papers, theses or dissertations.

For the introductory level psychology course, the first three levels of understanding are probably appropriate at most four-year universities. In addition, the next two levels may be appropriate for the honor section of introductory psychology or for very exclusive four-year universities. The last level is usually reserved for the graduate level. You are the one who must decide what level you want your students to perform. Do not be too optimistic about your students' abilities, but do not compromise your principles concerning class coverage and level either. Consult the faculty, undergraduate, and graduate students to help determine the level of the students and your class materials.

First Rough Draft: Course Objectives

Complete a first rough draft of the learning objectives for the class; allow these objectives to "sit" for a week or two. During this time, do not work on the course objectives. Many times the instructor's resource manual or student study guide will contain learning objectives emphasized in the text. These can be helpful in your selection process.

First Rough Draft: Teaching Schedule

The next phase of planning your course is to draft a teaching schedule for the course; this draft will force you to consider which objectives must be trimmed. This draft of a realistic time schedule should help reduce your learning objectives to a more realistic, teachable list. I like to use a desktop organizer/calendar that is about 16" x 22" to condense the teaching schedule materials. I like to see the overall fit of these different sections of the course and to compare different amounts of time spent on different areas. This method allows you to get a first sense of what the course will look like within the time constraints of the academic term. This large format calendar allows about 3" x 3" of working space per day. This space is very useful in getting a feel for the flow of the course and for writing detailed instructions about specific lectures or activities. Use a pencil for this preliminary round of scheduling; there will always be many changes both prior to the lecture and after the end of each lecture. An additional small pocket reminder or computer generated calendar is also useful for specific appointments and things to do for each day, but the larger format calendar is a must.

Textbooks

Now that you have a general sense of what the course is going to look like, it is time to consider the text(s) for the course. Currently there are a large number of texts to choose from in the introductory market. With the consolidations of publishers, this number has been reduced somewhat, but a reasonable number of diverse texts still exists. See Appendix E for a listing of current introductory psychology texts.

Choosing the Best Text

Ask other faculty members in your department for their input; they will all have their favorite text. Your department may have a standard text for all the sections. If this is the case, ask the introductory coordinator for the text currently being used in your department.

The Level of the Text

A very important consideration when choosing a text is matching the level of the text to that of the students. Many of the publishers' representatives that you will see in your first year of teaching will target you for a sales campaign because you do not understand the best methods for selecting the best text for your class. Following are some considerations when beginning the process of text selection: first, when will the text really be available to the class? A firm date, not a date like, by the fall term. Then when will all of the ancillary package be available? I ask for the test item file, student study guide and instructor's resource manual for each text that I am considering for adoption. Promises are easily made but often not kept.

By the time you are ready to select your text, you should have an idea of the level of your students. This level can be roughly divided into high, medium, and lower levels. (See Appendix E for levels of current texts) Ask your publishers' representative for a text appropriate for your level. On occasion, publishers' representatives will have a text that is not appropriate for your level but they will try to convince you to either adopt a text whose level is too high or too low. Resist these sales pressures. There are always several texts for each level available to choose from during each term.

Obtaining Examination Copies of Possible Texts

Now that you have achieved the status of faculty member, you can use the sample form in *Appendix A* as a guide to send to publishers to request an examination copies of texts. The departmental secretary will have a list of publishers and addresses to contact for these copies. When you send for an examination copy, your local publishers' representative will be alerted that you have been hired to teach psychology and are interested in adopting their text.

Meeting the Publisher's Representative

You can expect to meet regional publisher's representatives from the major publishing houses. This usually occurs in the first weeks of a new term. The publishers' representatives will be more than happy to assist you in selecting a text, particularly one from their company. These publishers' representatives typically work on a combination of salary/commission, and the adoption of an Introductory Psychology text is lucrative due to the typically large enrollment. Once you have met with your first publisher's representative, expect several others from different publishers. Your first several representatives will be interesting to talk to, but after the tenth in a one-week period you will probably tire of the constant "sell," which will vary from almost no pressure to a very hard sell. Depending on your personal response to sales pressure, time spent with these individuals may range from interesting and enlightening to boring and noxious. Realize that these representatives work very hard and are on the road away from family and friends much of the academic year. Be courteous, take a serious interest in their books, and take the time to remember their names, faces, and publishers. Many representatives will help with this memory process because they will almost always give you a business card with their phone number, address, and other company information. I write the month and year on the front of the card as a record of the visit. I then store all the cards together with a binder clip in a handy desk drawer. This record keeping is important because there can be a large turnover of publisher's representatives and you should remove old outdated cards from your file. Most of the representatives are very nice, interesting individuals and a kind word or sincere interest from you can make their work experience a little less tedious. If you have never lived out of a suitcase and travelled on the road for an extended period of time, you cannot appreciate how hard these individuals work.

During the Publisher Representative's Visit

Ask when the current edition of the text you are interested in will be available to your bookstore; many times publishers are somewhat overly optimistic about these delivery dates. Then ask what ancillaries are included with the text and when they will all be available; be specific, as ancillaries are notoriously late. This availability date is important because you want all the materials at the start of the class, not just the textbook. Not having an instructor's manual or test bank at the beginning of your first term can be a disaster.

Textbooks in Introductory Psychology are often revised on a three-year cycle. The major publisher's representatives will have a new (though usually only revised edition) text for you each year for your consideration for adoption. Many publishers would like you to change to a new text as often as possible, due largely to the used book market. If you find a text that you like, stick with it and with any luck, the updated editions will also be to your liking.

Factors in Text Selection

I always look first at the overall coverage of the text. Are all the appropriate chapters listed in the table of contents? Then I read some of the passages that are very hard for the students to understand. Review the chapters that your research emphasis is in to see how the material you know the best is covered. I then look at the layout. Are margins used for definitions? Are the tables and figures well done and useful to the students? Is color effectively used? How does the text "feel" in terms of a fit? Will the students like the text? I can still remember my first psychology text; I still have it. It was a book that consisted of only text; no pedagogy helped keep me awake. Today's students expect an attractive, interesting layout. All good texts strive for a comprehensive overall fit of color, artwork, and pedagogy. Always factor the publisher's representative into the equation when selecting a text. Is the representative going to get you a new computer disk for the test item file in two days when yours crashes? Are you going to be glad to see your representative when he/she comes to visit? Does the representative seem like the kind of person you can work with? These are important considerations. Remember, it is your choice; pick the text you want, and do not submit to sales pressures.

The Ancillary Package

In recent years the emphasis on the "package" has increased as different publishers strive for the best package; some of the items are of little use but most can be very helpful in your course. The following is a brief description of the items that you can expect to find in the text package.

Test Item File

At a minimum, a test item file should have 100 multiple choice items per chapter. Nice touches in the test item file are more items or additional editions. Essay questions, fill-in-the-blank, true/false and matching items also should be included. Make sure that your department has compatible computers to run the test item files. I ask for a demonstration disk, and I make sure their programs run on our equipment and that the software is designed to be used by secretaries, not computer science graduates. In the not-too-distant past, this compatibility issue was a serious consideration. Now most of the software will run on your computer but may still be very difficult to use.

Instructor's Resource Manual

Instructor's resource manuals are a tremendous source of valuable information on how to teach your course; you will use a good manual a lot and throw away a bad one. Ask the representative to send you a copy of the instructor's resource manual prior to adoption so you can preview this important item. Use this manual to help develop your course lectures.

Student Study Guide

Student study guides are an important resource for the students. They will lower their anxiety level about testing and are a good method of studying for examinations. Here again, the quality of student study guides varies, so ask for a preview copy. This study guide should be coordinated, with the test item file and the instructor's resource manual. If these ancillaries are not coordinated the students can be studying a specific emphasis while the instructor's resource manual and test item file are emphasizing something completely different. These ancillaries are always authored by different individuals; you can telephone or e-mail the authors with specific questions concerning these parts of the package.

Overhead/Slides

Overhead/slide packages are a must for large classes. I find myself using the chalkboards less and less, with much more emphasis on overheads. Students can see them better and once you have a set of good overhead transparencies or slides, your lectures are set; you do not have to write or draw the table or figure on the chalkboard for each class. Many publishers have two sets of these materials, one keyed to the text, which consists of reproductions of the tables and figures in that text, and many have a separate *Core* set that is generic to psychology. Again, some are excellent and some are very poor; ask for a preview from each publisher.

These items are what I would consider to be the minimum ancillary package. There will always be extras, many of which I find to be of little use, but you might investigate them on an individual basis. The "package" should be a major consideration in your text adoption decision. As a new instructor, you will use the package more than individuals who have more experience teaching psychology.

Ask the publisher's representative for a written estimate of the delivery date for these ancillaries. I have begun classes before receiving ancillaries. Late test item files are the worst, but missing any item is not acceptable. If you know ahead that any of these items will be late, you can plan your course accordingly or adopt a different text. Emphasize to the representative that you expect to have these materials when promised; be firm and demand realistic delivery dates.

After you decide on the text, ask your secretary to order the text through your campus bookstore. Be sure to include all the materials that you want ordered, such as students' study guides and additional readings or texts. Bookstores usually have a deadline for ordering texts. Many times this deadline is not the last day to order books for the next term, so ask your secretary for the real last day to order. If you can meet this bookstore deadline do so but do not be pressured into making a poor choice because of an arbitrary deadline. Remember, you will be using this text for at least one year.

Two Months Prior to Class

Begin to Develop Your Course Syllabus

Two instructors with the same text are likely to emphasize different aspects of the text, and you should start to think about the contents of your syllabus. Ask other instructors or your secretary for examples of past syllabi. These syllabi will give you a good format as well as the depth of presentation expected. See *Appendix B* for an example of the syllabus I use.

Number of Instructional Days in the Term

Consult your schedule of classes to determine the number of actual teaching days; there are holidays and special events when students will be excused from class. Do not forget that you will be giving examinations; at many schools these occur during regular class time. It is important to avoid scheduling examinations, either before or after important events or holidays. Students always want an early start for the holiday and study very little during holidays or special events like homecoming weekends. Try not to penalize students for enjoying college life; remember how much you enjoyed taking examinations.

Defining Lecture Length

One difficult aspect of developing a syllabus is to calculate how long your lectures will be. Most schools utilize a 50-60 minute schedule for Monday, Wednesday and Friday classes, and schedule 75-90 minute classes for Tuesday and Thursday classes. Calculate the number of lectures per topic in terms of the class length, and remember that you will likely teach both in the 50-60 minute and 75-90 minute time frames during your first few years in academia. Will you be very good at these calculated class period estimates? No; invariably you have too much material to cover in the class period. Try to schedule at least half a class period every two weeks to either catch up or lose time in the schedule. A lecture that is too short before a test is much better than having to try and cram 2 lectures into a single period. You can always have a review session if you are short of material.

Defining Examinations

In a typical semester-long course, I would recommend at least three and possibly four examinations over the course materials, excluding midterms (which are losing favor in many institutions) and finals. Student prefer smaller examinations over less material, possibility because if they receive a poor examination grade they are not doomed to failure in the class. Midterms and finals are usually set by the school; therefore, you must restrict your schedule to conform to these requirements.

Defining the Schedule

Should you be worried that you are not finished with your teaching schedule? No; several factors demand that you keep an open schedule as long as possible. First, the emphasis of the text material that you have chosen could change, according to your own wishes or due to outside constraints. You should attempt to stay as flexible with this syllabus as you can. I like to type a preliminary syllabus and hang it on my wall; as time passes, I usually will see improvements or changes to my original thoughts and can mark them in pencil on the original. I have very rarely used the first draft of a course syllabus. I have, on the other hand, printed hundreds of copies of the syllabus only to find errors or changes that I must make. Check with the secretary to see the time line needed to produce this syllabus and allow three extra days. In my upper division courses, I survey the class the first meeting day and modify my class schedule and syllabus according to the student population in the class and the needs of these students. I will add a lecture or two or introduce a topic the class has indicated they desire. If your class is small enough and your department allows for this flexibility, I would recommend this option of tailoring the content of the course to the needs and wants of the students. The students will see this as an attempt by you to allow student input into their education. You can still teach the course the way you want, but this student input makes for a better class. Of course, if you have a class of 100 or more students, then you really cannot use this option.

First Draft of the Syllabus

Produce a first rough draft of the syllabus and be as specific as possible as to details. Is there a holiday? Then list it. Be specific about dates, times and locations of all examinations. If recitation sections are held, be specific about locations and times. Leave as little to the students' imagination as possible but be as specific as possible. I usually do not like to add the times of films and videos to the syllabus because of the slippage factor (being too long or too short with your lecture material) in the lectures. The students are better surprised with films or videos; if you let them know you are showing one, many students might skip class that day, but of course the best students will attend. Guest lectures can be added to the syllabus, especially if you allow others from the school community to attend. When I have a guest lecture, I ask my students to invite any other students or faculty to attend. List all the texts required and recommended; include ISBN numbers. I usually put a copy of all materials for the course on reserve in the library; note this in the syllabus. Add any special circumstances, either yours or the school's. For example, is attendance required in your course, by you or the school? When will homework be turned in? Be specific. Where will it be returned? Note building and room. Where will grades be posted? Note building and room or area of the hall.

Types of Teaching Methods

Planning for class depends on the type of teaching method you are going to adopt. There are several different approaches; one possible choice is the "straight" stand-up lecture with no student input or interaction. This method is largely out of favor with both students and faculty, although some faculty insist on this method. A second choice is a more modern approach that encourages student questions and input, but this method can be restricted by the number of students in your class. I use as many demonstrations and examples of the principles under study as I can, since the more ways a student can be exposed to a principle the more likely he or she is to understand the principle. If possible, stay flexible and vary your presentation from day to day; lecture one day, conduct demonstrations or activities the next, and lead discussion the following day.

Other Course Requirements

Are there any required recitation sections, discussion sections, study sections or small group meetings? If there are, be sure to discuss with your introductory supervisor or chair how these sections are to be staffed and how these requirements are to be fulfilled. If these are not required by your department, you may want to integrate some of these alternatives into your teaching approach. Students often find alternatives to the straight lecture formats very interesting. The size of your section can be a limiting factor in the types and varieties of the alternative methods that you try, but give them serious consideration. See Chapter 7 for some suggestions.

Lesson Plan Pro's and Con's

During your career as a student, you have undoubtedly interacted with other students in the education department of your school. It may seem that these students and their instructors are obsessed with the lesson plan. You probably laughed at the prospect of assigning every minute of the class period to a specific topic or activity. The current question is whether you should use the dreaded lesson plan. I would say no. A college level course should be flexible enough to explore interesting topics and tangents introduced by students and not be constrained by an artificial system designed to engineer students through their education. Some of the best interactions and thinking the student will do is during these tangents. These tangents are a good place for students to get a glimpse of your personality and explore the field of psychology. Besides, how boring it would be to do the exact same lecture every term.

Begin to Write Your Lectures

History of Lecturing

Prior to the invention of the printing press, lectures were the main method of passing on knowledge. Professors or masters would read their hand written lectures to students; these lectures were then passed from professor to students, and when the student eventually became the professor, some current knowledge was added to the lectures and this information was passed on to the next generation of students. This method was far superior to the word-of-mouth method that had preceded it. In the word-of-mouth method, stories were told from generation to generation with no control over the original content. This method could explain some of the miracles of earlier times, owing to the simple conscious or unconscious elaboration of common events.

With the advent of printing and books, the lecture method has survived. Why? There are four primary reasons for the survival of the lecture method.

A Lecture Is a Contemporary Event

Since a lecture is a contemporary event, it can update the text materials in a course. Most texts in psychology will have a three-year cycle between editions. Add this to the lag time for journal publications and other texts and the most current the material in your text can be is three to four years old. I often present materials that I have just read in the newspaper or a journal minutes prior to class. The ability to stay current is an important aspect of the lecturing system. Although we would like to think that all lectures are updated each term, the sad fact is that many are not. I am sure in your undergraduate career you had a professor who read old, stale notes that were so out-of-date they were of little use. Do not let this happen to you; be current and update each lecture each term. I make myself and the student a promise to update each major lecture section each time I give the lecture.

A Lecture Has In-Depth Coverage

The lecture format allows not only for the transfer of information from one person to another, it also allows the demonstration of little-known relationships that may not be in the printed materials; many texts do not have the time or space to discuss specific topics at length and in depth, ranging from the introductory class to advanced classes. Additionally, the lecture allows conventional wisdom to be challenged, the classic theories with up-to-date research to be evaluated, and a new and different perspective on old problems to be discussed.

A Great Lecture Is a Great Lecture

If you have ever attended a great lecture, you will never forget it. I attended a lecture by Buckminister Fuller that was so inspiring I still remember it fifteen years later. Great individuals are sometimes great lecturers; if this is the case, attend as many as you can. Many schools conduct an invited lecture series; ask for a schedule of speakers. Great lecturers are so in love with their subject matter that they try to convey this feeling to the audience. When this happens, it is a great experience. Even we beginning instructors can strive to inspire the same passion in our students. When one good student decides to change majors and become a psychologist, it makes the effort worthwhile. You may develop into a good lecturer and even deliver a few great lectures; it is the passion for the subject matter that makes this difference.

Lectures Define a Commitment to Scholarship

Lectures can serve as a method of instilling what it means to be committed to a life of scholarship. Act as an example of this scholarly goal for the student who aspires to the academic profession by being a mentor to the student and instilling principles that have been passed down through the generations: honesty, ethics, and love for the discipline.

(Some of the material above is adapted from Allen and Rueter 1990)

The lecture format has survived, and now it is your turn to pass down the tradition.

Writing Your First Lecture

First Rough Draft

I start by using the rough teaching outline from the desktop organizer/calendar. In terms of your time line now is the time to start to write your first lectures. Realize that many of these first lectures will be changed as you see what works and what does not in the classroom. I like to use pencil for this first draft. It is really a bit scary to think you are the one who must choose what materials will be included in your class. I use other texts, graduate and undergraduate class notes, journals, and my research interests to develop these lectures. An additional source of inspiration for these beginning lectures can be found in the instructor's resource manual. Many will have short mini lectures already written for you. You can uses these mini lectures as a starting point and add your own material to them. Remember, these lectures are a reflection of your personality. Do not be afraid to show the students who you are; some will like you, others won't. You will remember the ones who like you and hopefully in time forget the rest. Every section of every term is different; there will be sections you cannot wait to begin, while others are like going to the dentist's office every Monday, Wednesday and Friday at 11am. Every instructor has his or her own set of biases that makes his or her teaching unique. In an introductory class everyone teaches the same basic material from different perspectives. The students will soon learn which instructors teach from which perspective and you will develop a following of students who both agree with and like your teaching perspective. Do not try to copy someone's style or approach; be yourself because it is much easier. Start to select the slides or overhead transparencies that you will integrate into your lectures and use these as the basic element from which your lectures are developed. Two months' head start on the lectures will give you time to refine each lecture and still stay ahead of other course commitments. Realize that you do not want to write all your lectures now but rather see what are the strengths and weakness of your style and lectures and modify your later lectures to enhance your strengths. I like to stay 2-3 weeks ahead of the class with my lecture preparations.

Structure of the Lecture

Make a skeletal structure or outline of the materials that you want to cover in your lecture. I usually try to outline the main points to be covered in the lecture. These main points should cover all the materials necessary to complete the lecture. Try to find an appropriate overhead or slide for each major topic and major sub-point. This may not always be possible, but as the years pass, you can add to your collection. Each main point can usually be subdivided into in-depth sub-points; it is your decision how many of the sub-points are to be covered in each lecture. At the introductory level, cover only the items necessary to complete a general understanding of the main point. Leave the subtle differences and depth of coverage for the upper division courses. If you do not adopt this strategy, you could be lost in an endless lecture on very minor points. Often during a very in-depth lecture at this level, the students will lose interest in the material.

Learning Points

You can decide if you want to use the learning points concept. The introduction of the main topics for the lecture in outline form is presented at the beginning of the class as an overhead or handout. Many students prefer this method because they can then fill in the material during the lecture and they will not miss any of the points that you wish to emphasize. A disadvantage to this method is that you must stay reasonably on track in your lecture and this gives you little room for student interaction. A possible compromise is to begin your teaching career with specific learning points and then make them more general as your lectures develop over time. You can also evaluate how well the students have assimilated the material by assessing the learning points at the end of the lecture. See Chapter 10 for more information of evaluation about the learning points.

Fleshing Out Your Lecture

Now that you have an outline of the lecture, use your training and experience to flesh it out. Decide how much of the lecture to write in your notes: every word you are going to say, brief phrases, or a single word to jog the memory of an important point. I usually suggest incorporating too much detail in the early draft form of the outlines of the important points. As you present this lecture over and over, there will be times when you can add or delete information in each section. I do this during the lecture when a new point or way of analyzing something comes up, typically through student input, when a funny saying works or when a student's question logically leads to the next section. During the lecture I update my notes with a colored overhead pen, usually because I have one handy and it stands out from the pencil notes. All of these *live* events should be recorded as they add new and interesting information that works. I also write comments like "fix this section," insert a big question mark, or simply cross out a section and write "skip" across it. I like to evaluate the flow of the lectures from the heat of the moment; this lets you know what really works in the classroom. When you learn what level works for you, the more you use and update your notes, the shorter the length of the original structure of the lecture notes will be; a single word may become a 15-minute section of the lecture. These lectures will evolve into something much better than what you began with. My notes are a mess to the average student. Some pages are so annotated that only I can understand what I have added, deleted or annotated. I find it reasonably humorous when a student asks to photo-copy my notes. I usually suggest they try a student instead.

Now use elaboration, which can consist of using statistics, making comparisons between different principles, offering contrast between different principles, using quotations as sources, or providing examples and illustrations of the principle under discussion. These are the details and the evidence for the lecture; these are the materials and details that students expect to learn in the class. If you use all the materials mentioned above as sources for these details, you will be amazed at how much *you* will learn from this course.

Using Audio/Visual Materials

These materials can include graphs, transparencies, films, videos, audio tapes, models, photographs, slides, maps, and any other materials you can bring to class that will help illustrate your main topics. I like to write in the margins of my lecture notes when one of these items should be presented in the lecture. Using a colored pen will help direct your attention to this note.

Lecture Strategies

My Method of Lecturing

A good way to plan your lectures is to tell the students what you are going to teach them, teach them the material and then summarize what you have taught them. If you use this format, the students will come to expect it and will be able to follow your lectures more easily.

Tell them what you are going to teach them.

You can provide an overview of the main structure of your lecture, either using a handout or on an overhead transparency at the beginning of the class. This material can be in the form of learning points. Students like this, especially if you always follow the plan. If there are detailed materials that must be copied from the chalkboard or overhead, make a photocopy and distribute the material to the class, which will save time in class and allow students to have the correct material and have a place to continue to take notes on the material from lectures.

Teach them what you are going to teach.

Spend the necessary time to make sure that the main points are covered and that the students understand these points. This may take the form of asking students questions, giving quizzes at the end of the class, or assigning short papers on topics covered in the lecture. You can also assume the students understand the materials, which they often do not, and have questions on the examination from the lectures. Do whatever satisfies you that the students understand the material. I usually pick several of the best students and use them as guides; if they look confused about a section of the lecture, I will repeat that section with different examples. If they look pleased, I continue.

Summarize what you have taught them.

Using the overhead or chalkboard, re-emphasize the main points of the lecture just prior to the end of the class period. Encourage individual students to stay after class to discuss any questions they might have about the lecture. These will typically be the best students in the class and are of great interest to the instructor; use these students as a gauge of the effectiveness of the lecture.

Some Final Lecture Tips

With this outline to organize your lectures, start the preparation for the first lecture. Use your own ideas and methods with these suggestions to form a standardized method of writing lectures. The more standardized, the more the introductory student will like the lectures. I keep my lectures in a file folder, where I number the pages and the overhead transparencies. (I dropped my notes on the floor last term and if I had not numbered the pages I would have been lost in my lecture.) Finally, close the file folder with a binder clip in case you drop the folder on the way to class. Always strive to keep your lectures organized; re-sort and clean your overheads, and update your notes prior to each class.

Other Course Considerations

Ordering and Planning Course Materials

Order films and videos, either through your library or rental outlets. Both usually give you a one-week use window. Make preliminary arrangements for any field trips. Contact several guest lecturers, typically someone you know who owes you a favor or someone you want to meet from the community. Indicate that you would like him/her for a specific guest lecture and plan for a specific week. Start to look at the logistics of the demonstration that you are planning and make preliminary attempts to secure any necessary equipment. If you must reserve these materials, try to keep the time frame as flexible as possible.

Special Needs Students

Your school will have facilities for students with physical or learning disabilities. The staff who work with these disabled students should be contacted and assured that you will cooperate with their specific program. Depending on your school, these individual students can be a significant percentage of the school population. Take the time to get to know each of the special needs students and offer any additional help you can. The students are starting at a disadvantage but in many cases will work harder to overcome these problems.

Four Weeks Prior to Class

The Teaching Assistant

By this time in the preparation process, your teaching assistant(s) (TA's) should have been assigned. If you have not met these individuals, set a formal meeting date to discuss both their and your role in the course structure. TA's are some of the best and some of the worst aspects of your psychology course.

On the plus side, TA's can assume the responsibility for a tremendous amount of the busy work that you will have in the class. Examples are checking rolls, making answer keys, posting scores, proctoring exams, showing films and videos, summarizing test results, and producing final summaries and graphs for your final grade determinations. They are also, in most instances, very nice individuals and often just a few years away from the position you now have. They will work hard, but they often need substantial guidance to understand the tasks that you wish performed. They usually have a very keen interest in learning how to teach psychology. Take the time to help these individuals learn how to teach; they are your responsibility.

On the negative side, at times it may seem that performing the TA's job yourself would be easier than trying to explain what and how you want an activity performed. Remember that being a TA has two major benefits: the first is that the TA learns from you, the faculty member, how to conduct a course and, secondly, in most cases, the TA's are also paid for their duties. Take the time to explain what you really want accomplished and then check the work to be sure the TA's have complied with your instructions. I have had both very good and very poor TA's; you should be able to discover the type you have very early on in the class. If your TA is of the poor type, be very careful to check all assigned tasks. TA's are like most of us in that when we are required to perform a task we will do a good job, but if left to own devices, we will often do less than our potential would indicate. Help your TA's remember they are the next new generation of instructors.

Assign the TA's to read the appropriate sections of the text, study guide, and course syllabus. Impress upon them the importance of being ahead of the students in the readings, assignments, and general understanding of the course materials.

Two Weeks Prior to Class

Set a Formal TA Meeting

Set a formal meeting for two weeks before classes start for the TA's to ask any questions they might have about the structure of the course. Clarify all questions at this time and have the TA's post office hours.

Check Text Materials

Check the bookstore to be sure that your text and ancillary materials have arrived and that there are sufficient quantities for your class. Many times bookstores will not have all the materials you ordered on the shelves by the first day of class and you must adjust your schedule. Put necessary materials on reserve at the library.

Contact your publisher's representative for any missing or low quantity items. By now you should have your ancillary package. Ask the secretary to run the test item file to be sure that it is compatible with your computer and that the disk was not damaged in transit.

Projected Student Enrollments

Many schools will register students in advance, sometimes months in advance. If this procedure is used at your school, ask the registrar for the projected enrollment for your section. This will allow you an idea of the number of students that you will be able to add to your section. At my university, the add/drop procedures begin the first week of the term, and up to 20 percent of the class may add/drop. If you do not track these add/drops, you can over-fill your class and have students sitting on the floor for your first examination. Another possibility is that you will under-enroll your class and in this case the administration might ask why your classes are not at capacity.

Visit Your Classroom

Check out the lighting arrangements, and know which switches turn off/on which light. There are typically two sets of switches in each room, in the front and back; find both sets. Check the heating/cooling systems, and/or the operation of windows. As you know, a very hot classroom is not conducive to learning. Check the operation of the projection screen and projection facilities. Investigate whether you will have to show your own films and videos or if there is a school service. If there is, take the time to meet the supervisor. Check the operation of the overhead projector, determine the distance the projector needs to be from the screen, learn where the cord plugs in and, most important, how to replace the spare bulb in the overhead projector; they always burn out during the term. If you cannot replace the bulb yourself, locate a back-up projector that you can use on short notice (minutes). The department will usually have an old overhead reserved for this purpose. Locate and test the microphone, if applicable. Then sit in the back row of the room and try to visualize what the students will see. Try to prepare your visual aids so that these students will be able to see and understand the visual aids. This will also give you a gauge of the size to write on the chalkboard; try different styles and sizes until you find the best for this specific room. I have found that the students who choose to sit in the last rows of the classroom are not as interested in the course materials, but the first time they cannot see the overhead, they will complain. I usually tell these complainers to move to the front of the class. Know the room and all the operations of the mechanical equipment. The first impression the students receive should be that you have been teaching in this room for several years, not that this is your first class. You will be nervous enough without trying to find the plug for the overhead.

One Week Prior to Class

Finalize

Finalize your syllabus, course and lecture outlines. Ask the secretary to produce any handouts that the students will receive the first day of class. Make any last minute decisions about the course. Remember, no matter how hard you try to make your first class perfect, there will be mistakes. Be flexible and correct the errors with a minimum of effort and lost time. Often a last minute change can be made in the form of an overhead that can be presented the first day of class.

Final Rehearsal

Begin the final rehearsal of your first lectures. Use a friend or colleague to practice the timing and delivery of your lecture. Use the actual room you will lecture in for this practice if possible. This will give you a feel for the acoustics of the room and how the mechanical components of the room work or do not work. It is much better to learn that the overhead is too large or too small for the screen at this stage rather than when 350 students are watching.

Relax and enjoy the rest of the week before classes start; your life is about to get very confusing very soon.

3

Structure of the Class

By now you should have completed lectures for the first several weeks and be planning and writing subsequent lectures. It is important that you keep at least three weeks ahead of the class in preparing your lectures; there are always unforeseen problems that could alter your schedule. An illness, a family emergency, or an accident could compress your time to prepare lectures. I also think that it is important to let these lectures *sit* for a couple of days before you finalize the content. You may have a better feel for what works in your lectures after you have presented the first couple of lectures. Be flexible and willing to change in order to maximize your first presentation of each lecture. Try to be prepared enough that most of the students will not know that this is your first lecture on a specific topic.

General Considerations for the Class

Guest Lecture Confirmations

Re-contact your first guest lecturer and set a specific date, time, and title. Occasionally, a guest lecturer will not be able to honor the commitment made earlier in your planning of the course. If the inability to honor the invitation is sincere, ask to reschedule for a later date. Often the guest will be happy to do so. This opportunity to reschedule also gives you the chance to judge the credibility of the guest. Guest lecturers offer the opportunity to have an expert in a particular field of psychology give a short but interesting presentation. Choose the guest carefully; he or she, for the most part, welcomes the opportunity. One advantage of guest lecturers is the ability to fill a gap in your experience. Select these individuals because they will, first, give the class a new perspective that you might not feel comfortable presenting and, second, they will give the student a break from your lectures and a chance to see a different lecturer. It is a nice touch to take your guest out to lunch either before or after the lecture. This does not have to be a $50 lunch at the best restaurant in town; it is the thought that counts.

Managing the Large Class

Classes Over 100 Students

One aspect of the large class that is often overlooked is that students, as a rule, do not like to sit through lectures. A student's interest level is usually the class period minus 10 minutes. This seems to be a universal constant. Try to use guest speakers, films, videos, and demonstrations as much as possible to augment and breakup your lectures. Keep student interest high and, thus, attendance at a maximum. This is very important. There are fewer events more disappointing than to come to a large class and see only about 30 percent of the class in attendance. You should strive to have all your students so happy with the class that they want to attend every period. This is often easier to accomplish in the summer session because you will have more motivated students.

Demonstrations in the Large Class

Demonstrations are a must because they do not involve direct student participation. Some volunteers from the class may be needed but the class as a whole does not have to participate. Some demonstrations are very short and can be used as lecture lead-ins, while others will take an entire class period. Use these demonstrations to add flavor to your lectures and break the straight lecture-only format. As you find good demonstrations, add them to your lectures but still try out new demonstrations each term. Demonstrations can be found in the instructor's resource manual of most texts.

Activities in the Large Class

Activities, on the other hand, are very hard to manage in a large class. They involve class participation and usually are not appropriate for the large lecture course. Even though activities are hard to accommodate in a large class, try a couple during your first term; this will give you a feel for the type of problems that you are likely to confront in future activities. Activities can be found in the instructor's resource manual of most texts.

Alternate Formats for Activities in the Large Class

An alternative that can be built into the introductory course at your school is the use of recitation. Each student signs up for a specific time other than the lecture time. Our department uses 2 1/2 hours of lecture and 1/2 hour recitation a week format. This allows us to have a recitation section meeting every other week. During these recitation sections we do activities, demonstrate principles, discuss principles from different perspectives, discuss the examinations, give practice examinations, and answer questions that are not generally understood from the lecture. The staffing of these sections can be trained, upper division psychology majors or paid graduates or graduate students. This use of recitation sections serves several functions for the introductory students. First, it allows the students in the recitation section to have a better understanding of psychology because we limit the size of the sections to 20 students. Many of the principles are discussed in the relatively small sections and thus are better understood by the individual student. Secondly, the recitation section allows students to have access to a "teacher" to ask questions and discuss topics in greater depth. Finally, this format allows students to meet other students and have more personal interaction in an otherwise very large lecture class. The undergraduate and graduate instructors receive several benefits from this recitation format. They are allowed to "teach" other students about psychology, although the department carefully monitors their teaching and second, they receive a feel for what it is like to teach. This first interaction with teaching can help them in their career choices. Finally, they can list this teaching experience on their vita when applying for graduate school or employment.

My department has recently hired teaching assistants who receive a salary to conduct these sections. Since these instructors are paid employees of the university holding a faculty rank, we can allow these assistants more latitude in what they teach. The benefits for the assistants who teach these recitation sections are several. First, they get to have primary control over their sections and gain valuable teaching experience. Second, they receive a reasonable salary and they can list this teaching on their vita when applying for graduate school or employment. Either of these two plans could work at your school. Discuss these types of alternatives with your course supervisor or department head.

Structured Journals in the Large Class

In addition to the recitation sections, my department also has instituted a structured journal writing component in our introductory course. This journal writing consists of two types of items. The first are structured items that are keyed to the text materials and are timed to coincide with the lectures. The students must read the text and attend the lectures to be able to write these journal entries. The students like these entries because they allow them to study the text materials a little at a time and force them to keep up with the readings. The second type of entry is the personal entry that is not keyed to the text or the lectures but rather is of a personal exploration nature, with each individual thinking about a specific aspect of psychology.

This format gives the large introductory class a more personal touch and is gaining favor around the country. The students like the recitation sections and the journals and so do the recitation leaders. If these types of changes are out of your control, you might suggest them to your introductory coordinator or department head.

Films in the Large Class

Films are a useful tool in the large class; they allow all students in the room to have a good view of the film. Unfortunately, many of the visual aids available today are not in the 16mm film format but rather in video. Many of the films available are very old, of 1975 or earlier vintage. Many sources for films can be found in the instructor's resource manual associated with your text. I would preview all films before presenting them to the class. I also discuss the fact that since most of these films are so old, the people dress "funny." I usually tell the students that this is how their parents dressed, especially if there is a very stereotyped "hippie" in the film. I will tell the students this is how their father or mother really looked before they were born. They always like this disclaimer. I do emphasize that the principles that are discussed in these older films are still relevant today and that many of the individuals and situations in the films are classics in the study of psychology. I tell the students to look past the "funny" clothes or hair styles and try to understand the principles that are being discussed.

Videos in the Large Class

Videos, on the other hand, can be very up-to-date, interesting, and contemporary. However, there is a major drawback to videos: many schools do not have large format projection video players, but rather TVs and VCRs. These have limited use because of the size of the screen and thus the number of students who can view the programming. A possibility is to show videos outside of the regular class time. Plan to have a smaller room and show the video several times each day. If you wish, you could keep roll or have questions on your examination. These videos can also be shown in the recitation or lab sections. A new and exciting technical innovation has occurred within the last five years that has allowed the cost of video projectors to be reduced below the range of $3000. If you can obtain the funding for a video projector system, it will greatly enhance your ability to show videos to large classes.

Handouts in Large Sections

Handouts in large classes can be expensive to produce for the quantity necessary, but they are useful. I find handouts worthwhile and the students like them. Handouts, such as outlines or summaries of your lecture, are always appreciated by the students. Disadvantages of handouts are the costs of production, your time assembling the information, and the problem of students who miss class and want a copy of the handout from a week ago. You will find yourself either carrying a pile of old handouts or having a line of students trailing you back to your office. A possible solution to the handout problem is to include them in the syllabus and sell the students these overheads at your cost through your bookstore.

Specific Problems of Large Classes

Classes of over 100 students have the additional problem of the background noise level. Very large classes can drown out your voice in the back of the room. Many students in the back of the room may lose interest because they cannot hear you; use the microphone when available. Students talking in large classes disrupt the class and annoy the instructor. One way I deal with the problem of talking during lectures is to ask the offending students if they would like to come down front and share their conversation with the rest of the class. A second method is to mention that the current section of lecture will be on the test or simply put up a new overhead transparency. A final method is to talk to the student offenders privately after class; a little fear goes a long way. Our school newspaper is delivered on Tuesdays and Thursdays. I always know when the newspaper has been delivered because the students are all trying to read the paper at the start of class. Ask them to put the paper away; be specific and forceful about this the first time it happens. One method that works is to not enter the room until you are ready to lecture and the class period has just begun. Try to enter from the front of the room near the podium, open your notes, and start to lecture. If you are consistent with your arrival time students will become accustomed to this method and will settle down more rapidly. Realize that if you lose control (students talking, rustling papers, reading the newspaper) of a very large class, it is hard to regain control in that class period. A final effective method is to suggest that today's lectures will be emphasized on the examination.

Learning Student Names in the Large Classroom

I find that it is almost impossible to learn the names of students in large classes. I do tell the students, however, that I remember most of their faces. I can make the distinction between students who have been in my class and those who have not. A year after a student has taken Introductory Psychology, I will see him or her in a grocery store and recognize the face; I always say hello. Not knowing the students' names is advantageous in that you cannot be biased in your grading if you do not know individual names.

Managing the Small Class

Advantages and Disadvantages of the Small Class

Small sections (30 or fewer students) have their own pluses and minuses. The first positive is that you will get to know each student's face and, possibly, name. Students like to have a personal relationship with the professor. Secondly, discussion is possible during the course of your lectures and we all know that many times the most interesting and important principles are developed during these class discussions. Small classes have a different feel than large lecture hall classes. I get the feeling that I am teaching to students, not just lecturing to a full auditorium. Several advantages of the small class are that eye contact can be made with individuals, students can't sleep in the back, there is less talking, and the students feel they are active participants, not simply going to the "show." Unfortunately, very few schools have the resources to fund small sections of Introductory Psychology or other upper division courses. If you have a small section, you are very lucky.

Learning Students' Names in Small Classes

Learning students' names can be accomplished by making a name/face association. I pick out some physical characteristic of the individual--style of clothing, hair style, accent, or other physical characteristic of the individual and then I make a short story using the face and characteristic. In small classes with a little practice you can learn most of the students' names when you see their faces.

A second method uses the fact that many students sit in the same area or even the same seat in a room each day of class. This second method of learning names of the students is to devise a seating chart with individual names of each student/seat and to ask questions during your lecture to specific students. This use of a seating chart may seem old-fashioned but it will have two effects. The first is that the students will have an impression that this is a more personal class and, secondly, the students will have to keep current with the readings to be able to understand the questions you ask them specifically. You could devise an extra credit point system for correct answers to lecture questions in a small class

Demonstrations in the Small Class

Demonstrations in small classes are really no different than in those of large classes except that students will have the opportunity for extended in-depth discussion during the demonstration. The logistics are the same for you in a small class.

Activities in the Small Class

Activities are a real possibility in small classes; there are many activities available for small groups. Some short five or ten-minute activities at the start of the class will involve the students in a concept or demonstrate a point and can be used as a lecture lead-in. Activities in small classes are fun for both the instructor and the students. Take the time to plan your activities and modify each after the class. Some will work nicely; others will be total failures. Some can be modified by you to fit your particular situation; try to establish a core list of useful activities. Many very good activities can be found in your instructor's resource manual associated with your text. An additional source for activities can be from social psychology instructors' manuals. You can ask your publishers' representatives for desk copies or seek out your departmental social psychologist and ask to borrow some of these manuals.

Journals in the Small Class

The type of journals mentioned in the large group section above could be instituted in the smaller lecture section. This is especially attractive because you will get to know the students from a different perspective as you read these journals, rather than having your assistants read the journals. You can have the students use the structured questions or make the journal more personal, even to the point of a daily diary of their thoughts.

Films and Videos in the Small Class

Films have no advantage in a small class, but videos do, primarily because most schools do not have the large format video projection devices discussed above, but rather TVs and VCRs. In a small class, the students can see the TV.

Handouts in the Small Class

Handouts in small classes can be more extensive, with less cost per section. You can use a variety of handouts to supplement your text but be careful not to violate copyright laws when preparing them. You can give the students handouts for homework and then go over it the next class period. Many of the most interesting new materials are not yet in print and can be introduced through handouts. You can be discussing rapidly changing events that happened within the last week through the use of handouts. Copies of newspaper articles are especially practical for this rapid turn around and discussion format.

Visual Aids in the Small Classroom

Visual aids are not as important in a small class. You can use the chalkboard in a small class; the students in the back of the class can see the materials. However, overheads are still very useful and the students in the back of the room can always see the materials. You can pass around photographs and other items and be fairly confident that they will be returned.

Managing the Class -- General Comments

When Things Go Wrong

No matter how hard you try to set up your class, there will be occasions when things will go wrong. Stay as flexible as you can and adopt the attitude that this is your first try at teaching and that these mistakes can be turned into a positive means of improving your course. The second time you teach the course, it will be much easier; the major mistakes will have been corrected. Additionally, the second time you teach the course you will be less nervous, although you will always be a little nervous. Adopt the attitude that this is your best first effort and improvements are sure to follow.

Night Classes

I have taught as many night sections of Introductory Psychology as the department can afford. I find these classes a nice change from the traditional day sections. You will get a very different mix of students; this is especially true if you are in a large city. The students in night classes are often employed during the day or are students who prefer to have more free time during the day to study, do research or recreate. I find the typical night students to be very motivated and ready to learn. These students come to class prepared and full of energy. Many of these night students are taking Introductory Psychology as their first class in college; they want to see if they like college and if they can perform at the college level. Most of these night students are very capable and enjoy an opportunity to learn. I find that many of these night students will become full time day students in the future. I try to encourage these night students as much as possible; they may not have attended college for any number of reasons, from dropping out of high school, raising a family, getting married, starting a job, or simply lacking an interest or motivation. These students are now ready to learn, quite a refreshing change from many of the day students. Help these night students with the bureaucracy of your school and encourage them as much as possible.

If you are the type of person who can accommodate a night class schedule, I would recommend trying a night class. Who knows how much fun you will have?

4

Meeting the First Class

Sure, I was excited when I got this job, but now it is 15 minutes until my first class meeting. Damn! I wish I hadn't accepted this job. Maybe I should go over to my classroom. They are starting to fill the room; guess I will go down in back of the stage. Let's see, I have my notes, class rolls, hair combed. Man, am I nervous. Let's see, what was it that I was going to start with? I think I will sneak a peek in the door. Oh no, I think there must be 300 students in there and they all expect me to teach this class. Too late to call in sick. What will I do? Hey, there is a student standing in the shadows. What is she doing back here? Miss, are you lost? First day in school and first class for you, huh? You say you are scared? Tell you what, let's both pretend we have been doing this for years and go in there and dazzle them, ok? Time to go; good luck to both of us. Throughout that term this young woman sat in the front row and we both had a great class.

The Beginning of a Teaching Career

Planning the First Class

Setting the Foundations for the First Class

How do you prepare for your first class? Realize that this may be one of the most stressful events of your life, especially if your section is a very large one. Most graduate schools emphasize research over teaching and now you are about to pay for this skewed emphasis. Any time you are in a new and unfamiliar situation, such as meeting new people, you are a little stressed, but conducting your first class with 300 students is really going to be stressful.

Some instructors deal with this stressful anxiety by handing out the syllabus and then leaving the class without any discussion. Sure, this reduces the instructor's anxiety, but it does little in the way of constructive usage of time. Since first impressions of you and the course are going to last a long time, take this opportunity to work on your anxiety and your fist impression. Remember, you have to come back at least 39 more times to teach this class. One method to reduce this stressful anxiety is to focus on the fact that you know the material in this course better than any of the students. You are the expert!

Give Them Structure

When students come to class, they expect some form of structure from you. They are typically new students and do not really know what to expect from college classes. The most important thing you can provide the first day is structure. Let the students know what is expected of them in terms of the class content, classroom behavior, and what they can expect from you in terms of teaching style. The students have come to the classroom wanting to know what the course is about and what kind of teacher you will be. Remember that the students are coming from diverse backgrounds throughout the community and country and will have different expectations of you and the course. They are all enrolled in other courses; some will be entering freshmen while others are graduate students. One of your tasks is somehow to shift this group of individuals from whatever state they enter the classroom toward wanting to study psychology. This can be harder than you think. There appears to be a lag time before students can really concentrate after a previous class; this time seems to be about 15 minutes. Your task is to shorten this lag time and get your lecture underway. I think demonstrations/discussions are a good method of re-energizing student interest in your subject matter. Sometimes an overhead transparency that requires the students to copy a significant amount of material as the first task of the period will facilitate this shift to thinking about psychology. I have found that its is best not to let the students continue to talk while you stand in front of the class. Use whatever technique that works, but gain control of every class and do it as early in the class period as possible.

Reducing Instructor Anxiety

Prior to the start of each class period, I like to take ten minutes to clear my thoughts; I just sit in my office, lights off, telephone off the hook, computer off, with the door mostly closed and relax. If anyone asks what I am doing, I tell them that I am meditating, which is partially true. I need this relaxing time to lower my anxiety level and prepare for the task ahead. Taking a walk, getting a drink of water, staring out the window or taking a final look at your lecture notes may work for you. Find out what relaxes you and use it just prior to class. I dislike it when a student comes to my office with a problem five minutes before the start of class, this interruption throws off my preparation and timing for the entire class. When I enter the classroom, I head directly for the podium. After reaching the podium, I look around the classroom and try to make eye contact with as many students as I can. Strange, yes, but this allows me to do two things. First, no matter how many times you enter a large classroom for the first class period, there is a level of anxiety. This pause to look at the class allows me to see if there are any familiar faces in the class. It could be a person you met in the student union building, at a party, or in the department. One face that you recognize will help lower your level of anxiety. Second, at this time I begin to pick out the individuals to whom I will direct my lecture. What do I mean *individuals*? There are 300 individuals in the room. One of the techniques that I use is to select 4 or 5 students in the classroom to direct my lectures to; pick students from different sections, left, right, front and back. How do you pick them? Your own personal taste dictates this, but I find someone who dresses differently or has a different hair style; this allows me to find this student at the beginning of each lecture. I use these individuals to monitor their note taking and adjust my speed of presentation so that my lectures are not too fast or slow. I can observe perplexing looks in these target individuals and go over difficult sections again. Bored expressions on these target students means speed this section of lecture up. Laughter at some of my attempts at humor are marked down in my notes for use in future classes. It is really weird; what I think is funny often is not, but students will laugh at different inane comments for years. These attempts at humor are nice to have as a break during boring sections of your lectures.

Making Personal Contact

After the first class meeting I always like to talk to as many students as I can right before my lecture starts. This may entail standing by the door just to smile and say hello to individual students as they enter. I also like to make a casual acquaintance with the individuals in the first two rows of the classroom. These are usually your best students and are often the non-traditional students. A problem with many classrooms is that they look the same; you will know you are in the right room when you see these front row students. The students like personal contact; they feel more like individuals. If I am early to a class, I do not stand in front of the class waiting for the starting time but rather walk around to different sections and talk to individual students, which reduces my anxiety and lets me meet more students.

Show No Fear

Do not show any fear of teaching the subject matter or the students will quickly learn not to respect you. Try not to admit that this is your first class on this subject matter. Act like you have been teaching this course for years. If you do not know the answer to a question, tell the students that you will research the best answer and answer the question the next class period. As you gain teaching experience, you will be able to synthesize answers on the spot, but remember: you may be the expert, but you are still human. Students have an intrinsic respect for professors; do not lose your class's respect the first day. Show no fear!

The Class Icebreaker -- What First?

This is it! No more fooling around. What first? Write your name and the course title and course number on the chalkboard. This may seem very simple, but it will relax you and the students will know they are in the right classroom. I always have a few new freshman who do not know the rooms or numbers and think that they are in a physics class. Additionally, most of the students in the room are seeing you for the first time; they can start to make the name-face associations between you, the course, and the room.

In a Small Class

Go around the room and ask each student his/her name, major, year, where he/she is from and what I like to call a "claim to fame"--bungee jumped last weekend, first hang gliding flight, made the football team, Truman scholar, foreign student, traveled over break-- anything they think is special about themselves. This gives you a chance to know the composition of the class by major and year and you can start to learn the names and faces of the students. This also puts the students at ease and allows them to get to know who is in the class and who they might like to meet.

In a Large Class

Ask for a show of hands by year: entering freshmen, typically at least half of the class, then how many sophomores, juniors, seniors and graduate students. This quick impression of the large class allows you to get a feel for the level of the class. Also ask for a show of hands for major; be general, like "engineering," not "civil engineering." This will give you a rough idea of the types of majors to whom you will be lecturing.

I always welcome the new freshmen and give them a short pep talk on how "*these are the good old days*." These are the days of great academic and personal discovery and they should be savored. I also make a few remarks about how these new students need to balance their academic work with other social aspects of college.

Hand Out the Syllabus

In both small and large sections, hand out the syllabus. I usually make an overhead transparency of the syllabus and go over each section; grading, when papers are due, examination dates, assigned chapters, and extra credit. Answer any questions the students have concerning the general format of the syllabus.

Give a Detailed Explanation of the Course

In addition to the syllabus, what exactly is expected from the students and how will they be evaluated? This should take the entire first period. During this time, you will be giving the students their first impression of your teaching style. The students will often evaluate this first encounter in terms of how enthusiastic you appear to be during your first meeting. Do not be phoney, but be sharp for this first class. The students want an objective class; be as fair as possible with the students and treat them as adults. A brief overview of the class will also give the students their first introduction to your lecturing style.

Explaining Grades

Grades are always a major part of the student's concerns. Be as objective and fair as you can with grades. You have been in graduate school for many years, often in a different part of the country, and you may not be familiar with the level and student expectancy concerning grades at your new school. Take the time to ask both students and faculty what is an average grade for this class, department, and institution. After you get to know the class better, tell them that it is not the grade that counts, but rather the knowledge they gain from the course. Evidence of this principle can be found in the Graduate Record Examination (GRE) and the job that you are now trying to prepare them for. They will hope they paid attention in all those undergraduate classes when the real evaluations come in the future, not some letter grade. Structure the course to be as fair as possible.

Care About Your Students

Students also want an instructor who cares about the students as individuals and attempts to understand their problems. I always think of the students as my responsibility and it is my duty to do as much as possible to help them through this first course in psychology. This may entail conferences in my office, help in finding tutors, calming the students prior to a test, or just understanding the problems of being an entering freshman or returning non-traditional student. I enjoy seeing *my students* several years later graduate from the university; many become acquaintances during their college days. See Chapter 8 for more details.

Do Not Bore the Students

Finally students do not want to be bored. Students already have plenty of boring classes in the large lecture situations; let yours be their best freshman experience. You do not have to be a stand-up comic, but try to lighten up the lectures with a little humor. This humor can take many forms, from jokes about college sports teams, politics, and local problems to overheads of cartoons from the newspaper. Have a little fun with the students; it will do both of you some good.

Things to consider when Structuring Your Class

The following are some suggestions about how to maximize the impact of your presentations when designing your class.

1. Come prepared. Do not let the class flow without structure. Have a lecture planned and stick to it. The use of learning points is a good method to give structure to the class.

2. Always start the class on time. If you are late, the students will learn when class really starts and they will start to come later and later to class. Make the first several minutes very important; talk about the next examination and give specific details about projects. Make the material relevant to the text so that students who are ready and taking notes will be rewarded.

3. Try to avoid open ended philosophical questions in large introductory classes. The students typically do not care about the meaning of life, animal rights or ethical applications of psychological principles. In smaller upper-division classes these types of questions can be very productive. Ask questions that do not require a large amount of background knowledge. These introductory students will not have the necessary background to answer very complex questions.

4. Respect your students. You have finally achieved some status in your academic area, but do not try to reduce your frustrations with other faculty during your graduate career by showing disrespect for your students. Remember, they are you several years earlier.

5. Establish that you are in charge of the class. Do not let students talk or be disruptive in class. Occasionally, there will be a student who asks questions that seem inappropriate to the main thrust of the class. If this student persists, ask the student to save his or her question for after the class. It is relatively easy for students to get their instructor off track and onto a tangent. Most students can figure out that this tangential material will not be on the examination, and some students will try to direct your attention from the lecture.

6. Use terminology that is appropriate for your students' level. Do this both in your lectures and in examinations. When 50 percent of the class asks the meaning of a specific term on an examination, you know that the level is inappropriate.

7. When writing your examinations for introductory classes, be as specific as you can. Make the questions easier than you think they need to be. You have just learned the material at a level the instructor must master, not an entering freshman.

8. Do not write tricky questions on your examination. If a student knows the material, he or she wants to receive credit for a correct answer. Do not be obscure in your wording or syntax.

9. When writing an examination, be sure that the material on the examination will be covered. I usually leave about 1/2 of a lecture off the examination to be sure I cover all the material. As you teach the class, you will learn how much material you can cover in a specific time period. It is always better to be short on the last lecture rather than long. You can always start the first lecture after an examination, but be sure that you tell the students where the material for the current examination ends in the class notes.

10. Minimize the turnaround time for test grading. If you are giving multiple choice questions, have them scored as soon as possible. With essay tests, I like to schedule the test for a Friday so I can have the test scored by Monday morning.

11. Encourage students to challenge any questions they do not understand or think they answered correctly on the examination.

12. Encourage students to check their answers against the key and their posted score. If there are discrepancies, again encourage the students to stop by your office to check their score.

13. Ask the students to either write down areas of the lecture that they do not understand or to come to your office to discuss areas that are not clearly understood. You can clarify any recurring questions at the beginning of your next lecture.

14. Encourage non-traditional students. These can be students over traditional age, foreign students, English as a Second Language students, individuals with special needs, and persons with both physical and learning disabilities. I like to take the time to help these students and encourage them as much as possible. In many cases, they are just starting and have relatively low self-esteem.

Introducing the Required Materials

The Text and Ancillary Materials

Introducing the text and ancillary materials is best accomplished by simply bringing them to the first class meeting. Hold the text up and explain that this is the only text that will work for this class, not the last edition of a friend's from a different class. Also have the study guide and any other ancillary materials you recommended or required for the course. If you have these materials on reserve at the library, which I recommend, tell the students their location and how long they may check out the materials. If you want a little humor at this point, say something like, "I put these materials on reserve so that if any of you have a course cancelled and you did not bring your psychology text, you can use the reserve text for a couple of hours of study." Many students will think this is funny.

The Add/Drop Problem

You will probably be flooded with students wanting to add your course. Is the course full? You should know this before the first class by checking the computer printouts available from your departmental secretary. Ask your supervisor what the departmental policy is for adding students to your class. Follow the procedure and use these procedures as a justification for not adding students. Many students will have desperate stories as to why they must add your class. If you have any discretionary power to add students, think about what is a valid reason to add the class, e.g., seniors needing the class to graduate, working single mothers, college sports team members, those needing a prerequisite for upper division classes, or new psychology majors. Decide the types of justifications you will allow and devise a method of selecting students who fulfill these requirements to add the course. If there are many students wanting to add the class and few seats left in class, conduct a lottery; at least this is a fair method. You will have a number of drops/no shows for each class. Ask your department chair or supervisor what percentage you can expect to be on your final roll at the end of the term and add the approximate number to fill the class. Be careful not to overfill a class, or you will have students sitting in the aisles at the examinations. Sign all drop slips and note the number for your records. Be firm with students who have missed the first class and want to add when they stop by your office; tell them the class is full. The add/drop system is very frustrating.

Evaluate Your First Teaching Experience

Return to your office and review your first day's performance in class. What were the high points? What makes you want to return to the next class? Also, what were the low points? How could you improve these low points? Write these suggestions down and put them in your introductory meeting folder. Next term you will already have improved your course and can make these changes. I use a folder for each section of lecture including the introduction to the class.

Go home and celebrate! But not too much; remember, you have to write next week's lectures tomorrow.

5

Examinations

Most colleges and universities use traditional systems of evaluating students. Included in these methods of evaluation are the use of examinations.

Ramblings about the Grading System

For many students the emphasis on receiving a letter grade next to his or her name on a transcript is even more obnoxious today than in previous generations of students. Many students believe that the short-term reinforcement of receiving a high grade in a course is the major reason for attending college. To that end, students will go to great lengths to receive a high grade in your course. On the first day of class when I mention grades, while discussing the syllabus, I tell the students that they all have one hundred percent of the course points and thus an "A" in the course. Now all the students have to do is not lose points on the examinations. I like the idea of subtracting points for errors rather than adding points for correct answer. So now to receive the coveted "A" grade all the students have to do is not lose any points on the examinations. I have often thought this minus points system would be a superior system.

Students are like any other organism in the Skinner Box. They will learn the minimum amount necessary to receive the reinforcement. The method that you use to structure your examinations can modify the students' behavior. If students learn that all they need to do is read the summaries an hour before the test, they will do only this. If they can get the notes from a friend and receive the grade they want, then that is what they will do. If a student can get the old test and pass the course, then that is what they will do. When writing examinations, you must try to modify these behaviors. One of your central tasks is to give the students a general overview of the material.

Several methods can be employed to assure attendance. The first is course points for attendance; this method may work in high school but probably not in many colleges. Home work can be based specifically on the material from the previous lecture, which can include developing test items for the examinations. I prefer to write items for the examinations that are specific to the lectures. I tell the students that one third of the items on an examination will be specific to the lecture. This reinforces coming to class and note taking. I try to write these items so that only the individuals who were in class are likely to get the correct answer, not the students who got the notes.

If your department or school has a policy of percentages equaling a certain letter grade, (A=90%, B=80%..) be sure you are aware of this policy and conform to it. In order to help alleviate tension on the first day of class and to give the students a feel for my teaching philosophy, I tell the students that the grades they receive are not important but the knowledge gained in the class is important. At this point, they usually laugh or at least want to. Eventually many of these students will understand that this short-term reinforcer of a letter grade is not all that a college education encompasses. A very good example is when taking the Graduate Record Examination (GRE). The GRE is a good example of being tested over what you know about a specific subject, not what your grade was in a course. The world of work also does not place any importance on the letter grade in a class, but rather how much you learned in the specific course. Your new employer will expect you to be competent in your field, and if you are not he/she will simply find a new employee who is. Some students won't listen, but tell them anyway. Many students will say they "need" the grade to get into graduate school, some professional school, or an upper division course in their undergraduate major. Perhaps we should have fewer professionals who "need" a grade this much.

You have, no doubt, just completed some aspect of your education and could have been one of these individuals who was too interested in grades. Let's see how good you are at telling students that grades are not the most important aspect of a college education.

Examinations

Types of Examinations

When considering the type of examination to give in your course, there are several factors that should be taken into account. First, consider the amount of time that you or, in the best case, your teaching assistant will have to spend in the preparation of the examination and then the grading of the examination. In my experience, I have found that there appears to be a negative correlation between the amount of time spent constructing the examination and the time grading it. For example, essay examinations may be one sentence long but it may take an hour to grade each student's answer, while a multiple choice question may take 10 minutes each to develop but involve no grading time by you or your assistants if you use computer scoring.

Many times the choice of the type of question on an examination is limited by the class size: large classes (over 50 students), multiple choice; medium classes (30 to 50 students), short answer, matching, fill-in-the-blank, or multiple choice; and for small classes (fewer than 30 students), essay questions are possible and you can also use a combination of the other methods mentioned above. In a large class, multiple choice questions are the only possible choice with the number of TA's available to many instructors. It should be noted that all alternatives that are practical should be used to evaluate the students. Evaluating a student's knowledge of as many aspects of psychology as possible is the most effective method of gaining a true representation of the actual knowledge of the student. The adoption of journals is an alternative method of evaluation that does have promise. I have tried to develop strategies to use students to self grade or grade other students' written work, although this can be very difficult. Finally, an additional consideration when selecting your type of examination is the level of the students as discussed in Chapter 2.

Construction of Examinations

Essay Questions

Essay questions should require the students to integrate the class notes and the text materials. Additionally, this type of examination will focus on the analysis of the problems being discussed and, in some cases, the applications of the principles that have been introduced.

Essay questions provide the most information about the depth of knowledge of the subject matter. The main disadvantages of this format are the amount of time needed to grade each student's examination, the focus of many essay questions, and the subjective nature of this type of evaluation. I have found that this form of evaluation should be limited to three items per hour. With essay questions, you will know the depth of knowledge of the students on a few select topics. This form of evaluation also has a subjective nature; the answers are not correct or incorrect but are shaded between the two. Students will often challenge points on essays examination because they believe that there may be several correct answers or lines of reasoning. The students usually feel a perfect score on an essay item is more easily attained than the instructor does.

Short Answer Questions

Short answer formats, which include short answer questions, fill-in-the-blank, and matching items are a good method of evaluation because they allow for a wide range of topic coverage; you may have up to 20 short answer formatted questions per hour. This breadth will give the first-time instructor the opportunity to evaluate how well the class is progressing in terms of the students' understanding of the principles introduced to this point. If possible this type of format can be developed to be computer scored.

Multiple Choice Questions

Your psychology package will include a test item file keyed to the text. This test item file is very important. In your initial evaluation of the "package" that is included with the text, you should spend time evaluating the test item file. I will not adopt a text until I have the current test item file in hand and I can evaluate how well the questions are written. Many test item files will break down the items in terms of difficultly: easy, medium and difficult. Additionally, some texts look at the type of information the specific item examines: basic knowledge, application, connections between chapters, or critical thinking. Many test item files are keyed to the text pages. This is helpful if a student challenges the item on the examination. I usually will not adopt a first edition of a text because the test item file is usually weak and the coordination between the test item file, student study guide, and instructor resource manual is weak. It is your initial task to evaluate this test item file or you may find yourself writing your own items. This is a task you should do for your lecture portion of the text, but it is an extra burden for the rest of the examination.

A new feature of Prentice Hall packages is the *Core Test Item File*. This test item file has been developed and has several interesting features. First, this test item file can be used with any text. These items are core items that cover areas common to all psychology texts. A second feature is that all the questions have been class tested and the summary statistics are presented with each item. Finally, this *Core Test Item File* gives the instructor a second test item file pool to draw items from. This *Core Test Item File* is also an excellent source of items that can be modified to cover materials in your lectures.

A second source of questions that is often overlooked is the students themselves. Ask the students to write their own items and submit them to you as part of a homework assignment. You can then choose the items that you like and use them on the examination. I usually like to limit these items to less than 25 percent of the items on the examination. These student-generated items will tend to be very subject matter specific and at a higher level than the items in the test item file provided by the publisher. If this multiple choice question writing is an option in your course or an extra credit assignment, usually only the better students will submit questions.

Number of Items for a Multiple Choice Examination

I have found that most of my introductory students can tolerate one item per minute for up to 60 minutes. Anything over this number and they have trouble finishing; anything less is too easy and could limit coverage of the material. I would rather have several smaller multiple choice examinations than a very long examination, and so would most students.

Using the Test Item File

The first thing I do when I receive my test item file is write or rubber stamp my name on the inside cover and on the outside edge of the test item file. Next, I decide where I will leave the test item file in my office for the school term. This is important because misplacing a test item file can be very frustrating while trying to construct an unbiased examinations. Did you lose the test item file? Did someone steal it? Where is it located now? These are not the kinds of questions you want to lose sleep over. A compromised test item file is worthless and cannot be used. I always put the test item file back in its place!

When I am choosing items for the test item file for my examination, I use a colored pen and write the school term, year, and section at the top of the first page of each section in the test item file. F95 (02)_____. Then I mark each item I want to include in the examination in the test item file with the same color pen. If you have multiple sections, use different colors for each section. This method is easy for the person doing the physical test construction and allows you to have a graphic representation of the items already used in the test item file. After I have the items marked, I count them and write the total with the same pen next to the term, year and section. I use the same test item file as long as I use the text; this helps reduce using the same items over and over and also lets you know when your test item file is used up. A major reason I change texts is that the test item file is used up. At my school we teach seven large sections a year and most test item files will be used up after one year, assuming no repeated questions. The use of the *Core Test Item File* can extend both the life of the usable non-repeated questions and the quality of your test items.

Computer Test Scoring

A good tip is to go to the test scoring center and meet both the supervisor and the individuals who do the computer scoring. If possible have them show you the facility and explain how the equipment works. Since many of these computer centers are located in the basement of the library, it is good to remember life in the basement of the library can get really dull and anyone showing interest in the scoring process will be remembered. Someday you may need to have a quick special run of test scores; hopefully, these staff members will remember your visit favorably.

Writing Your Own Multiple Choice Examination Items

For the first time instructor, writing your own multiple choice items may be very difficult. I would recommend writing these items only for your lecture questions in the beginning. When writing your own items, a good strategy is to limit the number of distractors (incorrect answers) to three. A four-choice item examination is enough to have questions that will probe the student's level of knowledge. I like to limit the use of "all of the above" or "none of the above" as the last alternative to a maximum 15 percent of the items and I try to be careful not to establish a pattern of having these items always being correct or never being correct. When writing your own items, be sure not to follow a pattern in your answers like using the "C" alternative as the correct alternative too much of the time. Make the correct alternatives as random as possible. After some practice, try writing a few questions from the text material. This is most easily accomplished by modifying current examination questions from the test item file. The *Core Test Item File* is particularly valuable because it contains statistics on each item and distractor. When you write your own items, be sure that the items covering material questions are a significant part of the materials in the text. Often I find myself being too specific when writing this type of item; the students will often perceive very specific items as unfair and not a good sample of their knowledge. Be sure to use language that is appropriate to the sub-field of psychology under study and the level of your students. We all become locked into our research fields and must make an effort to re-learn the vocabulary of the other sub-fields. Avoid trick questions; the students will not like them, although the best student will often get these questions. Don't make the items so difficult that none of the students can get the answer correct. Remember that a multiple choice item is designed to separate the students who know the concept from those who do not. If the item is too hard, no student gets the correct answer except the students who guess; this is the worst case. A difficult aspect of writing good multiple choice questions is writing good distractors, which are the wrong answers. Spend time writing the distractors; distractors are what separate the good students from the poor students.

How to Identify a Good Test Item File

When you receive your sample test item files from several publishers, how can you tell which is a good test item file? I use several criteria in the evaluation. First, I look at the number of items per chapter. One hundred is the minimum I would accept in a test item file. I then move to a chapter that the students have problems with. My students have problems with the physiological psychology and learning chapter. I then evaluate some random items. Some of the questions I ask can include ones concerning the correctness of the grammar and syntax. Is the level of the vocabulary similar to the text? Are the items evaluated it terms of , high, medium and low levels. Are they evaluated in terms of content, basic knowledge, and applications? Do the items contain many, all of the above or none of the above? Too many of this type answer many means the test item file author was running out of distractors or in a hurry to finish. Does this test item file have the same amount of coverage per topic as the text? I also like to evaluate the student study guide and the instructor's resource manual to see if they have been coordinated. A subjective question might be how does the test item layout look? Is it attractive? Are the answers associated with each question located on the same page? I hate turning to the back of the test item file to find the answers to the questions. Finally, how many editions has this test item file been through? The more the better is not always a good indicator, but it is better than nothing. I avoid first editions.

Writing Short Answer Questions: General Case

Writing true/false, matching, fill-in-the-blank, short answer, and oral items can be difficult for the new instructor. I would first try to locate examples in your test item file or student study guide and use these as a guide in your writing. If the questions are specific to your lecture, try a few of these types of questions on your first examination. As you gain experience writing these types of questions you will be able to expand the quantity and types you can use. Start off slow and see what works for you and your class.

I use the following information about examination questions as a guide for these types of items.

True/False Items

True/false items are difficult to write because the item must be 100 percent true or false. Any exception to the true or false case negates the answer. Students are very good at finding the one example that will negate your question. I should know; I was doing this all the time as an undergraduate. Try a few true/false questions and be lenient on individual exceptions when grading.

Matching Items

Of the two basic strategies with matching items, one is to provide the same number of matching items as answers; this is the easiest type of item, particularly when you do not know the last correct answers. The other alternative is to provide more answers than there are matching items; this can become a very difficult type of examination if properly done. Try a brief matching type question on your examination and expand as you become more familiar with the types of matching items that work best.

Fill-in-the-Blank

Fill-in-the-blank can be an effective method of testing; this is like a multiple choice item without the choices. These can vary from easy to extremely difficult, depending on your ability to write the items and the level of your students. Look in the student study guide for good examples of fill-in-the-blank items. These items are often used by the students as examples of test questions and should be used more in examinations.

Short Answers

Short answers are just that--short answers. You can limit the amount of space available for the answer on the examination and thus the length of the answer by listing several items per page and leaving the amount of space between each item as the only area for the answer. The short answer format should be used to ask very specific questions for which the students will need limited time and space to answer.

Oral Examinations

This is the most rigorous type of testing. You will always remember your oral defense. This type of evaluation can be used for small classes where the instructor wants to know the limits of the student's knowledge. It is very stressful for the students, but this method will let you see the limits of the knowledge the students have acquired in the class. Depending on class size, this could possibly be used as the final examination for the course.

How Many and What Type of Questions

Ask other instructors what types and level of questions they use in their examinations and use their response as a guide for your examinations. A nice mix of all the types of questions listed above will test all facets of the student's knowledge, but this method is impractical in most large classes. Experiment with the mix and find the best combination for you and your students. Remember, your first examination does not have to be perfect, so don't worry. When constructing examination items, try to plan ahead how these items will be scored. Can you use a template or computer scoring, or must you use the standard TA working on the weekend method? The more efficient you are in the planning stages, the easier the grading will be.

When to Evaluate

Timing of the Examinations

Students see examinations as a very important aspect of their education, probably due to their overemphasis on grades. In order to calm the anxiety that students often feel concerning examinations, I like to have several examinations each term. I will divide the term into thirds or possibly quarters with each section culminating in an examination; this allows for at least one examination prior to course withdrawal periods. If a student fails an examination for whatever reason, he or she can drop the course without penalty. This withdrawal period allows students to have a second chance in school rather than simply flunking out the first term. This early examination gives the students the opportunity to find out what kind of examinations to expect for the rest of the term and allows them to modify their study habits in order to maximize their examination scores.

After the first examination I offer students the opportunity to come to my office to receive some special study material I have collected over the years. These materials help students organize their studying and give them tips on how to study. I also can give them advice on tutors and study groups. These students are typically good students that want to learn but lack the skill; many improve drastically with the next examination. I track these students by asking them how they did on subsequent examinations.

Picking the Right Number of Examinations

Frequent short examinations (I prefer four or five per semester) are a better plan for an Introductory Psychology course as opposed to the older traditional format of a midterm and a final, which all students hate, including this former student. Several short examinations provide maximum feedback and a chance to change study habits in order to accommodate to the requirements you are placing on the students.

The Final Examination

Most schools still have some sort of final examination requirement, usually occurring after the conclusion of the regular teaching term. Many schools have dropped the compromise final exam, but your school may still require this examination. Check with your supervisor or department chair.

I prefer some form of a non-comprehensive examination for a final. I try to allow the students to choose the materials they prefer for their final; of course, this must be thought out in the planning of the course. One method is to group chapters not assigned during the course and then allow students to pick one group that is of special interest to the student. I like to have at least three groups of two chapters to choose from. An alternate method could be to have a group of additional readings the student could choose from for the final. Allowing the students to choose their final examination material is a nice touch. The students get to study some aspect of psychology that you did not have time to cover in the regular term. The students like this freedom to choose a topic of interest for further study. Although the logistics can be a little frightening with a large class, try this system. When using multiple topic finals, I ask the secretary to produce each individual examination on a different color of paper. I arrive at the final ten minutes early and set up chairs in the front of the classroom. The number of chairs is equal to the number of choices on the final. I then tape a sign to each chair stating the examination number or chapters covered by each final. I then put the corresponding examinations on the corresponding chairs. Then I hand out the computer scoring sheets (if used) and have each student mark an unused area of the scoring sheet with a special code, in case of a mix up of the scoring sheets. This code can be anything, but the number of the final examination group (e.g., 1,2,3,4) is the easiest. When the students have finished filling out the computer sheet I emphasize that the students **must** pick up the examination of their choice from the specific chair it is located on and (this is the important part) when they have completed the final, they must return the computer scoring sheet to the same chair. I use a little threat and tell them some of the horror stories of students who failed to comply and thus received a grade of "F" instead of an "A" because they put their computer sheet on the wrong chair. Be very careful that you have the correct computer scoring key for the correct pile of computer scoring sheets. I use a binder clip to separate the completed examinations with the answer keys on the top of each pile of computer scoring sheets. If you can, try this system of choice on the final; the students really like it.

Testing in a Large Class

Selecting the Type of Questions

With large classes you will almost surely use some form of multiple choice or objective computer-scored examinations. I always deliver the computer scoring sheet myself to the computer scoring center; these examinations are sensitive and should not be in any way compromised. During the planning phase of your course, at the computer scoring center, ask for the types of statistics you can expect to get with your examination scores. They will vary from school to school, but get as much data as you can with each examination. If your school can produce bi-serial r statistics, they can be useful in evaluating your own test items.

Cheating in the Large Class

Cheating can be a problem in the large class. I simply round up four or five TAs and instruct them to help proctor the examination. If you are lucky, the proctoring of your examinations will be considered part of the TAs' assignments and you will not have to attend the examinations. I would still attend at least the beginning of the examination period to make sure the examination begins smoothly. At the beginning of the examination I give the students a short "do not cheat" lecture intended to let them know what to expect if you catch them cheating. I have found that the sheer mass of the TAs' presence will stop most cheating. Also see Chapter 6 for more on cheating.

Testing in a Small Class

Selecting the Type of Questions

In a small class you can use any or all of the types of testing described earlier; the mix is up to you. In these small sections, I would suggest you avoid multiple choice items if possible. The other forms of evaluation give a much more complete picture of the student's knowledge of psychology. Additionally, I find that the better students like the more subjective forms of evaluation.

Cheating in the Small Class

In a small class you can proctor the examination yourself; I tend to trust students in the smaller classes because they are still individuals and they feel like they know you and that you trust them. To cheat in a small section is to lose the professor's trust.

General Considerations

Taking the Heat

After every (yes, every) examination, you are likely to have some sort of hostile aggression directed toward you concerning specific examination items. I have developed a system that works quite nicely for deflecting this aggression and turning it into a learning experience. I tell the students with challenges to write their name, student number, and section on a piece of paper, then the question they want to challenge. Next, I tell the students to look up the answer in the text or lecture notes and write a minimum of a paragraph explaining why their answer is at least as good as my choice. This response can include page numbers, quotes from the text or citations from lectures. Finally, I ask them to bring this paper to my office during office hours and we will discuss their questions. This system has several benefits to both the students and the instructor. First, the students have given the incorrect answer at least 95 percent of the time. With this system the students get direct, correct feedback about the concept which allows them to correct their incorrect cognition. These students realize they were initially wrong but now understand the corrected concept. The other 5 percent of the students who still do not like your choice of answer will comply and write down the requested paragraph of explanation. About 2 percent of the students will then show up for the discussion phase of this method. Of the students that show up probably less than half has a valid point and I will award them credit for the specific item on their examination.

But what a great system! I now have a record of why I gave the credit, so I put it in my course grades folder and the grade change stays in the folder until I make changes to my final grades at the end of the term. Yes, a great system! The students like it because you are fair, and it shows you care about the students' understanding of the principles of psychology. Instructors like it because it slows down some of the pressure of students from very large classes. The students get the correct concept and if you decide to give credit, you have a record for your files. Try it! Trust me on this one.

6

Grading

When you were preparing to teach this course, you developed a syllabus that detailed the course requirements. As you developed your syllabus, you took into account the course objectives, school and departmental requirements, and needs of the students. Now that this process has been established, it is time to evaluate the implementation of the course and the students through grading.

Managing the Evaluation System

Developing a Grading System

A grading system must be as fair as possible because students desire and deserve to be evaluated in an equal, unbiased way. Depending on the types of evaluation that you have decided on in the planning stages, these course examinations can range from totally objective multiple choice items to the more subjective essay questions. During any evaluation, the student should always be given the benefit of the doubt. I always err on the side of the student. Each class has its own unique needs and you should develop your system according to these needs.

The Mechanics of Grading

The File Folder Method

Even though this is the Computer Age, I still use the file folder method to keep track of the materials students generate during the course for small sections. Examples of what goes into each class's specific folder are: name lists and summary statistics for each examination (usually computer generated), makeup examinations, dean's excuses for missing examinations, extra credit summary sheets, and credit for successful examination question challenges. Make a separate folder for each section of your psychology classes. This folder should be stored in a safe place, as loss of these materials would be a disaster. Most of these documents are one of a kind and are difficult to replace. Depending on your level of paranoia, you might decide to make a photocopy of these materials. I like the individual student computer sheets and/or examinations to be stored in my office, though not always in a neat and orderly manner. The better your system for finding specific student copies of individual examinations, the better. You will have, on occasion, students who think there is an incorrect score on their individual examination, particularly computer-scored examinations. I have know of two computer scoring errors in the last ten years. However, I have experienced numerous student-generated errors, for example, using a hard lead pencil, not filling in the scoring sheet dark enough, skipping items, and writing in the margins, to name a few. Above all, you must reassure the students that your records are correct. The best method to assure the student that your records are correct is to hand-score their examinations while they are present. Compare the student computer score sheet or examination to the posted answer key. All of these materials are stored in my file folder until the final test is completed, and then I post the changes to the final computer files.

The Computer Method

Several of my colleagues use various computer programs to organize their grades. Most major publishers will include a grading program with their texts. For a small class, using these programs can be a good method, but posting each entry to the computer program can take a lot of time and effort. I prefer to have the computer scoring center keep track of my examination scores until after the final and then update and print a summary sheet for all the students. Check with your test scoring service to see what your options are. In my department, we can interact with the main frame computer with our office computers. We can download all the student files to floppy disks and annotate the files with extra credit, recitation points, journal points, and any other corrections that are necessary prior to printing the final grade list. Spreadsheets are also useful in managing large amounts of data. These computer scoring center files are secured and you will need the passwords or unkeying programs to access these scores. If possible, use this method to save the time of posting and totaling the scores by hand. Ask your supervisor or department chair for programs currently in use in the department.

Examination Item Security

In my large classes, I let the students keep their copy of the examinations. The logic is simple; if someone wants to compromise the questions in the test item file, they will find a way, so I simply give the questions to everyone. If students would work as hard studying the materials as they do trying to scam the testing system, they would be better students. So rather than have the fraternities and sororities be the only ones to have the old examinations, I give the entire school copies. I also have the old test on reserve in the library for students that are not connected to the old test market. Be sure to have the answers to the old test on reserve also .

The Demand for Fast Turn-Around Time

Many students expect rapid turn-around times for examination scores. In order to deal with the problem, I post the answer key immediately after class, in the same location where the examination scores will be later posted. The students can then take their examinations and compare their responses to the answer key to find their score on the examination. I find that about 20-30 percent of the class will check the answer key immediately after the test.

Use the following to help determine the turn-around time for your examinations.

Multiple Choice and True/False Examinations

With computer-scored multiple choice and true/false tests, the turn-around time can be as short as 1 hour, but overnight is usually a safe upper limit.

Short Answer Format Examinations

With short answer, matching items, fill-in-the-blank and essays, the turn-around time is dependent on the number of items and the teaching assistants at your disposal. A good tip is to schedule your examination on a Thursday or Friday so you or your assistant will have the weekend to complete the grading. It is important to have as fast a turn-around time as possible. When constructing the examination, I like to plan for the scoring of the examination. Part of an examination could be scored by computer. Templates can be constructed for fill-in-the-blank and matching items. Try to make the scoring as easy and efficient as possible.

Essay Examinations

Essay examinations take the most time to grade and, depending on the level, may be very time consuming. After your first examination, you will have a better feel for the amount of time required but I would recommend at least 10 minutes for each essay question per student.

These guidelines are intended to give you an idea of the time involved in grading examinations.

Use of TAs for Grading

Try out your TAs by letting them grade a portion of your examination; be sure to be specific as to what you expect from them in terms of grading. Check all of the TAs' work; most of them will try to do a good job but often will grade too severely. I give the TAs feedback about their performance and suggest changes to make them more efficient and accurate. After you are confident that the TAs are grading in the manner that you expect, allow them more and more responsibility. I spot check their grading to be sure the quality remains high. If there are any questions concerning grades the TAs have produced, I am the final authority. If the students have *any* questions concerning a grade on an examination and cannot resolve it with the TA, you must make the decision concerning the grading. I always give the student the benefit of the doubt in these disputed grading situations. I tell my class at the beginning of the term that I will have TAs grading examinations and that any problems are to be brought to my attention.

Posting Grades

Check with the school regulations to see how scores are to be posted. These rules vary from school to school; at my university, student identification numbers are the accepted practice.

Establish a central location to post your examination scores; outside your office door is not the best place since there is a possibility that there will be some disgruntled students after each examination. Also, the other faculty in the office hallways will not appreciate 350 students jammed into the hall trying to find their examination scores. Perhaps your department has a specific location for posting scores. Always use the same location after the first examination. I leave the previous posting up until the hour before the next examination. I am still amazed that some students will look for their last examination score just prior to the next examination. After posting grades, I put the mean and standard deviation on the summary sheet and then mention the mean and standard deviation in the next class.

Criterion vs. Class Curve Grades

The question often arises, "What does an 87 mean?" Of course, the answer depends on the type of grading plan that you developed in the planning stages of your course. You probably chose either a criterion system or a class curve system.

The Criterion System

The criterion system requires the students to perform at a predetermined level for a specific grade. A typical system uses the following distribution: 90% = A, 80% = B, 70% = C, 60% = D and 59% and lower = F. Of course, this system has advantages and disadvantages. On the plus side, you can integrate the final grade criteria into your syllabus and the students know exactly what level they must obtain for a specific grade. A disadvantage is that the level of your examination can be either too easy (everyone gets an "A") or, more likely, too hard (everyone gets a "D" or worse). For a new instructor to use this system, he or she must be careful that the level of difficulty of the examination is appropriate to the level of the students and goals for the class.

The Class Curve System

The class curve system allows the instructor to choose the grade-cutoffs *post hoc*. After looking at the distribution of scores, the instructor can either make the grade cuts by percentage of grades -- 15% = "A", 30%= "B", etc. -- or make the grade cuts by the often naturally occurring trimodal distribution. I plot the data to see the type of distribution for each class. If your class is large enough, the students will typically cluster into three distinct groups (trimodal)-- A, B, and C with the D's and F's trailing the distribution. The class curve system is a good method of establishing grades but it is hard to explain to the students that you just "decide" what the grades are based on the distribution. You will also get more hassle from students who are on the cut line of a grade than if you use the criterion system. I often use the criterion system so the students know the levels of performance required and then reserve the right to lower the cut-off percentages depending on the examination scores. I tell the students in the initial class description if I am going to use this system and additionally, that this system forces the students to compete against each other for a grade, not a predetermined cut-off. With the curve system if a student lets another student cheat, he or she is really hurting his or her chance for a good grade.

Extra Credit

Course Extra Credit

You may decide to allow your students do some projects that you did not plan for at the beginning of the term; offer these tasks as extra credit. Perhaps students wish to explore topics in greater depth; this can provide them with extra credit. One point--be sure that all the students have equal access to the extra credit points and that these points really are extra credit. Add them to the totals only after the grades have been established.

Final Grades--Paper to Paper

Processing Final Grades

At most schools, the administration has not yet developed a system that allows for direct computer input of grades. This often means that you will print out a grade sheet from your computer and then hand copy the grades onto the official registrar's grade roster. This task can be time consuming and boring and can often be more efficiently accomplished with two individuals. Be very careful not to make errors; students with lower grades will always be in your office the day after grades are posted. An even worse problem are the students who get a higher grade and, of course, never report the higher grade. Many schools allow grade changes only in an upward direction, for example, "B" to "A". So the student with the higher incorrect grade must keep the higher grade. Use your TAs to help with the final transformation, but be involved in the work yourself; you are the responsible individual. Double check all grades; find and correct missing examination grades, extra credit, and any other problems that arise. Call the registrar's office for help with the technical problems that arise; you are sure to have grades for students who are not on your roll and students on your roll without grades. Take the time to get this right; this is the last chance to correct any errors. Sign all copies and date each page of the roster as requested by the registrar. If your department does not keep a copy of the grade roster, make a copy for yourself. Be sure to check with the department secretary for the due date for your final grade rosters. Do not be late; students may receive late grade reports and the individuals posting the grades at the registrar's office do not like late grade reports.

Dealing With and Eliminating Cheating

Defining the Parameters of Cheating

Cheating is a constant problem; many times new students really do not understand all of the ways they can be accused of cheating. To help eliminate or curtail this problem, my university has an orientation for all incoming students which attempts to define cheating. Additionally, I always spend some time before the first examination or assignment to reinforce the notion of cheating as defined by my school. If you do not spend this time and the occasion arises that you must accuse an individual of cheating, often the cheater will say he or she did not know he or she was cheating. The most obvious types of cheating include copying another's examination, using crib sheets (many variants), stealing examinations or using a stolen examination from a file system, and/or having another student take his/her examination (a real possibility with a class of 350 students). A myriad of other methods can and will be tried. Laboratory reports are often a source of cheating and can be plagiarized or the work can be done in groups; a good TA can often spot these attempts at group work. Class papers can either be re-typed with the new author's name added, or computers can just make the name change when one pushes the print button. Thoughts can also be plagiarized. Students can use previous writings submitted without references. A final method are paper mill papers. The students simply calls a 800 number and give the subject and credit card number and the paper is in the next day's am express shipment.

What are the best methods to deal with the problem of cheating? The following are a few suggestions you can use to prevent the most common types of cheating. You may discover other types as you continue in your career; be sure to be as fair with the students as possible in resolving these problems.

Copying Other Examinations and Crib Sheets

Instruct your teaching assistants to proctor the examination very closely and warn potential cheaters. Tell them to watch for students using crib sheets or copying from another student's examination. Make cheating as difficult as possible. Ask students to sit in every other seat, if possible. I use parallel forms of the same examination, by randomizing the questions and using two forms of the examination. One of my favorite methods is to print the same examination on different colors of paper and tell the students they are different examinations; this only works once though. If you suspect a student of copying , warn that student. If it persists, confiscate the examination and have the student stay after class. After the examination has concluded, explain the consequences of cheating to the student. This might mean an "F" for this examination, or for the course or, it could mean dismissal from the school. Check your school regulations or faculty handbook for specific procedures and policies. Be very sure that the individual student was cheating; it is best to have at least one (two are better) of your TAs see the incident. Remember, the student may appeal your decision, and you have the least political clout in the department. Be sure.

The Use of Compromised Examinations

The use of compromised examinations to make a "file" of examinations is widespread on most campuses. The solution is to simply change the items for each examination and announce that procedure to the class. Many individuals will not believe you until the first examination, but then they will. Another solution is to try and control the items on the examination. This can be accomplished by giving a number to all examinations and having the students record this number on their examination; after the student turns in the individual examination, check to see if any of the pages are missing. Maintaining a secure test item file is very difficult. This is one of the major reasons that I change texts often: I need a new test item file.

Physical Theft

Physical theft of examinations prior to the class period can be handled in several ways. Count or number all the examinations and store them in a secure area of the department office. Additionally, the computer disks containing test item files and examinations should also be in this secure area. If the examinations are left in your office, do not leave them in public view and be sure to lock your office when you are not there. The possession of a copy of your final examination two days prior to the examination time can make a student rich and famous.

Having Another Student Take the Examination

Require student identification cards for admission to the classroom and have each student sign his/her name at the top of the examination. This substitute student can be a larger problem than you might think, especially in classes where the text and the class notes stay relatively constant. Be sure to mention that the identification cards will be required for admission in the two class periods prior to the examination and in the syllabus. You should be prepared for students who forget their identification cards; one possible strategy is to have the students take the examination and sign the top of the examination and write their identification number. After the examination and before you score the examination, have the student produce his or her identification card and sign a piece of paper in your presence. The student rumor mill will have the news out very quickly that this form of cheating will not work in your class.

Copying Laboratory Reports

The copying of current laboratory reports is very hard to stop; I would allow the students to work in groups and then grade at a higher level.

Recycled Term Papers

Term papers that are re-typed and re-submitted are hard to spot. This is especially true for papers from other sections or schools. If you have any questions about the authorship of a paper, ask the student to bring in the rough draft and the research materials. Do not allow too much time for the student to produce these materials. Non-quoting of references is always a problem and falls in the gray area; use your judgment as to what is copied and what is the use of an idea in the student's own words.

Paper Mill Papers

To stop the use of paper mill papers, assign specific topics that are not likely to be in the paper mill catalog. Assign specific referenced articles or books and instruct students to incorporate these materials in their papers. Paper mill papers are easier to spot than you might think; they are usually vague and never address any specific issue.

After the Cheating Incident

Your school has a written policy for cheating; obtain a copy and read the procedures. This material can either be a separate document or in your faculty handbook. You must follow the specific procedures very carefully because students can challenge your decision and it is your responsibility to prove they cheated. Be sure to have at least one other credible witness. Document the incident and report it to the department chair or course supervisor at once.

How to Administer Examinations

Instructions to the Students

You should clearly indicate whether or not students should guess on the test items, the time limit for the examination, and any other directions appropriate to your examination. I remind the students where the answer keys and computer sheets will be posted at the beginning of the examination. Finally, I would mention the procedure for challenging examination questions (see Chapter 5). With multiple choice test items, I emphasize that the students are to choose the best alternative. I print this statement as a heading on the examination. Many students will try to think of any single specific incident that will make the correct answer invalid; emphasize that the intent of the examination is not to trick students. I have developed a lecture on test taking and studying strategies, which I usually give at least two weeks prior to the first examination. Many entering freshmen have poor study skills; this type of lecture can be very helpful in maximizing their performance on examinations. Many schools have instituted student retention programs; this lecture can be part of this retention program. Ask your introductory supervisor or department chair about this program.

Administering the Examination

If the examination requires a computer scoring form, tell the proctors to pass out the form from both the front and back of the class at the same time. The students in the back of the class can feel cheated because they did not have the same amount of time for the examination as the front of the class. Emphasize how you want the form filled out and the specific areas you want filled in. Announce when the examination will conclude and where students can find the answer key and grade posting. Pass the examinations out in the same manner as the computer scoring sheets. Be as flexible as possible in your testing situations and expect the worst. For example, I have given examinations where I did not have enough copies for the class. What to do? I took several of the examinations, tore off the last half of the pages, and gave them to some of the students with instructions to do the last half first and then raise their hand. By the time the students doing the first half are done, the proctors can switch the halves. Panic, but it worked out. I once had my former secretary staple the wrong last page on an examination; use the same type solution as above. Remember that you have to appear to be in charge even though everything is crashing down around you. If a problem arises and cannot be successfully resolved, ask the specific student affected after the examination if this problem affected his/her grade. Most will say that it did not; if it did, offer a make-up examination.

Encourage Student Questions

I always encourage students to question any aspect of the grading procedure they do not understand. If a student thinks the computer scoring sheet is incorrect, that student should come to my office and we can check the answer. If the student thinks an essay question was graded inappropriately, he or she should come to my office to discuss the problem. I also tell the students that mistakes are occasionally made and that a grade that should be an "A" can turn out to be an "F" by accident Students should always question anything they do not understand. They should not be afraid to come and talk about the problem; you cannot overemphasize this point.

How to Avoid Problems with Examinations

The following suggestions can be implemented as a part of your examination routine. If you follow these procedures, you are less likely to have problems with your examinations. Anything that cuts down the confusion during the examination process is helpful. Try the following suggestions and modify or add your own to the list.

1. Make the answer key and scoring key early and recheck it prior to the examination.

2. Make more examinations (10 percent) than you think you will need. Often there are blanks or unreadable pages or the secretary can miscount. It might seem wasteful, but you will end up using most of the copies and you can always recycle the rest.

3. Bring more computer scoring sheets to the testing site than you think you will need. Returning to your office at the beginning of the examination is one of the worst things that can happen.

4. Make sure your proctors know what you expect from them during the examination. Emphasize that exams are serious; there's no fooling around during the examination.

5. If you have any last-minute corrections (spelling errors or additions/deletions) to the examination, write them on the overhead or chalkboard and call the students' attention to the changes.

6. Designate a clearly defined area where students must turn in the computer scoring sheets and/or examinations. Tell students ahead of time whether they can keep their individual copies of the current examination.

7. I re-read the examination during the testing period, answer all the questions, and compare them against the student answer key and computer scoring key. If you find errors in the scoring keys, you should correct them on the spot.

8. Post the key *after* the examination. If students learn that you post the answer key on the way to class, they will show up 10 minutes late with some answers memorized.

9. Personally take the computer scoring sheets directly to the scoring center; to lose these sheets is an unbelievable hassle.

10. Post the computer scores or examination scores as soon as possible in the predetermined location.

11. Be flexible. If there is a fire alarm, ask students to leave their examinations on their desks and leave the room. What if the lights go off? Try to have some form of orderly evacuation. If you think the examination has been too disrupted, cancel it and schedule a new examination for the next class period. Re-write the examination and hope the roof does not fall in next time.

Make the Examination Fun

Examinations are a necessary part of most college requirements. Rather than dread these examinations, you can look at them as a challenge. They are hard to write, hard to administer, and always challenging to score. Students hate examinations; do your part to instill in these students that examinations can be a fun challenge of their knowledge of psychology. If students can begin to think of examinations as a difficult game show on television, such as *Jeopardy*®, then they might enjoy them more.

7

Alternate Forms of Evaluation

Alternate Forms of Evaluation in the Classroom

These alternate forms of evaluation are intended to supplement the traditional examinations that are given in most schools. Students often like these types of evaluation; you should try to incorporate as many as you can into your course.

Large Classes

In a large class, your options for alternate types of evaluations other than the examination mentioned in Chapter 5 are limited. This limitation is primarily controlled by the number of students; any number over 100 makes alternate forms of evaluation very difficult. Additionally, the number and experience of your TAs can be another limiting factor. An alternate form of evaluation that we use at my university is an interesting model that is being used more throughout the academic community. It entails the use of a large lecture section with smaller recitation sections. This type of structure permits forms of student involvement that do not fit the large course format. At my school, the lecture portion accounts for 85 percent of the course and the recitation sections are 15 percent of the course content. Recitation sections allow for the use of the small personal-type group interactions that students like. See the examples of the types of activities that students can be involved with in the small class section described below.

Small Classes

In small classes or recitation sections, many strategies can be used to involve the students in their learning process. Of course, these alternate methods can be evaluated and given course credit. Try to incorporate as many of these activities as you can in your course; the students like the variety. Use the following types of activities as a starting point for your own ideas.

Case Study

Use case study materials during the class period to evaluate an individual problem. One strategy is to pass out the case study materials at the beginning of the class period and have the large section break down into small 5-or 6-student groups. Ask each group to discuss the case using the lecture and course materials. The intent is to evaluate the individual case study using the tools obtained from the class. If you wish, you can designate a variety of different case study stations where the case studies are different; then after an appropriate amount of time, rotate the groups to the new stations. Students like to look at individual case studies and try to use the information from the course. To evaluate the students, instruct the groups to prepare a short paper and/or presentation for the next class meeting. Evaluate the presentation and/or paper as a group project.

Role Playing

Role playing is a useful strategy for students to gain a feeling for what it must be like to be a different individual with behaviors other than their own. Try leading the class in a role playing exercise; you can be a major player in the exercise. Instruct each student to role play being homeless, a drug addict, a convicted murderer on death row, a person with AIDS, a schizophrenic, or a president of a university that has just received a 25 percent reduction in funding. Use your imagination and use situations that are current and relevant to your students. The closer the roles are to real life, the better. Assign a paper and evaluate each student's paper on what the student has learned from playing the different role. Students will gain useful insights into problems that they otherwise might not be exposed to.

Debate Teams

Debates are an interesting format which can involve the entire class. Form student teams and choose a side on a current topic in psychology. Use any subject that is current and as local as possible; be creative. These debates should be guided by you, the moderator; be careful not to let the debates turn into a shouting match between rival viewpoints. This format is valuable because the students get a different perspective than they would through the standard lecture format. A nice touch is to let the students evolve into groups and pick their own topics, either the pro or con side of the issue. Then reassign the groups to the opposite viewpoint that they have selected. They will hate it at first, but will gain valuable insights about aspects of the topic that they have not yet explored. This method will also help dissolve false stereotypes and misinformation about the subject area. Evaluate the thoroughness of each group's preparation. Additionally, ask the groups to perform a self-evaluation of its individual members. This self-evaluation can be performed by using a form that allows each student to grade another student's effort, input, and contribution to the group's project. The good students like to have the power to evaluate their group members, while the poorer students do not like this type of evaluation.

Panel Discussions

Panels are an additional form of alternate evaluations. The students can form their own panels or you can suggest several topic areas. The students can prepare and present the panel discussion to the rest of the section. Typically each student becomes an "expert" in a sub-area of the topic. The depth of presentation can be very interesting to an introductory course. Evaluate the group presentations as a whole. Instruct the groups to use the self-evaluation process described earlier.

Simulate Group Decision-Making Processes

Tell the students to form groups either by themselves or using your direction. Suggestions for decision-making groups are a military unit in a war situation, a large corporate board trying to make product marketing decisions, a group of athletic coaches plotting a strategy for the next game, or any group with a group goal. Each group must try to reach a group decision on the problem. Then if you have a lecture on the Groupthink process as discussed by Janis (1972), present this lecture. If you do not have a lecture on this topic, this would be a good time to develop such a lecture. Have the students analyze their group decision in terms of the Janis model and look at the ways their decision went right or wrong. This project could take more than one class period to complete, but it is worth the effort; many of these students will be in similar types of group decision-making situations very early in their careers. Evaluate using a group paper on the group decision-making problem encountered by the group. Have each group use the self-evaluation process described earlier.

Small Group Discussions

Pick controversial topics in psychology and then break the class section into small groups (5 or 6 students) and assign each group to discuss the problem and come up with a group consensus about the topic. Then ask the groups to present their findings on the topic; some debate will surely follow, both between and within the groups. Discuss the advantages of parallel versus independent decision making. Emphasize the point that variant ideas are often the best ideas to come out of these activities. These variant ideas often lead to interesting discoveries; use examples like Watson and Crick's discovery of the DNA structure. Evaluate the groups as a whole and in terms of individual participation. Instruct the groups to use the self-evaluation process described earlier.

Brainstorming

Brainstorming is designed to give the students an opportunity to produce as many ideas as they can in a limited time frame. Brainstorming can either be performed in groups or by individuals. Again, pick topics that are controversial. Explain to the students that they are not to be judgmental of their ideas during the first phase of this session. Later the class can evaluate the different approaches to the problem. There will be several ideas that are repeated, but the more interesting ideas are likely to be the novel solutions to the problem. Discuss the latest research on the effectiveness of this method. Evaluate each group as a whole in terms of participation. Groups should use the self-evaluation process described earlier.

Lecture Summaries

Assign specific students to summarize your previous lecture into a 5-minute oral presentation and present it to the class at the start of the period. Use this summary to measure how well your lecture was understood. This process also allows the students to get a different perspective on the materials they encountered in your last lecture. Answer any questions the students have and clear up any misconceptions. Evaluate individuals on oral presentation and depth of understanding of the previous lecture.

Student Oral Reports

Assign students to present oral reports to the class. The topics of the reports should be gently guided. I usually require instructor approval of the topic. Some students will have inappropriate topics and you should guide them into an acceptable area. These reports will give the students valuable experience with oral presentation. The class will receive information on topics that they have had little or no exposure to in the course. Additionally, the level can vary with these student reports so the students will receive a very different level of information than they are used to in the lectures. Evaluate individuals on oral presentation and depth of understanding of the material.

Student Individual Oral Examinations

Ask students to present individual oral examinations on specific topics in your office or other appropriate venue. Evaluate the depth and breadth of knowledge of the subject material. This method also allows for immediate feedback.

(This classification system was partially adapted from Allen and Rueter 1990).

These methods are primarily designed for small classes or recitation sections of larger classes. Their use represents a different approach from the traditional testing format usually employed in most courses. The students will like these types of evaluations. You can use these in a combination with other traditional forms of evaluation to add interesting features to your class.

Alternative Evaluations: Large and Small Class

Another major group of alternative evaluations suitable for the large class without recitation groups or the small class consists of written assignments that students complete on their own time.

The Classic Written Assignment

Assign each student to write an essay, from a short two pages to a maximum of 20 pages. The primary limiting factor in the length of the essay is the amount and quality of TAs you have access to in your department. If you have a small class, you can read all of these essay assignments yourself; in a large class, you must have support. Topics should be open but must have instructor approval. I help the students with references for materials, where to look for specific articles, journals, books and suggestions as how to start their essays.

Structured Journals

The use of structured journals keyed to specific materials in the text and lectures is a valuable method of insuring that students keep up with the reading assignments. The students will have to think about the issues you present to write their journal entries; evaluate the entries in terms of your lectures and the text materials. The students will like this form of evaluation because it allows them to work at their pace, to think about issues in psychology, and use these journal entries as a method of studying for tests.

Unstructured Journals

Assign the students to write on topics they feel are important to them personally. Explain that these entries must be focused on the context of the materials encountered in the text and lectures. This type of journal entry allows students to think about personal problems or situations in a new light--psychology. These types of journals are best evaluated on a submitted/nonsubmitted basis, because there can be no right or wrong answers.

Diaries

Instruct the students to keep unstructured daily diaries of their personal experiences and feelings. This form of exercise encourages students to think about what they have done and how they feel. These types of writings are best evaluated on a submitted/nonsubmitted basis, because there can be no right or wrong answers

(This classification system was partially adapted from Allen and Rueter 1990).

Some of the projects mentioned above will fall into the category of collaborative assignments, with groups of individuals working on a common project. Be sure to be very specific as to what you expect from this effort. Give examples and feedback about the projects. How you evaluate this type of written material is up to you; course points, pass/fail, or credit for turning the assignments in are all alternatives.

Many students prefer this type of evaluation over traditional examinations. A mix of both the traditional and the alternative evaluation is probably the best method for most instructors. As you gain experience with your teaching, try different alternate forms of evaluations to see which works for you and the students. Do not be afraid to experiment with these alternatives.

8

Interacting with Students

Understanding Students

When interacting with students, it is important to know the capabilities of the students you are attempting to teach. If you are new to the school, ask other instructors for their opinions about the students and their capabilities. Determining the appropriate level to teach the course materials is always a difficult problem. Teaching at a high level will lose students of modest abilities, but teaching at too low a level will lose students with greater abilities. Finding the correct presentation level of the material may be one of the more difficult aspects of adapting to your new teaching position. If you are a former undergraduate at your school, you will already have a good idea as to the level of understanding of the students. I have found that many new instructors tend to teach at levels that are too high in their first classes; they also assume they will be able to cover more material than they really can. Knowing the capabilities of the students can be critical to the success of your course.

Finding the Level

Go to the registrar's office and ask to see the summary statistics of the test scores and profiles for the entering freshman class, since these individuals are the majority of the students you will have in your Introductory Psychology classes. This material can also be useful for upper-division classes. These statistics should include ACT and/or SAT scores along with other local forms of high school evaluation. Pay particular attention to the ACT and SAT scores; these are national tests and can be used as a rough measure of the incoming freshman class's ability. Look to see how your school ranks in the national norms.

Compare the ranking of your current school with your previous undergraduate and graduate schools. This comparison is a rough measure of the differences in levels at which you were taught as an undergraduate/graduate and the target level of your teaching. Adjust your expectations of your students' academic abilities accordingly.

Another major source of information comes from TAs, other instructors, and your introductory course supervisors. Take the time to meet with these individuals and ask specific questions about the abilities of the students and the level of instruction that other instructors have adopted in the past.

Another source of knowledge about students' abilities are the students themselves. If your course starts in the fall term and you are on campus over the summer, go to the freshman orientation meetings and talk to the new entering freshman students. Ask specific questions about what they expect from your course, your department, and college in general. These students probably will not have specific answers, but you can gain a feeling for how the students will perform at different levels of expectation. If possible, sit in on a few representative introductory lectures given by other instructors in your department and other departments at your new school. These lectures may not be the most interesting ones you have attended while in college but they are a valuable source of what the students expect from a class in terms of level.

Relating to Students

One of the skills you will have to develop in order to be an effective teacher is the ability to relate to the students, both at the professional level and the social level. With undergraduates, you will interact mostly at the professional level but with graduate students there can be more social interaction. The following are types of students you are likely to meet in your first class. At large state universities like my own, the diversity of students can be tremendous; there will be traditional, shiny-faced freshmen, older vocational rehabilitation students, returning housewives, returning graduates looking for career changes, high school drop outs, former military personnel, laid off construction workers, and even former homeless individuals. Overlay this diversity with the ethnic, racial, economic, religious and regional influences and the mix of students is enormous. I like the diversity of the students in the public university school system. These students do not all dress and act the same. The mix is always refreshing; when you first walk into the class, there are *individuals* there, not row after row of clones.

The following attempt at a classification system of students is intended to subdivide students into major specific types that I would expect you to encounter in the classroom. This classification system resembles the trait system of classification of characteristics used by psychologists in the 1950s. Many students will show some of each classification but few will have only one. Use this stereotyping system to look at the types of students you are likely to meet. I would draw on this information to devise a plan to deal with these "types" of students before you meet them. Knowing how to deal with specific student types prior to encountering them in the classroom is very helpful. You should think of specific responses to the types of problems these students can generate. Additionally, decide how you are going to deal with a room full of a specific "type" student.

This list of stereotypes is not intended to offend any individual but rather to give you a sense of the types of students that you may encounter in your classes.

The Self-Motivated Student

Self-motivated learners, found more likely among juniors and seniors than freshman, are able to formulate their own educational objectives. Most self-motivated students are able to think creatively, participate in class easily, and feel comfortable socially with instructors. Such students prefer independent study, self-paced instruction, problems requiring independent thought, self-designed projects, and student-centered classroom settings. Self-motivated students, while not in need of day-to-day attention, do require an intelligent and caring mentor to ask questions and to provide encouragement. If you can find the time to sponsor a student of this type, the rewards will be great. Many times these students are taking introductory classes late in their academic career; they may find the material at too low a level.

The Respectful Student

Respectful learners enjoy taking college courses and have great respect for their professors. They ask good questions in class and often seek out the professor for additional information. They are innately excited about learning, and they pursue new knowledge with vigor. Respectful learners are a joy for the instructor. They can be counted on to be eager participants in class discussions and to be leaders in small group activities. Frequently an older non-traditional returning student fits this type. These students will often sit in the front rows of the classroom; they do not want to miss anything. These students rarely miss class lectures.

The Submissive Student

Submissive students expect the instructor to tell them what to do. They expect to come to class, to sit quietly, and to take notes. They neither expect nor desire to interact directly with the instructor. While some professors may welcome a classroom full of submissive students, taken to an extreme this type of student offers little intellectual or emotional satisfaction for instructors. Whatever the method used, the instructor needs to encourage submissive students to present their own views rather than simply regurgitate the ideas presented to them. These students often like to get "lost" in the crowd in the center of the classroom; they feel secure when no one can see them.

The Paranoid Student

Paranoid students are like submissive students in that they want to be spoon-fed. The main difference is that they are afraid they will miss the feeding. Paranoid students live in fear that they will miss something; they therefore constantly ask the instructor to repeat definitions and concepts. Paranoid students frequently are competitive and exhibit high levels of ambition, anxiety, and suspicion. These students will often "hang around," either after class or in the hall, or they will walk with you back to your office. It is easy for professors to become irritated with paranoid students since they interrupt the instructional flow to request that information be repeated or more fully elaborated than the rest of the students in the class. Paranoids also imply that the instructor is out to get them by being vague or that the instructor intends to be picky by testing for trivial information. These students are frequently the first at your door to challenge examination questions and often the last to admit that they are incorrect. When dealing with paranoid students, the instructor should assure them that tests will involve major concepts and will be fair. Sample questions from previous tests may even be distributed to all class members to assure the paranoid that all is well. You will often find paranoid students who want to know the correct answer to question #47 from a previous test. I assure these students that this item will not be on the current examination, but they insist that this information will give them an advantage. They are likely to increase the frequency of interactions as the examination draws near. I have had calls at home at midnight asking for the answer to an examination question I gave 12 months earlier; I usually just say the answer is "C" and leave the phone off the hook. Having done as much as possible to calm the paranoid in class, the instructor should ask the persistent paranoid to stop by after class so that his or her questions may be answered without taking up class time. Since the paranoid student thrives on praise, the instructor may wish to provide some when it is deserved. This type of student will fight to get a front row seat in order to demand your attention.

The Silent Student

Many undergraduates are the silent type. Fearful of saying something stupid, they choose instead to remain silent. They blend into the background as much as possible during the class period. The instructor should not ignore or give up on silent types but should instead attempt to create a friendly and supportive classroom atmosphere that will encourage these students to participate. Instructors may have students discuss questions or issues in small groups so the silent-type will be more likely to participate. In whole-class discussions early in the semester, the instructor may ask such students questions that call for a yes, no, or other limited response. Later in the semester, after the student has acquired confidence, questions calling for an elaborated response may be asked. Be careful not to push too hard with these students; they will usually simply try to escape the situation. Being lost in the crowd is what makes these students feel good; they tend to sit in the middle of the class in order not to be noticed.

The Partying Student

Students who are "party-ers" enjoy the social aspects of class. Party-ers love to talk. Often this student functions in class as the social leader. Additionally, these students view classes as meeting places rather than learning environments. They are attention-seekers for whom social concerns are more important than intellectual matters. Party-ers can perform ably in class if they are given what they seek: attention. Instructors can let party-ers distribute handouts, organize a schedule for student oral reports, or present a summary of a previous class period. By giving party-ers recognition, instructors can provide the necessary motivation for them to achieve intellectual goals in addition to social ones. These students usually sit toward the back on the side of the class in the company of like-minded students. This position allows them to talk during class and exit rapidly so they can begin the "party" immediately.

The Unprepared Student

Some students simply lack what it takes to make it in college, due at least partially to a lack of preparation. The unprepared student may lack necessary study skills, career direction, interest in the subject matter, or, possibly, native intelligence. Some may even be in college at their parents' insistence, rather than their own desire. These students in past decades were often in school to avoid the military draft. The instructor's responsibility is to get unprepared students to counseling services, to remedial services, and to other testing and tutoring services on campus. In many universities, information about such services is included in a handbook of student services. When such information is not freely available, instructors may request it from the Dean of Students' office or your departmental secretary. This student will usually sit in the back of the classroom so that you will tend not to ask him or her questions.

The Social Isolate

This student never interacts with any of the other students. He/she comes to class, sits quietly, and takes notes, never offering any input. When the class is over, the student leaves as soon as possible and never socializes with the other students. These students may even dress differently from the other students. They are very hard to interact with, as they just seem to disappear when given the opportunity. These students will usually sit on the side of the classroom as far away from other students as possible. Dealing with this type of student is difficult, primarily because they are never around. Interact with the student as he or she enters the room; try a comment about the last class or the readings in the text. Any gesture will help break the ice and possibly start to develop an environment more conducive to learning. Many times the student will fade into the class and you will never see him or her again, but an effort should be made to let the student feel at ease with the professor.

The Preoccupied Student

Students may be preoccupied with non-academic pursuits: Greek activities, intercollegiate athletics, work, dating, family, drinking, or pumping iron. Second-semester seniors are notorious for "senioritis." This is the feeling that they have had enough of school and that it is time to party before entering the "real world." You may have several in your class. Preoccupied students may come to the instructor with a veritable plethora of excuses for late papers, nonattendance, or shoddy work. One instructor's strategy in dealing with preoccupied students is to let them know that they are not going to get away with their behavior--that their grades will suffer if they do not start attending class regularly and doing the assignments. Once the instructor has established the policy, it must be enforced. However, preoccupied students usually do not care; they only need a "D" in your class to graduate and probably have already interviewed or obtained a job. They sit anywhere they want and change seats throughout the term in order to maximize their last contacts with other students.

The Terrorist Student

The terrorist treats college professors with hostility, cynicism, and detachment. Terrorists are habitual rebels who sit in the back of the class, make cutting remarks, and generally disrupt class proceedings. Terrorists are frequently juniors or seniors who are taking required freshman-level classes and who feel that the class is beneath their dignity and ability. I always ask this type of advanced student why they waited to take this "stupid" class until now; they usually do not have a good answer. Instructors who are victims of terrorists cannot ignore the situation since terrorists can destroy the learning environment for all the students. The most civilized way to deal with a terrorist is to arrange a private conference. During the conference, the instructor should openly express how the terrorist's actions affect the class. Approaching a terrorist on a person-to-person level sometimes causes him or her to behave in a decent manner. This strategy is not, however, universally effective. When a terrorist persists in expressing contempt for a course, the student should be told to drop the course. As a last resort, the instructor may ask the course supervisor, then Dean of Students, or the student's academic adviser to speak with the terrorist in a firm manner.

The Left Wingers

These students express the political view of the left; they are fewer number than in recent decades but are still a viable force in class. Use these students as sounding boards for class discussions. Often these students will dress differently than the average student. These students are frequently a valuable resource for portraying a radical view point.

The Right Wingers

Because of political changes in recent years, I have seen an increase in right wing students that express views always thought more appropriate for their parents' generation. These individuals will be vocal and have an opinion on almost any subject discussed in class. Many of these individuals will mimic the current political or entertainment guru of the right wing. These students are also a valuable resource to the professor, for class discussion and to deliver the right wing line. I like to involve the left and right wing students in discussion of national and regional topics. This is usually more fun for the left winger, but use discretion and do not allow the discussion to get too personal or over excited.

The Politically Correct

These students are always politically correct, often to a fault. They strive to be the least offensive persons in class. Many students will not have the same views as these students but will very rarely confront PC students for fear of being viewed as politically incorrect.

The Bad Student Athlete

This student type is often more concerned with staying eligible for the season than learning anything in your class. They rarely attend class, their coaches are constantly concerned with the student's grades and often will send grade progress reports which require your time to respond. It appears these students' coaches are more concerned about their athletes' eligibility to play their sport than the students' education.

The Good Student Athlete

These students are attending school on an athletic scholarship and are making the most of the opportunity. They not only perform well in their athletic event but are very good students. They have major time commitments to their sport but will strive to be very good students. I will help these students with scheduling conflicts and work with them and their coaches to maximize their performance in class.

The Trust Funder

Dresses nicer than you do, drives a better car than you do, and lives in a nicer part of town. These students have life made and know it. They are in school not to find a career but rather because their parents are paying them to attend. They are often more interested in the current snow conditions, wave conditions, or weather forecast than your class. These students always get what they want because they have always been able to buy it. This may be the first time that they have to apply any effort for a reward, in this case, a grade in your class.

The Deadhead

This type of student dresses like his or her parents did or wanted to in the 1960s. Often very bright students who wish they were born 30 years earlier. When these students apply themselves, they often are the better students in your class. With the recent death of Jerry Garcia this type student may vanish until the *new* 1960s.

The Out-of-It Student

These students may have emotional difficulties or may display abnormal behaviors that allow them to attend college at only a minimal level. Often as academic pressures increase, these students' behavior becomes more erratic and less predictable. They can withdraw late in the academic term because they simply cannot handle the pressure. Work with these individuals as much as possible to try to get them through your class. Many of these students will be the "Incomplete" in your class that is never made up.

The Amorous Student

These students think for whatever reason that you are available for romance. These students must be told very early in their explorations that it is inappropriate for an instructor and student to become involved. They will often come to your office hour, stroke your ego, and in general make you feel good. But remember Nancy Reagan: Just say no!

The Physically Handicapped Student

Make all attempts to mitigate any problems these students have, whether it is access to the classroom, or time needed to get from class to class. Call your school disabled students services office to ask if there are any additional areas that you can help with.

The Learning Disabled Student

These students have a disability that does not allow them to function well in the academic environment. In many cases these students have to be tested for their disability and will have a card certifying their disability. They may require more time for tests, special quiet testing areas, require readers, or need any number of other services. Contact your learning disabilities office and ask for the current policies for helping these students. Do as much as you can to help these students; often they will be very motivated. One disadvantage these students will also have is that other mainstream students may resent their perceived advantages in testing and evaluations situations.

(The types of students were influenced by Allen and Rueter 1990)

Use this classification system to understand the motivations of the students. Additionally, your understanding of the "types" of students in your class will enable you to deal more effectively with their behavior and perhaps modify their behavior, if necessary. Add to this list of "types" as you encounter them.

Students are your responsibility; you must help all these various types maximize their potential for receiving a college education.

E-mail me any additional types of students that you encounter at upyfw@gemini.oscs.montana.edu

Interactions with Students Out of the Classroom

You face a new uncharted course as you leave the classroom and enter the less well-defined area of conduct with students out of the classroom. A broad general rule is to remember how you interacted with faculty members when you were an undergraduate.

Office Hours

Always be available during your posted office hours. If you are not going to be able to keep your office hours (attending a conference is a good example), announce the times you will not be in your office. During illness or emergencies, ask the department secretary to post a note on your office door explaining why you will not be in your office.

Conducting Your Office Hours

How you should conduct your office hours is a subject that concerns many new instructors. During posted office hours, you should be in your office--not somewhere else--willing and able to help students. Do not be engaged in a project that cannot be set aside, like writing a book. Do not talk on the telephone for the entire hour. A former colleague of mine would talk on the telephone for the entire hour, long distance, while several students waited in the hall. When he finally got off the telephone, it would be time for class and he would tell the students to come back later and rush off to class. This is extremely poor form; the students are the reason you are in your office! Read the introductory text or do other light work that can be interrupted.

Be friendly to the students in your office; ask them to have a chair and show real concern for their problems. On occasion you will have students with personal problems that you cannot or should not handle. Know the proper school referral policy and send these students to the appropriate agent on campus.

During your office hours, you are likely to have a few publishers' representatives visit; this will happen primarily at the beginning of each term and during text decision time. Give the publisher's representative the same courtesy that you do to students, but realize that these individuals have second priority. If a student is waiting to see you, excuse the publisher's representative and take care of the student's needs. The representative knows that this is what you should do and he or she will understand.

During many of your office hours, no one will come to visit. I like to schedule my office hour right before class meets. This allows me to go over my lecture notes and catch up on my reading. As examinations near, the frequency of visits will increase, so plan to see more students who have specific questions about examinations.

Rules You Should Never Break

You must be very careful never to exhibit any questionable conduct with students. One of the most sacred rules in academia is to refrain from using your position to gain favors from students. This includes anything from football tickets to sexual favors. Never put yourself in a position where someone can question your integrity. The best way to accomplish this is to leave no doubt about your intentions. A good policy, for example, is to always keep your door partially open when a student is in your office. Rumors are a very nasty thing to stop, even when they have no basis in fact. Be fair; above all, never give any consideration in the area of grades to students you like or find attractive. Even a false hint about unethical behavior can mean the end of your teaching career. Do not even think about any unethical behavior. If you do not already have a copy of the school rules on sexual harassment and instructor's conduct, get one and read it.

Conduct Off-Campus

You may meet students off-campus or at other functions not associated with the school. You should not shun them, but realize that they are still your students. Do not put yourself in a position you may regret. You do not have to act like a monk, but realize that your new position dictates a certain level of conduct. Do not date your students; just don't do it. Dating your students is very bad form.

The Day of the Examination

It amazes me when I hear of the high number of tragedies that occur on examination day. I can remember going into the department office the morning of my first examination of the fall term and being greeted by the department secretary who said that she wondered what type of tragedy would befall the students today; she was waiting for the phone to ring. There are occasions when real problems will occur; one of the best policies, and probably the most fair, is to have an outside agency decide if an excuse is proper. My university directs the dean of students to make those decisions and issue excuses for absences from examinations. Some students will realize that they have a conflict with your examination (a student may be on the golf team, for example); have that student pre-arrange his or her absence with you so you can write a make-up examination. Be as flexible and fair as you can with students; most will not try to take advantage of the situation.

After the examination, you are likely to get upset students who say they are going to flunk out of college because of your test. Assure them that they probably will not flunk out of college; ask them to see you during your office hours the next day. At this meeting, discuss study strategies and other resources available at your school.

Campus Resources Available to the Student

You will become aware of students who will need extra academic help. I always encourage students to stop by my office any time and talk about problems they are having with school. Most campuses offer a variety of services for students with academic problems. To find out what is available to your students, start with your own department's services and then look up others listed in the campus telephone directory.

The following is a list of services available to students at most schools.

Student Records

The first resource is likely to be the college or university office that supervises freshman students. This office maintains student records and assigns advisors. At many schools a large portion of the students will be enrolled in the college of general studies which performs the same functions. Often services like tutoring programs are coordinated through these offices. Some schools are making these records available to advising faculty on-line.

Writing Centers

Sometimes called writing labs, and probably staffed by members of the English Department or Composition Program, the writing center offers assistance on a variety of writing problems. Because the staff in writing centers is often highly qualified, we recommend referring students with writing problems.

Tutoring Services

On many campuses, the most highly organized tutoring services are probably those provided for student athletes, Greek organizations, or learning disabled students, but other campus organizations may offer voluntary tutoring programs or serve as clearinghouses for more informal peer tutoring arrangements.

Counseling Programs

These programs offer assistance for students with academic or emotional problems severe enough to require such an approach. This program may include a learning resource center or testing program to help students develop better study skills or test-taking behaviors and services to help students set educational goals and plan careers. Additionally, there may be emotional counseling available.

Research Services of the Library

It is a good idea to make yourself aware of research services available at your campus library. Depending on the size of its collection and staff, the library may offer individual term paper conferences, presentations about specific resources to classes, and computer-assisted searches. Much of the traditional library service is or will be converted to on-line services. Discuss these new services with the appropriate individuals in your library.

Reading Programs

Most schools have a separate reading program or lab to assist students in developing the reading skills crucial to good academic achievement. There may be individual staff or off-campus organizations that specialize in these type of problems.

Professional Services

In many college towns, students have access to professional editing or research services. Often typing/word processing services will offer editing assistance. You probably want your students to use editing services.

Student Health

Most campuses have a student health service designed to take care of student health needs. There may be occasions that arise when you will want to refer students to this health service. These problems can range from minor to severe. Be aware of the service that the students can expect.

Mental Health Center

Many campuses also have some form of mental health facilities. These often are associated with the psychology, counseling or medical departments on campus. You are likely to encounter several students who indicate a problem in this area. Be aware of these service options and refer any student who needs the services.

=====

(Some of the components in this list of services are adapted from Seelbinder and Landstrom 1990)

Your familiarity with the services available will help you to make appropriate suggestions to students who may need help or who may ask you to direct them to other resources. Encouraging your students to seek additional help may at times present a problem. Some students may feel you are abandoning them; you will have to reassure them, making clear the limits you face.

9

Interacting with the Faculty

Dealing with Faculty

Your Place in the Big Picture

Knowing that you are at the very bottom of the political/power totem pole can foster a healthy attitude. As you look at the faculty in your department, realize that they are the final authority in judging your performance. Each school has some formal vehicle for student evaluations of your teaching ability and some form of faculty annual review for your performance. However, much of the real evaluation is often not accomplished using a formal procedure but rather using an informal evaluation of you by the other faculty members. Do not be paranoid, but realize that you are always being evaluated. Be cordial and be yourself.

Faculty Stereotypes

There are several definitive types of faculty you are likely to meet. The following is an attempt to list the types of faculty members you can expect to meet. Use this information to help direct your interaction with the faculty. Knowing what to expect will allow you to make preliminary decisions as to how you might act in certain situations; besides, it is fun to see how many you can recognize in your department.

87

The Big Gun

This individual is a full professor, with very high status on the campus, who is well known in the research community and is probably known nationally. This is the person you always thought you wanted to be. You will often find that to attain this level of status these professors have totally devoted their lives to the study of psychology, often to the exclusion of family, social interactions, friends, and even personal health. They are usually too busy to have much interaction with you as a new instructor. Big guns typically teach very little and usually only at the graduate level. They normally have the maximum political clout in the department and school.

The Small Gun

This individual is probably a full professor approaching the end of his career who never reached the level of achievement that was expected. This person is not renowned for teaching or research but does an adequate job in both. He may have devoted much of his recent energy toward school committee/administration work. This person can be a good ally and will have the time to discuss aspects of your teaching. He will usually have moderate political clout in the department and school.

The Non-Tenured

These are the individuals who are trying to do everything all at once. They have good teaching evaluations from students, interact with the senior faculty socially, do as much research as possible, and try to publish enough to be tenured. They usually burn the candle at both ends and have little spare time. They can be a good source of information as to what the power structure is in the department. The non-tenured usually have little political clout.

The Post-Tenured

Many faculty exhibit a post-tenured depression. This may be evident in their teaching and, particularly, in their research. They have finally made it and are taking a breather before starting in the promotion cycle. They are usually good allies and have increasing political clout.

The Promoter

This faculty member is back at the grind, in both teaching and research. He is trying to increase his status and rank in the school. The promoter is a good ally for the present and future and someone you can ask about specific do's and don't in the department. This individual can often help with questions concerning teaching. Political clout is medium and rising.

The Disgruntled

The disgruntled faculty member hates the department; he may have just been denied tenure and is probably leaving the department very soon, either voluntarily or otherwise. This individual is often the sour grapes type and is best avoided. He may have negative political clout.

The Administrator Current

This is the current department chair. The current chair has a tremendous amount of power over your life. In many schools, this individual has the final hiring authority and a major input in the tenure process. This person, with committee input, will also write your annual review; realize that the current chair has tremendous political clout in the department and school.

The Administrator Past

This faculty member was the department chair at some time in the past. The administrator past has returned to the ranks of the faculty and may or may not be happy with the situation. As the chair, he had a light teaching load but is now required to do more teaching and research. This person can be a valuable resource for understanding the workings of the department and the school. This individual may have higher aspirations in the school and may be a Dean some day. Political clout can vary but is usually at a high level.

The Absent Member

This individual, for a number of reasons, is not physically present very much; he is usually tenured. This absence typically has something to do with a consulting business he is running. Absent members perform at a minimum level in the department and are off with their other work most of the time. They often will use the school to legitimize their outside interests. Clout can vary but usually is on the low side.

The Dinosaur

This individual is also known as deadwood and is usually older; he may have been productive in the past but is not now. He is tenured and abusing the tenure system; he is simply drawing a paycheck. This person performs at or below expected standards for a faculty member in the school but realizes that there is usually little that can be done about his behavior. This person demands the most support, TAs, travel, release time and does virtually nothing for this special treatment. This person believes that his rank allows for his special status. In every department I have ever been associated with, there is at least one dinosaur. His political clout is usually negative with active members; as in the past it is best to avoid dinosaurs.

The Adjunct

This person is not on a tenure track line in the department. This individual works on term or yearly contracts. Trying to hang on by the thinnest of margins, the adjunct must be the best teacher in the department, since there is usually no research commitment. Since this individual is judged on a different scale than the rest of the faculty, she tries to be better at teaching than any of the other faculty because her job is dependent on it. The adjunct's teaching load is always higher than the tenured faculty because she is a teaching specialist and typically does not do research. Always the first to go in short money times, the adjunct can help you tremendously in your teaching. Political clout varies but is usually low.

The Mole

He is there but he is not in sight. This individual comes to work, teaches his classes, and disappears. Often he comes to his office or to do research but rarely socializes with the faculty or students. This person is best left alone, if you could find him in the first place. Political clout on the low side.

Just Leaving

This faculty member is about to retire, usually after a long career at your school. With tight budgets, the norm of the 1990's dictates that many of these pre-retirees are given very good inducements to retire early. Some take the offers and others refuse wanting to continue in the comfort of high rank and status in the department and school. These interesting individuals will often give you valuable insights into the workings of the department that others would not. Political clout is usually on the high side.

The Emeritus

In many schools the emeritus holds a very high status. This retired individual often was an internationally known researcher or teacher. This person wants to keep active in academia and usually has an office in the department. If you can approach this individual, you may gain a valuable ally for future interactions with the administration at your school. This individual often knows many of the highest ranking individuals in the administration, so a phone call from this person can be worth a lot. Political clout very high.

The Other New Guy

This person is very much like you: brand new, shiny, fresh out of graduate school. Often this person is a candidate to be a good friend. You might share many of the same interests, sports, music or politics that the rest of the faculty may not. A good friend can help you through the tough times and may some day have high status and political power.

The Bizarre Member

This individual is tenured, and that is good for him. This person has at least one severe personality/major psychological problem and can barley function in real life let alone teach and do research. On the days when he is off his medication he will be even more bizarre. The only thing that keeps this person around is tenure. Negative political power.

The Burn Out

Like many stars, they burn brightly for a short time. This person was on the fast track but has fallen off. Now content to teach the minimum and do some research. Losing political power.

The Incompetent

This person has always been incompetent in both teaching and research but barely managed to get tenure and now is a permanent fixture in the department. The students do not like this person because they can see through to his incompetence. Lower political power.

The Grant Guy

This person has a large grant and has had funding for many years. This person can be very well known nationally and internationally. Teaches little but does excellent research. This person is a lot like the big gun, only with a very large grant. High status.

The Grant Guy, Lost

Same as above, but has just lost his funding, which he has had for many years. Now he faces the prospect of coming back to the ranks of the teaching faculty.

The Mentor

This the person you have been looking for. This person is a very good teacher, is well connected on campus, and conducts a good research program. What makes this individual most important is that he is willing to share his success with a new instructor like yourself through the meandering process. This person should be courted, and she will help you through your career. Political clout high.

This list of stereotypes is only partial; you will find many others in your department. This list is intended as a practical guide to help guide your interactions with these faculty members. Remember, these are the people who will decide if you stay or leave your present position.

There will be departmental factions that may try to recruit you; stay as politically neutral as possible--be apolitical.

Complete the duties that are required for your position. Volunteer for additional departmental or school duties if appropriate and you have the time in your teaching and research schedule. Many schools look at service to the community and school in their tenure and contract negotiations. See Chapter 12 for a more detailed discussion.

Dealing with the Staff

Head Secretary

The head departmental secretary has a tremendous amount of power over your future in the department. In many departments this individual decides what gets done when. If you are on the wrong side of this individual, your teaching can be adversely affected. Be cordial and professional in your interactions.

The Working Secretaries

These are the individuals who do the daily work, type exams, make handouts, take messages, arrange classroom assignments, order textbooks, and process all the paperwork for the department. Do not make unreasonable demands on these individuals, like demanding a test be typed and ready in two hours. If you can use a word processor and have access to one, do as much of this kind of work as you can. These secretaries may be younger and more friendly than the head secretary, but remember where the power is. Treat these individuals with respect; their job is a hard one with little reward. Send flowers on National Secretaries Day and take them out to lunch once a year.

The Techs

They are the individuals who run the laboratories, storerooms and animal care facilities. These are usually interesting individuals. Introduce yourself; you will need their assistance in the future.

School Staff, Bureaucrats

These individuals are not related to the academic area of the school and are often referred to as the "administration." Depending on their level and function, they can be very helpful or very obstructionistic. They are the paper pushers. Lower level paper pushers are usually more helpful than their supervisors since they are the ones who do the work and know the system. The best strategy for dealing with this segment of the staff is to make sure you comply with their paper deadlines and stay out of their way as much as possible. They will only need to know your name and the fact that you are always prompt with your paperwork. Their job can be very difficult especially concerning grade deadlines, graduation deadlines, and transcript evaluations, so do your best to be on time.

Interacting with the Staff

As a new instructor, you may find that you have more in common with the secretaries and technical staff than you do with the faculty members. They are often younger, more personable, less stressed, and more fun to interact with than the faculty. Remember to temper your interactions with these individuals. You are now a faculty member and must act accordingly.

Use these suggestions about types of individuals you will meet in the department and school to guide you in selecting the appropriate behavior for different situations. It never hurts to have an idea of what to expect in your new environment.

Professional Development

The major national meetings on psychology include the American Psychologist Society (APS), the American Psychologist Association (APA) Division Two, and the National Institute on the Teaching of Psychology (NITOP). These are the major national meetings whose sections are devoted to the teaching of psychology, with NITOP dedicated to the teaching of psychology. Many regional meetings have specific sections on teaching. Consult your regional conventions for details.

The following is a listing of major conferences and addresses. For further information contact each individually.

American Psychological Society Teaching Institute. Contact Doug Bernstein, Department of Illinois at Urbana-Champaign, 603 East Daniel Street, Champaign, IL 61820.

Annual Conference on Undergraduate Teaching of Psychology. Contact Judith R. Levien, Department of Psychology, College of Technology, State University of New York at Farmingdale, Farmingdale, NY, 11735.

Division Two/Council of Teachers of Undergraduate Psychology. Contact Stephen F. Davis, Psychology Department, Emporia State University, Emporia, KS 66801.

Mid-America Conference. Contact Joseph Palladino, Department of Psychology, University of Southern Indiana, Evansville, IN 47712.

Midwest Institute. Contact Pat Puccico, Department of Psychology, College of Dupage, Glen Ellyn, IL 60137.

National Institute for the Teaching of Psychology (NITOP). Contact Doug Bernstein, Department of Psychology, University of Illinois at Urbana-Champaign, 603 East Daniel Street, Champaign, IL 61820 or conference coordinator Joanne Fetzner by e-mail at jfetzner@s.psych,uiuc.edu.

Northeast Conference. Contact Barney Beins, Department of Psychology, Ithaca College, Ithaca, NY 14850 or e-mail at beins@ithaca.edu.

Southeast Conference. Contact Bill Hill, Department of Psychology, Kennesaw State College, Marietta, GA 30061.

Southwest Regional Conference. Contact John Hall, Department of Psychology, Texas Wesleyan University, Fort Worth, TX 76105.

Ursinus Conference. Contact Eileen M. England, Psychology Department, Ursinus College, Collegeville, PA or e-mail eengland@ursinus.bitnet.

10

Evaluating Your Teaching

A major event in your academic career is the continuing evaluation of your teaching. Evaluations can come in several forms, from the formal to the causal. The faculty is, although they may not admit it, evaluating you constantly. Much of what you say and many of the actions you take are being appraised. The faculty may not make a formal evaluation of your classroom behavior and general conduct as a faculty member until it is time for a formal contract to be renewed or for the typical annual review. You should not be paranoid about this constant assessment of both your behavior and personality, but rather realize that everyone is evaluated at the beginning of his or her career in this manner. The faculty wants to see if you "fit in" with the department. On the other hand, you wish to see if this department is where you might want to spend the next 40 years. So be yourself and enjoy this first experience of teaching, but conduct yourself in a professional manner at all times.

Formal evaluations can be expected in the form of committee reviews or departmental annual reviews. These consist of submissions from you of materials about your teaching effectiveness, research, publications, and service to the school and community. Sometimes committees will visit your class to assess your teaching. A committee or the department head will write a report and forward it to a higher authority on your progress in the department. This evaluation processes is a traditional method of securing contracts, tenure, promotions, and raises in academia. Be sure to provide an orderly presentation of your materials; be prompt in supplying the requested documentation and provide everything requested. In a way, this may be the least noxious method of evaluation; you provide the major portion of the materials and you are judged on your performance, one would hope, in an objective manner. Personal appraisals by the faculty are factored into the equation at this point, but the major portion of the evaluation should be objective.

Student Evaluations

Formal Student Evaluations

Major components of the evaluation process are student evaluations of your overall classroom performance. Many departments or schools will have standardized evaluation forms which utilize years of normative data on your department. Check with your supervisor for the correct evaluation form and ask if there is a preferred time for administration. The formal evaluations will often compare you with school norms on many factors involved in teaching. In some cases, your evaluations might even be compared to state or national norms.

Informal Student Evaluations

Students are constantly assessing college teaching informally. Casual positive comments like, "Dr. Lynch is the best teacher in the introductory course; be sure to take his section" are common. Negative evaluations are also common. "Grey's class is a waste of time; he knows nothing; skip it if you're smart" or "Peterson doesn't know anything except his research, and all of his classes are the same material despite the course title." These are the types of assessments that are used by many students when selecting a psychology section. Although these evaluations are informal, they have a way of getting back to your supervisors and department chair. On many campuses, student organizations have independent directories of faculty teaching effectiveness, ease of grading, and how interesting the faculty member has been in the past. These data are usually for sale in a small booklet. After your first year, buy a copy of this booklet to see how you have fared.

Stereotypical Faculty Styles

Students can also classify instructors into stereotypes; these can be both positive and negative. You should be aware of these different types and strive to be seen as a positive type instructor in the students' eyes.

Negative Instructor Styles

Instructors who display an ineffective teaching style are often unaware of the impression they give to their students. First-term instructors are frequently shocked by end-of-course student evaluations. They had assumed that all was well with their teaching and that their students both liked and respected them. Among the styles that students do not like or respect are the following.

The Bore

In the classroom of the boring instructor, the most interested and active person present is the instructor, who talks on and on about *the* facts, concepts, laws, or precepts. Since the instructor is doing all, or almost all, of the talking, the class period passes rapidly for her; however, the same instructional period may seem endless and boring for the students. Few students have a 50- to 60-minute attention span. Few lecturers are sufficiently dynamic, creative, and entertaining that student attention may be sustained for such a period of time. What instructors must understand is that most undergraduate students do not share their love for the discipline, yet. The bore merely presents the material to students; no attempt is made to relate the information to student needs and interests. In turn, the students doze, doodle, daydream, read the student paper, talk or do homework for another class. But, being enamored of her own voice, the bore never notices. If you are this type of instructor you had better be tenured or teaching required courses.

The Boor

A boor is a person who is lacking in social skills. Instructors who are boors treat their students in a rude, cool, or distant manner. They belittle student questions; they interrupt student responses; they show little respect for student ability; they smirk instead of smile. The most offensive of boors are instructors who are arrogant about their own intellectual achievements. They treat students with great disdain since they consider the undergraduate incapable of the high level of intellectual exchange the instructor values. Not all instructors who are perceived as boors are arrogant, however. In many cases, instructors who are shy or apprehensive try to conceal their uncertainty by showing little of their personalities to students. In the process they seem overbearing, haughty, and distant. They communicate to students that they do not wish to establish cordial interpersonal relationships. Students will take the boor's class but will not recommend it to other students; they will usually take this class because it is the only section offered.

The Flake

The flake suffers from terminal disorganization, he is the classic absent-minded professor. Instructors who are flakes have difficulty getting to class on time. Once they get there, it takes them a long time to get everything sorted out. Lecture notes fall to the floor. Tests the students expected back are back on the instructor's desk. That desk reflects the personality of its user: layers of clutter everywhere, barely a spot available for work. It doesn't take long for students to recognize that an instructor is a flake. In addition to looking flaky, the flake is intellectually disorganized. Assignments are made in a haphazard fashion. Information is not presented in a clear and straightforward manner. Students will take advantage of this disorganization by turning in assignments late, saying the instructor lost assignments when they were never turned in, and generally taking advantage of the professor's inability to organize himself.

The Fake

Instructors are sometimes assigned to teach or assist in courses outside their areas of primary expertise. When this happens, it is expected that they will expend considerable energy in mastering the subject matter before attempting to teach it to others. Some instructors, however, decide to take a shortcut through the preparatory process by keeping a few pages ahead of the students and by "winging it." Typically the fake doesn't succeed. When an instructor doesn't know the material, students can tell: factual errors are made, questions are avoided or answered in an evasive manner, information is presented in a hesitant or halting fashion. There is no substitute for knowing the material. To accept a teaching assignment is to take on the obligation of becoming appropriately informed. If you find yourself in this position, take the time to master the material or turn down the assignment. A competent instructor of psychology should be able to teach *any* undergraduate class with 6 months' preparation. This assumes that the instructor will take the time to master the material. As you progress in your career, you will be asked to teach classes in which you may not feel totally at ease with the subject matter. Take the challenge to explore new areas that you may only have roughly explored in your earlier training. Many times this "forced" learning will lead you to new and exciting teaching and research areas.

The Wimp

A wimp is a wimp. Instructors who are wimps are highly uncertain about matters of pedagogy. They make assignments in a tentative, unsure manner. Assignments often sound more like questions than statements. Wimps refuse to accept responsibility for the courses they teach. When students complain about course content, procedures, or expectations, the wimp is likely to say, "I don't like it either, but that's the way the department wants it done." Undergraduates soon learn that a wimpy instructor is a person to be manipulated rather than respected. Students maneuver the wimp into modifying assignments, changing due dates, and wasting class time by justifying course content and procedures. Do not be a wimp, take a position and defend it. It may not always be the correct position but at least have a position.

The Never Changing

This instructor is still teaching the same materials he learned in graduate school 25 years ago. For this reason, psychology effectively stopped the day she graduated. The same tattered, non-updated notes are used every term. The same false rigor is used to cover her incompetence each term. This instructor tends to be very rigid and dogmatic in her style of lecture, thus trying to cover for her lack of current knowledge. Students recognize the lack of competence of this instructor and have no respect for her. Students will only take her class if it is required and it is the only section available. Tenure is the only thing that keeps this instructor in the classroom and employed by the school.

The No Content

The students come to class; the instructor shows up; his mouth moves, but nothing of substance ever comes out. Some students will like this instructor because he tends to grade easily to hide his lack of competence, and he can be entertaining. The only psychology the students learn is from the textbook, if the instructor has one.

The Phoney

This instructor is a competent instructor in the presentation of the materials but is not interested in the students or the discipline. The phoney can be typified as the smile-and-firm-handshake type. This instructor will smile and act friendly to the students when he is really not at all interested in them. Students will take his classes, but will not respect or interact with him in informal situations.

===

Positive Instructor Styles

The following are some of the types of instructors for whom students have respect and whom you should emulate.

===

The Eccentric

Certain instructors are effective because their exceptional intellect commands the attention and respect of their students. Such instructors have excellent verbal fluency and elaborate ideas in vivid language and imagery. They are often a bit unorthodox in appearance and behavior. Why not? They are college professors. Because of their dedication to the study of psychology, they may give little attention to dress and personal grooming. They develop mannerisms that set them aside from others; they may pace back and forth as they speak or they may lead a class discussion while sitting cross-legged, guru style, on their desks. But it really doesn't matter. Students like and respect eccentric instructors.

The Entertainer

Some instructors are successful because they are entertaining. They are gifted storytellers and they use language in creative and humorous ways. They dominate the classroom because they like to be the center of attention. But their students don't care. They build illustrative materials from the lives of students. Entertainers take a personal interest in students because they want to adapt their "material" to their audience's interests, needs, and senses of humor. Students will line up to take a class from the entertainer.

The Basic Competent

Some instructors are effective because they have basic teaching competence. They don't display the intelligence of the eccentrics or the humor of the flashy entertainers. Still, they get the job done. The basic competent is the reverse of the flakes; they have clear goals in mind and they communicate their expectations to students in a clear manner. They set and adhere to deadlines. They grade and return work promptly. They are efficient in leading class discussions. When presenting information, they are straightforward. They are never tardy to class. They are always in their offices during announced office hours. They are dependable.

The Helper

The helper places high time demands on herself. Helpers go out of their way to ensure that their students will do well. They hold extra office hours before major assignments are due. They hold evening review sessions before tests; they invite students to call them at home with questions. Helpers are basically nice people who treat their students with respect and who are, in turn, liked and respected by their students.

The Mentor

The mentor is a wise and trustworthy person. Mentors teach by example. They have exceptionally high standards of scholarship; they demand a great deal of themselves and, consequently, expect a great deal of their students. Mentors serve as role models of the skills and habits of inquiry they seek to impart.

Professor Personality

The students love this style; the professor has an out-going personality, and both students and faculty like this person. In and out of the classroom, this individual is always "on," up beat, and happy. The material in class can vary in quality and quantity, but this person still always gets the highest student evaluations.

(This classification system was influenced by Allen and Rueter 1990).

While this system for categorizing instructor styles is stereotypical, it does represent the range of styles one finds among instructors in a large department. Instructors may, of course, possess characteristics from two or more of these categories. The important point is that instructors need not be locked hopelessly into negative styles. Instructors can change their style as they acquire experience.

Students are very good at picking out the "type" of instructor you are. Strive to be a positive "type"; this can best be accomplished by being honest with yourself and the students. After your first course evaluation, see which of these types you appear to be. Work to change negative attributes and enhance positive styles.

Questions Concerning Student Evaluations

Questions often arise about formal student evaluations and how they can affect you. Since these evaluations often carry tremendous weight in both your department and your school, it is very important to consider the following points.

Are Student Evaluations Valid?

This *is* the fundamental question. If student evaluations really are a measure of your effectiveness in the classroom, then they should be used as a method or evaluation for retention and promotion. But if they are not a valid measure, what is the point of these evaluations? What do they really measure? Student evaluations are weighted heavily in most departments only behind grants and research papers. More research into the validity of different formal evaluation instruments is needed at all schools. Many schools have "standardized" evaluations that are neither standard nor valid. Many of these instruments have simply evolved from past failed attempts to evaluate the faculty. The individuals with good evaluations get promoted and gain influence, while those with low ratings may not receive tenure or promotion. It makes sense that the people in power like the instrument that gave them good ratings and, at least partially, the power.

At the other extreme are national evaluations of teaching. In the education department at many schools, students are obsessed with passing the national or regional teaching tests. These tests will either guarantee them a job or not, based on their rank order. These evaluations are the evaluation process carried to the extreme.

Are Students Qualified to Evaluate?

Some of the common concerns of faculty regarding student ratings are whether the students are qualified to evaluate. Do they have the proper perspective? Many faculty say that this knowledge and the ability to evaluate can only be gained through experiences outside of the classroom in the real world. Basically, students do not know what they need to know to evaluate their teachers. I tell students to think about ethical issues, but I realize that many will not have the time or the inclination to do so while they are in college. I suggest that they might have time to think about these problems later in their careers when these ethical issues come up. I have had former students call me on the telephone to discuss issues that I brought up years earlier. They sometimes find themselves in an ethical dilemma. We can all remember the teachers whom we really hated while we were in college as undergraduates. In many cases, those teachers were the ones who demanded the most from us at a time when we were not ready to produce the required results. Now we look back and think that this class was one of the best we had in college. I wish I had taken more classes from that "tough" instructor. So at least in the short term, the instructor who is easy on the students in terms of grades and classroom behavior may receive higher marks on student evaluations, but probably not in the long run. If you are trying to get your contract renewed or receive tenure, this may be a concern. You can be easy with grades and expectations and receive high evaluations from the students, but cheat the students in the long run. A difficult problem. Maybe an alternate method of asking students for evaluations five years into their careers would be a better method.

Are Students Expert Enough to Evaluate?

Students do not know enough about the material to tell if the instructor is good or not. An important point to remember is that the students come to you with very little knowledge of psychology. You are the expert and choose what is important; you can slant the presentation any way you want and they will not know it. To do a proper evaluation, the students would have to already know the materials, which they do not. Again, the five-year post-graduation evaluation may be the answer.

Effects of Personality Factors in Student Evaluations

Another problem often perceived by the faculty is that the students rate instructors on personality factors, not on what they learned in the classroom. I am sure that we can still remember certain professors who had abrasive personalities or were boring, and we probably rated them lower than individuals with friendly outgoing personalities. One suggestion is to be as interesting in and out of the classroom as you can. Do not be a phoney, but realize that personality factors can affect your student evaluations.

Factors Affecting Student Evaluations

Characteristics of the Instructor

Gender of the instructor plays little role in the evaluation of the course. Younger instructors are often rated higher than older instructors. This is possibly due to a closer fit in social variables and understanding of the behavior of younger students. Knowledge of subject matter is not sufficient for high evaluations, but you must provide an interesting presentation of the material and get the student excited about the class and the discipline. A boring associate professor in a suit and tie just does not cut it anymore. Remember, you were sitting in the same seats as your students four or five years ago; try to do a better job than some of your professors did.

Student Expectations of the Class

Probably the most important factor is whether the students expect the class to be a good class or not. If students have heard good things about the class, then they are more likely to rate the instructor highly. The class standing of the students also appears to have an effect on the rating of the instructor. Entering freshmen will rate an instructor higher than graduating seniors, probably due to the unfamiliarity of the rating system in the freshman year. Most other physical variables about the instructor have little influence.

Maximizing Your Evaluations

In order to maximize your evaluations, several factors should be considered. These suggestions are offered as a method of understanding what the students consider important in the class and in the instructor.

Be Prepared

Be prepared and have a thorough knowledge of your subject matter. Be as prepared as you can for each lecture. This may entail attending other upper division classes if you are weak in an area. Additional reading in a particular sub-field can also help.

Be Fair

Be fair to the students in all aspects of the class, from grades to answering questions. Treat the students with the respect they deserve. Err on the side of the students. Do not do anything that will be perceived as favoring one student or group of students over another.

Dress Contemporarily

Do not dress too differently than the students; a suit is usually out of place on most campuses these days, at least in the psychology department. Similarity in dress will let the students believe that you are approachable. I can remember being totally frightened at the prospect of having to talk to a professor in a suit and tie when I was a freshman; but then, that was a long time ago.

Show Real Concern

Show real concern for the students as individuals and try to understand their problems. Try to remember the types of problems that you had when you were a student. School is often not just what is happening in the classroom; be aware of student needs.

Stick to Your Schedule

Do what you say you are going to do, when you say you are going to do it. Stick to your schedule; students at the introductory level like structure. If the only constant in your class is the schedule, then that is a start.

Follow Your Syllabus

Follow your syllabus to the letter. Do not add any additional requirements. Do not delete any assignments; some students, the better ones, might have already completed some of the assignments.

Be Friendly

Be friendly and do not abuse the power of your position. Some new instructors can become enchanted with their new status and abuse their new power. Be as friendly with students as your personality allows.

Be Fun

This does not mean that you have to be a stand-up comic, but be as light as you can. This introductory class is one of the only times the students will have the opportunity to have any fun in the classroom; most classes get too serious beyond the introductory level. Let the students have a feel for the discipline and a look at your personality. Besides, you are going to have to teach this class for many years; would you rather have some fun in the classroom or just read your notes?

Evaluate Me, Not the Course

On evaluation day tell the students to rate you as an instructor, not the course content, textbook or the examinations. This simple strategy will increase your student evaluations in a positive direction.

Emphasize the Importance of Evaluations

On evaluation day tell the students that your evaluations are used for tenure, promotion, and salary increases. Emphasize that these are very important evaluations to the department, school, and to you personally. Indicate that you read every comment and modify the course the next time that you teach it based on your evaluations. They are important!

Taking these factors into account, you will, first, become a better instructor and, second, these factors will help maximize your student evaluations.

Other Methods of Evaluation

Student Letters of Recommendation

You may not need them now, but in the future written student evaluations of your performance in the classroom may be necessary for tenure and promotion, contract renewal, or applications for awards. In many instances, the students, usually of your choosing, will be asked to submit written evaluations of your classroom performance. This is similar to the student letters of recommendation you are asked to write: a nice turnabout. Pick several students from each class and ask them if they would consider writing these performance evaluations at some future time. If they say yes, keep track of their addresses and telephone numbers for future reference.

Student Oral Evaluations

Oral evaluations can be both very informative and at the same time difficult. If you are good at receiving criticism, invite students to stop by during your office hours to discuss directions that the class could take in the future. Also ask the students what they like and dislike about your teaching. Ask how you can improve your teaching. You will probably only have a few students show up, but they will be your best students: listen to them; they have good ideas.

Anonymous Student Evaluations

Provide a suggestion box for your class; this can be accomplished by dropping a sealed letter in your departmental mail box. Most of the comments will be useful in helping with minor adjustments in the class. These suggestions can be incorporated into the next term if they are good suggestions. Be prepared for the terrorist student to take the opportunity to take a cheap shot at your class and you; have a thick skin. I can remember reading my first 250 formal class evaluations and finding 95 percent were positive. But there was one very negative evaluation: I can still remember that evaluation. It was probably from a terrorist student.

Faculty Teaching Evaluations

Invite your supervisor and all other interested faculty to attend your lectures. If you want to live a stressful life, see your uninvited department chair in the third row when you are really not as prepared as you would like to be for that day's lecture. These faculty members, as a whole, will decline for various reasons. But the few who do show up will be valuable in shaping your future teaching. Ask faculty members for evaluations of your teaching and specific suggestions that you can use to improve your teaching. The faculty members who respond will probably also be the better teachers in the department.

Self-Evaluation

Evaluating Verbal and Non-verbal Messages

The ability to correctly evaluate verbal and nonverbal messages in the classroom can be a major part of your success and continued betterment of your teaching skills. Students will communicate different messages for different levels of performance in your lectures. If your lecture is very interesting and well presented, the students will smile, laugh at your jokes, ask questions, take notes, and present a general demeanor of having a pleasant experience. This is a positive, rewarding environment for the professor. Professors dream of this kind of response from the class. On the other hand, when a professor is unprepared, the material is seen as not interesting. If the instructor appears not to enjoy the material, he or she may be greeted with sleeping students, yawns (one will start the whole class yawning), frowns, late students entering the room during the lecture and, my favorite, the blank stare. This is also a type of dream: a nightmare. When you have a lecture like this, upon returning to your office, immediately evaluate what you can do to improve this lecture: more overheads, fewer overheads, a demonstration or activity, a short video presentation at the beginning or end, or a total re-write of your lecture, with a new emphasis on the materials. It is important to "fix" this lecture immediately, or it will go back into the file and come out next term just as bad.

Student Behavioral Evaluations

As you gain more experience during the term, you should start to look at other subtle nonverbal cues that the students will exhibit in the classroom. The ability to attend to these cues and then evaluate and modify your lecture is very important. This can usually be done through classroom experience. The following is an attempt to give you a shortcut on assessing these behavioral cues.

Student Behavior Just Prior to the Beginning of Class

Are they talking to each other and, if so, are they talking about the class or some social interaction they had over the weekend? Do the students just sit and wait for class or read the student newspaper? If they just sit and wait, this could be an indication that you are not inspiring the students in this class. Do the students talk to you before or after class? Before the class starts I pick out a "lucky" student of the day and either sit next to the student or stand and talk to this student and any others nearby; I like to spread out this "luck" and see how the students feel about me and the class or life in general. This will give the students the feeling that you care about them as individuals.

Student Behavior When the Class Starts

Do the students put away the newspaper, stop talking to each other and begin to take notes? Do they continue with a negative attitude about the class lecture by not being prepared to take notes and continuing to talk? Do they have questions about previous lectures? Do the students act interested and ready to learn?

Student Behavior during the Class Period

Do the students listen intently to your lecture and take notes? Are there questions during the lecture? Are most of the students awake and functioning, or are they simply going through the motions? Are the students fidgeting in their chairs? Are the students eating and drinking soft drinks during your lecture or doing other class homework? A good class is one that takes notes and asks appropriate questions. At the end of the class, do the students start to get ready to leave 5 minutes early, or 10 minutes early, by shuffling their papers and putting on their coats?

Student Behavior after Class

Are students coming down to ask questions about the material in the lecture, or do they just all leave by the quickest route available? Do students smile when they see you on campus and stop to talk or just stare straight ahead and not "notice" you? Does anyone stop by during your office hours to discuss the material in class or talk about problems in general? Do the students give you the respect inherent to your position in the school? Do the students use positive terms to describe you and your course to their friends?

These are the types of behavioral evaluations that the students give you each day; you should pay attention to these cues and adjust your classroom presentation to bring out the positive side of these cues. If you constantly find negative answers to these behavioral questions, this may be the time for a major modification of your teaching style and content.

Self-Evaluations of the Class and Students

Your attitude toward the students is an important aspect of self-evaluation. Use the following questions to analyze your attitudes toward the students. Be honest with yourself when answering these questions.

Do You Respect the Students?

Do you find yourself thinking of the students as being stupid and only there so you can do research or other creative activities ? Do you think teaching is the evil you must put up with to have the school resources at your disposal? Do you criticize students for incorrect answers to questions in classroom discussions? Are you very sarcastic about the performance of the students? Do you see them as a necessary means to a paycheck?

Do You Respect the Course and the Discipline?

Are you enthusiastic about the course and does it show in your presentation? Do you criticize the textbook, course director, or enforced departmental format in class? Do your lectures transmit the importance of the subject matter to the students, or is this just another stupid freshman survey course? How much do you really respect the discipline and how does this show in the course?

How Well Do You Communicate with the Students?

Good communication requires good organization. I always go over my lecture notes just prior to class; that is why office hours just prior to class are good. I clean overhead transparencies, arrange the lecture pages and re-read the material, and then update with new materials obtained since the last term. Any time I find new material on a topic I add it to the front of my lecture folder on the topic. This allows me to integrate the material before the next class. I can add new transparencies or any other information that will improve the lecture. I then take a binder clip and clip the materials closed. I also like to number the pages of the lecture notes in case I drop the folder; the worst day of your life is when you are trying to sort out your notes in front of 350 students who are becoming more and more restless as you struggle to remember which part of the lecture goes where. When lecturing, do you communicate with a clear, interesting, and accurate message to the students? Can they understand what you are trying to say? Do you make eye contact or do you look down at your notes and read? I find myself looking less at the students since I have gone to a more integrated format that uses a lot of overhead transparencies. I look at the overhead projector too much and have to make a point to make eye contact with the students. Do you stand in one place all the time? A podium is a nice crutch but can you leave it? I make myself walk around the front of the room and, depending on my mood, I may walk all around the room and even sit down next to a student and continue to lecture from there. I usually carry around one page of notes and leave the rest on the podium; this can make class more fun!

Do You Really Care About the Students?

Do you try to learn student names in a small class or at least faces in a large class? Do you portray an air of friendliness and indicate that you are approachable? I encourage the students to come and see me anytime they can find me, not just during office hours. I like students to come up to me off campus and say they took my class and that they remembered me. It is a positive reinforcer to have someone give an unsolicited positive comment. Do you encourage questions both during and after lectures? If you discourage questions early on, you will probably not get many for the rest of the term. Is this the kind of class you want? Are you the type of instructor you would have enjoyed as a student? I remember as a student hating lectures presented by boring people who did not care about the students or the discipline. I made a promise that if I was ever in the position to do a better job, I would. Surprise! I finally have the chance and I try my best to make my classes the best on campus. You should aspire to the same goal.

If you find yourself answering these questions in a negative manner, it may be time for a major re-evaluation of your aspirations in the teaching area.

Improving Your Teaching

Understanding the Need for Improvement

When I first started teaching I thought my course was a very good course; now many years later, I realize that it really was only moderately successful. You will be able to make giant improvements in your teaching in the first few years. A first step is that you must recognize that improvement is possible. Knowing you can improve is half the battle. The other half is a constant striving to improve your presentation, content and attitude. You must look with a critical eye toward the weak aspects of your course. If you deliver a weak lecture because you are not an expert in the field of psychology, read more on the area or sit in on an upper division class on the subject. This improvement is up to you. Identify the areas that you should work on and do the work. You will be amazed at what you really do not know about psychology.

Ask for Help from Your Colleagues

Discuss the course with your colleagues, course supervisor, or department chair for suggestions and ways to improve your performance in the classroom. Many of these veterans of the teaching wars will be happy to share some of their secrets of success. Ask to visit other instructors' classes and observe first hand the strategies that other instructors use to teach psychology. Attending other sections can be especially helpful in improving your course.

The strategies and habits that you develop in these early courses will set the pattern for the rest of your teaching. Strive to be the best instructor in your department and, if you fall short, evaluate your weaknesses and then work to improve your shortcomings. Remember, next term you get a fresh start and a new class of students.

11

Computers and Communications

In the Beginning

I think back to the Dark Ages when I wrote the first edition of this book in 1991. A lot has changed since that time, particularly in computers and communications. In the last decade, locations like Bozeman, Montana have moved from the obscure to the mainstream. The ability to travel to and from areas like Bozeman has seen major improvements. I can be on the West Coast in three hours or the East Coast in five. Also major improvements have occurred in the areas of communications and computers. This chapter will outline some of those changes since they will affect your teaching and professional development.

Old Computers

As I sat down to write the first edition of this book, it took a while for my Zenith 8088 to warm up. The operating speed of 6 Mega Hz was pretty fast at that time at my institution. When this machine was purchased, we were led to believe that the 10 megabyte hard drive would never be fully utilized. I typed in the command word and the computer started to load the MS-DOS Word 4.0 word processing program. I knew that I would have five minutes to think as the computer ground away at this large task. Finally, the program was loaded. No reason to look for the mouse; it had not been invented for this machine. All the commands were key strokes. Five-and-a-quarter inch low density disks were the norm and were very fragile. The 13-inch monochrom, green and yellow monitor was especially inviting as I started the first edition. Printing was always interesting. I walked my floppy (they really were) disk down to the main office, loaded MS Word, up-loaded the chapter to be printed, hit the correct key strokes, and waited for all the fonts to be down loaded, 10-20 minutes in many cases. But I was smiling. Why? I had just given up my Apple IIe and stepped into the computer revolution with my 8088!

The Modern Era

Current Computers

In the last five years, computer hardware and software have made incredible strides. I now sit at my 486/66, with 500 megabytes of memory and realize that I am still not at the high end. Pentium (586) processors running at over 100 megahertz with one gigabyte memory 6x CD ROM readers and large (19-20 inch) thousand color monitors are the norm.

Along with these new computers have come new operating systems, like Windows and Windows 95 that make running any number of different applications easy. How you interface with these new computer applications can affect your teaching significantly. In the following section, I will discuss some of the major applications available at most schools.

The Internet

With the advent of the personal computer in the mid 1970s, the potential for tremendous growth in communications began. Local networks had been in place since that time, with much of the research being sponsored by the military on how to build larger networks. Since 1983 the Internet has grown from a small experimental research project to the largest network of computers in the world. The Internet is in essence a collection of networks and routers that function as a single, large network. The Internet reaches sites in governmental, educational, and commercial organizations around the world.

The World Wide Web (WWW)

The World Wide Web (WWW) is an advanced browsing service (this browsing is called surfing by some individuals). This Internet service organizes information by using hypermedia. Each document contains embedded references to images, audio or other documents. The WWW was first developed to allow physicists around the world to share information. The power of the WWW is that it allows information on one computer to be linked to other computers. In essence, you have the information on every computer in the WWW at your command. By simply clicking on a highlighted reference on your computer screen, you have access to the material on that distant computer.

Your school probably has access to the Internet; if this is the case, be sure to get an address and an account and start a home page as soon as possible. If your school does not provide this service, you should acquire a commercial service.

Come Visit Our WWW Site

One of the first problems many new users of the Internet have is where to start. You can access the Montana State University home page by typing **http://www.montana.edu/** This will access our home page and from there the world is available. One of the nice features about this site is its links to many other sites. By clicking on the netsearch button, you can access several different search engines. These will allow you to access many different sites. By scrolling to departments and clicking on "psychology" you can access **http://www.montana.edu/wwwpy/** which is the psychology department's home page. From this site, you can access various faculty home pages, including my own at **http://www.montana.edu:80/wwwpy/fwpage.html.** I will have an annotated listing of the most up-to-date and interesting sites that I can find. Stop by and check out a picture of me, and my campus, and leave a message or comment on this edition of the book. From the Montana State University home page many of the more useful psychology sites can be accessed. This home page is all you or your students will need to get started on the Internet.

Prentice Hall publishers can be accessed at **http://www.prenhall.com.** This address provides an expanding list of useful and interesting information.

E-Mail

E-mail is one recent development that can greatly impact your career. In the not too distant past, a letter from Bozeman would take 4-5 days to reach a destination in the United States, often weeks overseas. Now via e-mail this time is cut to seconds. If you have a question concerning some aspect of teaching, the textbook, or your research, simply e-mail the individual. If he or she is at the computer, you will receive a reply in minutes, not weeks. In our department all the faculty use e-mail and most of the departmental business is conducted via this paper-less mode. Memos between the head and the faculty are sent via e-mail, and meeting times and assignments are likewise sent via e-mail. All communications are stored not in a wasted space filing cabinet but rather on the hard disk of our computers.

There are many different types of e-mail interfaces your department or computer center can give you, as well as the necessary address and software to access this wonderful modern communication application.

Bulletin Boards

Many different chat lines are available through both school (local) and commercial (national) services on almost any topic you can imagine. Through these bulletin board you can find just about any type of information you want. A good example are teaching tips (TIPS); to subscribe send the message SUBSCRIBE TIPS <Your First Name> <Your Last Name> to E2PSYSOU@FRE.FSU.UMD.EDU. TIPS is an interesting bulletin board on tips specific to the teaching of psychology. This single site can generate from 10-25 messages a day! A very large amount of time can be consumed using these services. See an article in *Psychological Science*, Vol. 6, No. 4 July 1995, by Kelley-Milburn for some excellent sites and a thorough background on resources for psychologists.

Browsing the Internet

One of the major tools for accessing research and teaching materials is Gopher. This system uses easy-to-follow menus and is a major source of information. This system can be accessed through the MSU home page along with several other browsing programs.

Electronic Journals

Several journals are currently available, and an increasing number are being added. Some of these journals are or will be available only electronically. Following is a short list of places to start:

Psyche, psyche-1 on listserv@nki.bitnet: SUB psyche-1 <your first name> <your last name>.

Psycholoquy, a refereed electronic journal with an emphasis on cognitive science, neuroscience, behavioral biology, linguistics and philosophy. To subscribe, listserv@pucc.bitnet: SUB psyc<your first name><your last name>.

PSYGRD-J, a journal dedicated to publishing articles from the graduate student perspective in psychology. To subscribe, listserv@acadvml.uottawa.ca. SUBpsychgrd-j<your first name><your last name>.

Data Bases

Several methods of searching data bases are also available. Some are free and some require a subscription fee. These include services such as *PsychLit, Current Contents, Carl Uncovered,* and *Eric.* By browsing or searching the Internet, you can receive information on these services.

Psi Chi, The National Honor Society in Psychology

This organization was founded in 1929 at Yale University for the purpose of encouraging, stimulating, and maintaining excellence in scholarship and advancing the science of psychology. Psi Chi is open to undergraduate and graduates, men and women. Psi Chi is a member of the Association of College Honor Societies and is an affiliate of the American Psychological Association (APA) and the American Psychological Society (APS). Psi Chi's sister honor society is Psi Beta, the national honor society in psychology for community and junior colleges. There are currently over 840 senior colleges and universities with active chapters in the United States. For more information, contact the Psi Chi National Office, 407 East 5th Street, Suite B, Chattanooga, TN 37403 or e-mail psichi@utcvm.utc.edu.

If your school has an active chapter, this is a good way to become associated with the best students in your department. If your school has either an inactive or no chapter, a good way to fulfill your service commitment to the department would be by starting a chapter.

Communications Services

Individuals who do not have access to the Internet through their school or who want access in their homes can subscribe to commercial companies. These include *America on Line (AOL)*, *Compuserve*, *Prodigy* and *Microsoft Network* and are the major services available. Check your local telephone book for listings of other providers in your area.

United Parcel Service (UPS) and Federal Express (FedX)

I am still amazed that I can deposit a parcel at 5 p.m. in Bozeman, Montana and it will be delivered virtually anywhere in the United States the next morning by 10:30 a.m., and for under 15 dollars; what a deal. The US mail still requires 4-5 days to many locations and has no method of tracking your letter. This increase in the level and speed of communication time takes weeks off the correspondence between individuals. There are other services, but these two are the major ones. Check your local telephone book for others.

The FAX

Within the last five years, the FAX machine has moved from a curiosity used only in large companies and departments to a necessity for most individuals. This is the fastest and often least expensive method of sending documents that do not require an original. Locate your department FAX and review the operation and billing procedures.

Journals

Two of the best are *Teaching of Psychology*, Lawrence Erlbaum Associates, Publishers, 365 Broadway, Hillsdale, NJ 07642, and *The Teaching Professor,* Magna Publications, Inc., 2718 Dryden Drive, Madison, WI 53704. Other very good journals can be located in Appendix D and F.

Computer Magazines

The following is a brief listing of the major magazines dedicated to either computers or the Internet.

Internet World, Mecklermedia Corp., 20 Ketchum Street, Westport CT 06880.

Mac World, 501 Second Street, San Francisco, CA 94107.

Multia Media, PC World Communications Inc., 501 Second Street #600, San Francisco, CA 94107.

New Media, P.O. Box 1771, Riverton, NJ 08077.

PC Computing, P.O. Box 58229, Boulder, CO 80322.

PC Magazine, One Park Avenue, New York, NY 10016

PC World, PC World Communications Inc., 501 Second Street #600, San Francisco, CA 94107.

Wired, PO Box 191826, San Francisco, CA 94119

Video

The use of video recording technology can be useful in the classroom. You can play pre-recorded tapes, and a possible additional use is to record your lectures for your own review. You can see the positive and negative aspects of each lecture and can improve each lecture. You can also document your teaching for tenure and promotion. A good demonstration would be to show clips from your first attempt at a lecture and your progress several years later. Videos can document improvement in your teaching.

Wild Waste of Time

Despite the information and fun that can be found on the Internet and the World Wide Web, a note of caution. These services mentioned above can be a tremendous consumer of time. Once you are on-line and surfing the Internet, you may spend valuable time that could be directed to either teaching or research. Additionally, if you are on a commercial service you can pay a lot for the services, typically based on a minimum number of hours per month and a dollar per hour fee after the minimum. Be careful not to spend too much time and money doing non-productive work.

12

Final Thoughts

The Big Three

Major consideration must be given to how you will distribute the finite energy that you have during your first years as a faculty member. In most schools there are three components to a successful instructor: research, teaching, and service. Depending on the size and emphasis of your school, these three components must be adjusted.

Research

Research is what most of us are taught to do in graduate school. Your speciality can be in any field of psychology, this is what you are the expert at. Along with research comes the most important area: grants. If you can secure some grant funding in the beginning of your career, you will have a substantial head start on other new faculty members. Many public institutions are morphing into a hybrid public/grant funded institution. Reliance on grant funding to back-fill the ever shrinking funding from the public sector is a common scenario in higher education. The use of these funds at an ever-increasing rate to fulfill the mission of the school is an interesting use of research funds. Individuals with grant funding are in a position to receive special consideration when it comes to tenure and promotion. If you can get funding early and in a substantial amount, you are in a good position.

Teaching

How to teach is what you probably were not taught in graduate school. Teaching is what many of us want to do at our school. This book attempts to help on this journey. At many research institutions, teaching comes in a distant second in importance. You can be the best teacher in your school and never be promoted to full professor. But at the same time, you must be a good teacher to become tenured. The mix between research and teaching can be interesting; the best researchers get grants and buy out of teaching. They can be the best teachers, but they are also the funded researchers. In some cases, teaching faculty are deemed to be at a lower level than research faculty.

Service

This is the area that many of us like to spend our time. Service can be to the school in the form of committee assignments, directors of programs, search committees, tenure and promotion committees, faculty advisor to honor societies, or work on the faculty governance body--all the things you do that you do not get paid for. In the community, this service can come in the form of volunteer work for non-profit agencies, free clinics, youth organizations, or charitable organizations that enhance the community.

Many times individuals believe that this service commitment is an important commitment not only to the school but the community. However, in some cases, the school does not have the same perspective. Many a faculty member has not been promoted or tenured because he or she invested his or her energies in the service area at the expense of the research and teaching areas.

Balancing the Big Three

The balancing of research, teaching, and service depends on your school. If you are at a large university, this is fairly easy; research, teaching and service in that order. A small private liberal arts college? A two-year junior college? Then what? Look at what most of the younger faculty do with their time. Ask your chair for some direction. Ask your colleagues in the department. Get as many opinions from diverse sources as you can. Your department will have some sort of promotion and tenure document that will give you official/formal requirements but in some cases these requirements do not always fit the real requirements exactly. Know the parameters and adjust your mix to fit these as well as possible.

The End

After reading this book describing how to find your way through the maze of teaching your first psychology class, I hope the task will be easier. Throughout this book, I have attempted to share my experiences in teaching with the hope that this knowledge will give you a shortcut to becoming the good instructor you want to be.

The following is a summary of an article by Michael J. Strube (1991), that does a good job of summing up general rules for effective and ineffective teaching; this list of do's and don'ts is an interesting final look at the strategies in teaching psychology.

Ten Rules for Effective Teaching

1. *Develop clear goals, objectives, and course policies.* These provide the blueprint for the class. Develop both process (or "how to") goals and outcome (or "where to") goals. The goals and objectives you use should be communicated to the class in a carefully and clearly written syllabus. All aspects of the course (e.g., textbook, assignments, exams, papers, discussions, and evaluations) should follow from the course goals. Students should never be mystified by any aspect of the class.

2. *Know your teaching environment*, and use it to enhance your teaching and the students' learning.

3. *Know your material.* There is no excuse for being unprepared.

4. *Facilitate positive relationships* with your students. Take the time to get to know and understand them. Be sensitive to their needs. Treat them honestly, and be flexible in handling their problems. Recognize that each student is an individual with a unique perspective. Never belittle a student for expressing a viewpoint or attitude.

5. *Effective teaching involves effective communication* that motivates. Enthusiasm and organization are two critical components of effective teaching. Provide structure to the material and engage the students through clear examples, applications, anecdotes, and a variety of presentation (e.g., guest speakers, audiovisual aids, discussion groups, student presentations, etc.).

6. *Try to teach students how to think.* The facts fade quickly from memory, but the rules for good thinking can be used anywhere and at anytime. In particular, train students how to evaluate ideas critically and present ideas clearly. Train students how to express themselves effectively in speaking and writing.

7. Each lecture, as well as the entire course, should tell an engaging and *coherent story*. A good story has a beginning, a middle, and an end. It has a plot that is logically consistent and binds the facts and characters together.

8. Students should be provided *valid, reliable, and frequent evaluation* of their progress toward the course goals. Given the problems with any one method of evaluation, several methods should be used so that students have ample opportunity to demonstrate what they know.

9. *Know yourself*. Be aware of your teaching strengths and weaknesses. Evaluate your teaching frequently, and use several methods. Find an effective teaching style that is a natural extension of your personality (i.e., be yourself).

10. *Have fun*. Teaching and learning should be enjoyable. Allow spontaneity, and encourage a spirit of play.

Take the time to plan your course and present the best effort that you can. Take the time to evaluate the content and style of your course; after this evaluation make every effort possible to improve your mistakes. The next time you teach this course it should be much improved.

Pass on the experiences of your education to the next generation of students. Some of your first students could be your colleagues in the future.

Good luck on your teaching career; remember, have fun!

Appendix A
Text Request Form
School Letter Head

Publisher Name and Address   Date

Dear Publisher:

Please send me a copy of _____, _____ Edition for possible adoption in my Psychology ____ class, for _____ Semester/Quarter 199_ . Please also send any ancillaries available with this text.

Class Name: Introductory Psychology

Class Number: _____

Present Text: _____

Number of Students per section: _____

Telephone Number: _____

Office Hours: _____

Text Needed By: _____

Decision Date: _____

Committee or individual decision :_____

Thank You

Your Name
Your Rank

Appendix B

PSYCHOLOGY 100S (01)

SCHEDULE OF IMPORTANT DATES

EXAMINATION #1	October 2: Chapters 1, 2, 3 & 4
EXAMINATION #2	November 6: Chapters 5, 6, 7 & 8
EXAMINATION # 3	December 6: Chapters 9, 10, & 11
FINAL EXAMINATION	December 17th, 6pm

GENERAL INFORMATION

OFFICE	305 TRAPHAGEN HALL
OFFICE HOURS	MWF 1-2 pm, MW 5:30-6 pm
PHONE	994-5172

ESSAY DUE DATES

October 10, November 11, & December 17. Due in class at the beginning of the period.

Appendix C
Psychology Teaching Resources

General Psychology Teaching References

Allen, R.R., & Rueter, T. (1990) *Teaching assistant strategies: An introduction to college teaching.* Dubuque IA: Kendall/Hunt.

Benjamin, L. T., Daniel, R. S., & Brewer, C. L. (Eds.) (1985). *Handbook for teaching introductory psychology.* Hillsdale, NJ: Erlbaum. A collection of articles from *Teaching of Psychology*, including general issues and various activities.

Benjamin, L. T., & Lowman, K. D. (Eds.) (1981). *Activities handbook for the teaching of psychology.* Washington, DC: American Psychological Association.

Charles, C. M. (1992). *Building Classroom Discipline* (4th ed). White Plains, NY: Longman.

Diogenes, R., & Vestal, L. B., (1994) *Prentice Hall Critical Thinking Resource Manual for Psychology.* Upper Saddle River, NJ: Prentice Hall. Available through your Prentice Hall Representative.

Gardner, R. M. (1980). *Exercises for general psychology.* Minneapolis: Burgess.

Gleitman, H. (1984). Introducing psychology. *American Psychologist, 39,* 421-427.

Hock, R. (1992). *Forty studies that changed psychology.* Upper Saddle River, NJ: Prentice Hall. Available through your Prentice Hall Representative.

Johnson, G. R. (1995). *First steps to excellence in college teaching.* Madison, WI: Magna Publishing.

Johnson, M., & Wertheimer, M. (Eds.) (1979). *The psychology teacher's resource book: First course.* Washington, DC: American Psychological Association.

Herb, D. O. (1974). What psychology is about. *American Psychologist, 29,* 71-79.

Keller, F., & Sherman, J. (1974). *The Keller plan handbook*. Menlo Park, CA: W. A. Benjamin.

Magnan, R. (1990). *147 practical tips for teaching professors*. Madison, WI: Magna Publishing.

Makosky, U. P., Whittemore, L. G., & Rogers, A. J. (Eds.) (1987). *Activities handbook for the teaching of psychology*. Vols. 2. Washington, DC: American Psychological Association.

Makosky, U. P., Whittemore, L. G., & Skutley, M. L. (Eds.) (1990). *Activities handbook for the teaching of psychology*. Vols. 3. Washington, DC: American Psychological Association.

McKeachie, W. J. (1986). *Teaching tips: A guidebook for the beginning college teacher (8th ed)*. Lexington, MA: D.C. Heath.

McKenzie, S., & Cangemi, J. P. (1978). What new students in introduction to psychology really want to learn: A survey. *Journal of Instructional Psychology, 5,* 5-7.

McLeod, R. B. (1971). The teaching of psychology. *American Psychologist, 26,* 245-249.

Neff, A., & Weimer, M. (Eds) (1989). *Classroom communications: Collected readings for effective discussion and questioning*. Madison, WI: Magna Publishing.

Parrott, L. (1994) *How to write psychology papers*, New York: Harper Collins.

Pettijohn, T. (1994). *Sources: Notable selections in psychology*. Guilford, CT: Dushkin Publishing.

Pregent, R. (1994). *Charting your course: How to prepare to teach more effectively*. Madison, WI: Magna Publishing.

Radford, J., & Rose, D. (Eds.) (1980). *The teaching of psychology*. New York: John Wiley & Sons.

Ryan, J. B. (1974). *Keller's personalized system of instruction: An appraisal*. Washington, DC: American Psychological Association.

Schoenfiled, A. C., & Magan, R. (1994). *Mentor in a manual: Climbing the academic ladder to tenure*. Madison, WI: Magna Publishing.

Silverstein, B. (1982). Teaching a large lecture course in psychology: Turning defeat into victory. *Teaching of Psychology, 9,* 150-155.

Smith, R. A. (1995). *Challenging your perceptions: Thinking critically about psychology*. Pacific Grove, CA: Brooks/Cole.

Walker, E. I., & McKeachie, W. J. (1967). *Some thoughts about teaching the beginning course in psychology*. Belmont, CA: Brooks/Cole.

Weimer M., Parrett, J., & Kerns, M. (1988). *How am I teaching: Forms and activities for acquiring instructional input*. Madison, WI: Magna Publishing.

Weimer M., & Neff R. A. (Eds.) (1990). *Teaching college: Collected reading for the new instructor*. Madison, WI: Magna Publishing.

Appendix D

Psychology Journals

Advances in Neural and Behavioral Development. Ablex Publishing Corporation, 355 Chestnut St., Norwood, NJ 07648.

Advances in Personality Assessment. Lawrence Erlbaum Associates, Inc., 365 Broadway, Box 237, Hillsdale, NJ 07642.

Advances in Psychology. Elsevier Science Publishers P.O., Box 211, 1000 AE, Amsterdam, Netherlands.

Advances in School Psychology. Lawrence Erlbaum Associates, Inc., 365 Broadway, Box 237, Hillsdale, NJ 07642.

American Academy of Psychoanalysis Journal. John Wiley & Sons, Inc., 605 Third Ave., New York, NY 10058.

American Association of Suicidology. American Association of Suicidology, 2459 S. Ash, Denver, CO 80222.

American Association of Mental Retardation. American Association of Mental Retardation, 1719 Kalorama Rd., N.W., Washington, DC 20009.

Consciousness and Self-Regulation. Plenum Publishing Corp., 233 Spring St., New York, NY 10013.

Contributions in Psychology. Greenwood Press, Inc., 88 Post Rd. W., Box 5007, Westport, CT 06881-9990.

Contributions to Residential Treatment. American Association of Children's Residential Centers, 440 First St. N.W., Ste. 310, Washington, DC 20001.

Corrective and Social Psychiatry and Journal of Behavioral Technology Methods and Therapy. Martin Psychiatric Research Foundation, Box 3365, Fairfield, CA 94533-0587.

Counseling Psychologist. Sage Publications, Inc., 2111 W. Hillcrest Dr., Newbury Park, CA 91320.

Cultural Context of Infancy. Ablex Publishing Corporation, 355 Chestnut St., Norwood, NJ 07648.

Current Issues in Psychoanalytic Practice. Haworth Press Inc., 12 W. 32nd St., New York, NY 10001.

Current Psychological Research and Reviews. Transaction Periodicals Consortium, Rutgers University, Dept. 2000, New Brunswick, NJ 08903.

Current Psychology. Psychological Press, Box 309, Hendersonville, TN 37075.

Current Topics in Human Intelligence. Ablex Publishing Corporation, 355 Chestnut St., Norwood, NJ 07648.

Current Topics in Learning Disabilities. Ablex Publishing Corporation, 355 Chestnut St., Norwood, NJ 07648.

Developmental Psychology. American Psychological Association, 1200 17th St. N.W., Washington, DC 20036.

Developmental Review. Academic Press, Inc., Journal Division, 1250 Sixth Ave., San Diego, CA 92101.

Developments in Clinical Psychology. Ablex Publishing Corporation, 355 Chestnut St., Norwood, NJ 07648.

European Journal of Social Psychology. John Wiley & Sons Ltd., Baffins Lane, Chichester, Sussex PO19 1UD, England.

European Monographs in Social Psychology. Academic Press, Inc., 1250 Sixth Ave., San Diego, CA 92101.

Foundation of Thanatology. Foundation of Thanatology, Foundation Book & Periodical Division, Box 1191, Brooklyn, NY 11202-1202.

Foundation of Thanatology Series. Charles C. Thomas, Publisher, 2600 South First St., Springfield, IL 62717.

G.E.J. Newsletter. Grief Education Institute, 2422 S. Downing St., No. 1, Denver, CO 80210-5812.

Gestalt Journal. Center for Gestalt Development, Inc., Box 990, Highland, NY 12528.

Groups: A Journal of Group Dynamics and Psychotherapy. Association of Medical Group Psychoanalysts, c/o David Weisselberger, M.D., Ed., 185 E. 85th St., New York, NY 10028.

Handbook of Psychology and Health. Lawrence Erlbaum Associates, Inc., 365 Broadway, Hillsdale, NJ 07642.

Individual Psychology. University of Texas Press, Box 7819, Austin, TX 78713.

Infant Behavior and Development. Ablex Publishing Corporation, 355 Chestnut St., Norwood, NJ 07648.

Institute for Consciousness & Music Newsletter. I.C.M. West Press, c/o IMI, 8600 Foundry St., No. 2028, Savage, MD 20763-9514.

Institute for Psychoanalysis. Chicago Institute for Psychoanalysis, 180 N. Michigan Ave., Chicago, IL 60601.

Interbehaviorist. c/o Edward K. Morris, Ed., 2035-D Haworth Hall, Department of Human Development, University of Kansas, Lawrence, KS 66045.

International Congress of Graphoanalysts. International Graphoanalysis Society, 111 N. Canal St., Chicago, IL 60606.

International Journal of Comparative Psychology. Human Sciences Press, Inc., 71 Fifth Ave., New York, NY 10011-8004.

International Psychologist. International Council of Psychologists, Inc., c/o Dr. Carleton Shay, Ed., Educational Foundations Dept., California State University, Los Angeles, CA 90032.

Journal of Biodynamic Psychology. Biodynamic Psychology Publications, Boyesen Institute for Biodynamic Psychology, Centre Ave., Acton, London W.3, England.

Journal of Black Psychology. Association of Black Psychologists, Box 55999, Washington, DC 20040-5999.

Journal of Business and Psychology. Human Sciences Press, Inc., 72 Fifth Ave., New York, NY 10011-8004.

Journal of Child and Adolescent Psychotherapy. Rivendell Foundation, 5100 Poplar Ave., Ste. 2820, Memphis, TN 38137.

Journal of Child Psychology and Psychiatry. Pergamon Press, Inc., Journals Division, Maxwell House, Fairview Park, Elmsford, NY 10523.

Journal of Child Psychotherapy. Association of Child Psychotherapists, Burgh House, New End Sq., London NW3 1LT, England.

Journal of Clinical Psychology. Clinical Psychology Publishing Co., Inc., 4 Conant Square, Brandon, VT 05733.

Journal of Cognitive Psychotherapy. Springer Publishing Company, 536 Broadway, New York, NY 10012.

Journal of College Student Psychotherapy. Haworth Press, Inc., 12 W. 32nd St., New York, NY 10001.

Journal of Communication Disorders. Elsevier Science Publishing Co., Inc., 52 Vanderbilt Ave., New York, NY 10017.

Journal of Community Psychology. Clinical Psychology Publishing Co., Inc., 4 Conant Square, Brandon, VT 05733.

Journal of Comparative Psychology. American Psychological Association, 1200 17th St., N.W., Washington, DC 20036.

Journal of Consulting and Clinical Psychology. American Psychological Association, 1200 17th St., N.W., Washington, DC 20036.

Journal of Cross Cultural Psychology. Sage Publications, Inc., 2111 W. Hillcrest Dr., Newbury Park, CA 91320.

Journal of Educational Psychology. American Psychological Association, 1200 17th St., N.W., Washington, DC 20036.

Journal of Experimental Psychology: General. American Psychological Association, 1200 17th St., N.W., Washington, DC 20036.

Journal of Experimental Psychology: Human Perception and Performance. American Psychological Association, 1200 17th St., N.W., Washington, DC 20036.

Journal of Experimental Psychology: Learning, Memory, and Cognition. American Psychological Association, 1200 17th St., N.W., Washington, DC 20036.

Journal of Experimental Social Psychology. Academic Press, Inc., Journal Division, 1250 Sixth Ave., San Diego, CA 92101.

Journal of Near-Death Studies. Human Sciences Press, Inc., 72 Fifth Ave., New York, NY 10011-8004.

Journal of Nonverbal Behavior. Human Sciences Press, Inc., 72 Fifth Ave., New York, NY 10011-8004.

Journal of Occupational Psychology. British Psychological Society, St. Andrews House, 48 Princess Rd., E. Leicester LE1 7DR, England.

Journal of Organizational Behavior Management. Haworth Press, Inc., 12 W. 32nd St., New York, NY 10001.

Journal of Personality and Social Psychology. American Psychological Association, 1200 17th St., N.W., Washington, DC 20036.

Journal of Personality Assessment. Lawrence Erlbaum Associates, Inc., 365 Broadway, Hillsdale, NJ 07642.

Journal of Personality Disorders. Guilford Publications, Inc., 72 Spring St., 4th Fl., New York, NY 10012.

Journal of Phenomenological Psychology. Humanities Press, Inc., Atlantic Highlands, NJ 07716.

Journal of Psychohistory. Atcom, Inc., Atcom Bldg., 2315 Broadway, New York, NY 10024-4397.

Journal of Psychophysiology. Oxford University Press, Walton St., Oxford OX2 6DP, England.

Journal of Psychotherapy & The Family. Haworth Press, Inc., 12 W. 32nd St., New York, NY 10001.

Journal of Rational-Emotive and Cognitive-Behavior Therapy. Human Sciences Press, Inc. 72 Fifth Ave., New York, NY 10011.

Journal of Religion and the Applied Behavioral Sciences. Association for Creative Change Within Religious and Other Social Systems, Box 219, Frederick, MD 21701-0219.

Library of Analytical Psychology Series. Academic Press, Inc., 1250 Sixth Ave., San Diego, CA 92101.

Lifestyles. Human Sciences Press, Inc. 72 Fifth Ave., New York, NY 10011.

Memory and Cognition. Psychonomic Society, Inc., 1710 Fortview Rd., Austin, TX 78704.

Minnesota Symposia on Child Psychology. Lawrence Erlbaum Associates, Inc., 365 Broadway, Hillsdale, NJ 07642.

Modern Psychoanalysis. Center for Modern Psychoanalytic Studies, 16 W. 10th St., New York, NY 10011.

Naropa Institute Journal of Psychology. Naropa Institute, 2130 Arapahoe Ave., Boulder, CO 80302.

National Character Laboratory Newsletter. National Character Laboratory, 4635 Leeds Ave., El Paso, TX 79903.

National Psychological Association for Psychoanalysis. Psychological Association for Psychoanalysis, Inc., 150 W. 13th St., New York, NY 10011.

Parenting Studies. Eterna Press, Box 1344, Oak Brook, IL 60521.

Pathways. Educational Society, Box 5719, Takoma Park, MD 20912-0719.

Pavlovian Journal of Biological Science. J.B. Lippincott Co., E. Washington Sq., Philadelphia, PA 19105.

Pediatric Mental Health. Pediatric Projects, Inc., Box 1880, Santa Monica, CA 90406-1880.

Perception. Pion Ltd., 207 Brondesbury Park, London NW2 5JN, England.

Personality and Individual Differences. Pergamon Press, Inc., Journals Division, Maxwell House, Fairview Park, Elmsford, NY 10523.

Personality and Social Psychology Bulletin. Sage Publications, Inc., 2111 W. Hillcrest Dr., Newbury Park, CA 91320.

Personality, Psychopathology and Psychotherapy. Academic Press, Inc., 1250 Sixth Ave., San Diego, CA 92101.

Personnel Psychology. Personnel Psychology, Inc., 9660 Hillcroft, Ste. 337, Houston, TX 77096.

Population and Environment. Human Sciences Press, Inc. 72 Fifth Ave., New York, NY 10011.

Population and Environmental Psychology Newsletter. American Psychological Association, Division 34, 1200 17th St., N.W., Washington, DC 20036.

Progress in Behavior Modification. Academic Press, Inc., 1250 Sixth Ave., San Diego, CA 92101.

Progress in Experimental Personality Research. Academic Press, Inc., 1250 Sixth Ave., San Diego, CA 92101.

Progress in Psychobiology and Physiological Psychology. Academic Press, Inc., 1250 Sixth Ave., San Diego, CA 92101.

Progress in Self Psychology. Guilford Publications, Inc., 72 Spring St., 4th Fl., New York, NY 10012.

Psychological Bulletin. American Psychological Association, 1200 17th St., N.W., Washington, DC 20036.

Psychological Review. American Psychological Association, 1200 17th St., N.W., Washington, DC 20036.

Psychology. Pennsylvania State University, McKeesport Campus, University Dr., McKeesport, PA 15132.

Psychology Today. American Psychological Association, 1200 17th St., N.W., Washington, DC 20036.

Psychometrika. c/o Cynthia Null, Department of Psychology, College of William and Mary, Williamsburg, VA 23185.

Psychonomic Society Bulletin. Psychonomic Society, Inc., 1710 Fortview Rd., Austin, TX 78704.

Research in Organizational Behavior. J.A.I. Press, Inc., 55 Old Post Rd., No. 2, Box 1678, Greenwich, CT 06836-1678.

Review of Behavior Therapy: Theory & Practice. Guilford Publications, Inc., 72 Spring St., 4th Fl., New York, NY 10012.

Review of Existential Psychology and Psychiatry. Box 23220, Seattle, WA 98102.

Review of Personality and Social Psychology. Sage Publications, Inc., 2111 W. Hillcrest Dr., Newbury Park, CA 91320.

Sage Series in Cross Cultural Research and Methodology. Sage Publications, Inc., 2111 W. Hillcrest Dr., Newbury Park, CA 91320.

Saybrook Review. Saybrook Institute, Graduate School and Research Center, 1772 Vallejo St., San Francisco, CA 94123.

Soviet Psychology. M.E. Sharpe, Inc., 80 Business Park Dr., Armonk, NY 10504.

Teaching of Psychology. Lawrence Erlbaum Associates, Inc., 365 Broadway, Hillsdale, NJ 07642

The Sports Psychologist. Human Kinetics Publishers, Inc., 1607 N. Market, Box 5076, Champaign, IL 61820..

Spring. Spring Publications, Inc., Box 222069, Dallas, TX 75222.

Springer Series in Cognitive Development. Springer-Verlag, 175 Fifth Ave., New York, NY 10010.

Appendix E

Introductory Psychology Texts

The following is a listing of most texts currently in print as of summer 1995. These texts are listed in relative level of presentation.

High Level	Upper -Middle Level	Middle level	Lower Middle Level	Low Level
Atkinson & HB	Bernstein & HM	Baron A&B	Crooks & HB	Coon - West
Carlson & AB	Crider & HC	Benjamin & PH	Feldman & McG	Feldman & McC
Gleitman - Norton	Roediger & HC	Davis & -PH	Gerow - HC	Huffman & Wil
Gray - Worth	Bourne & HB	Dworetzky-West	Laird - HM	Kagan & HB
Zimbardo - HC	Seaman & PH	Gleitman Basic	Lefton A&B	Lahey - WCB
Shaver & Mac	Santrock - WCB	Kalat - B/C	Morris PH	Haber & McG
Sternberg & HB	Weiten - B/C	Myers - Worth	Ornstein & HBJ	Morris Ess - PI
	Wortman & McG	Sdorow - WCB	Santrock -WCB	Wood & B/C
		Smith - West	Papalia & McG	Plotnik - B/C
		Wade & HC	Peterson - HC	
		Worchel & PH	Rathus - HBJ	

Appendix F

Teaching and Research Resources

The following is a selective, but reasonably complete, list of journals in psychology and related fields, such as behavioral science, cognitive science, communication science, neural science, and psychological medicine. I have mainly included English-language journals; the non-English journals that are included are obvious from the title. I have classified the quality of each journal in terms of the selectivity, or rejection rate, whenever I felt somewhat qualified to do so. Note that this is a rough average for articles published in each journal; the quality of some articles may be lower or higher.

Key to Journal Ratings:

**** Known to be a very high-quality, very highly refereed (very selective) journal.

*** Known to be a moderately high-quality, moderately highly refereed (moderately selective) journal.

** Known to be an intermediate-quality, slightly refereed (somewhat selective) journal.

* Known to be a low-quality, nonrefereed or only slightly refereed (very unselective) journal.

No rating indicates that I am not familiar with the journal.

invit Invited articles only.
mag Magazine.
news Professional newsletter.
new Too new to rate.

Following each journal title, I list the Medline abbreviation, if known.

Rat.	Journal Name abbreviation (if known)	Medline
***	Acta Psychologica	Acta Psychol
	Addictive Behaviors	
	Adolescence	
**	American Behavioral Scientist	
	American Journal of Community Psychology	
***	American Journal of Clinical Hypnosis	Am J Clin Hypn
**½	American Journal of Mental Deficiency/Retardation	Am J Ment Defic
	American Journal of Psychiatry	Am J Psychiatry
	American Journal of Psychoanalysis	Am J Psychoanal
**½	American Journal of Psychology	Am J Psychol
**½	American Psychologist	Am Psychol
mag	American Scientist [very good articles]	
***	Animal Learning and Behavior	
**½	Annals of the New York Academy of Sciences	Ann N Y Acad Sci
**	Année Psychologique	Année Psychol
****	Annual Review of Psychology	Annu Rev Psychol
news	APA Monitor [professional issues, employment ads]	
***	Applied Cognitive Psychology	
**	Applied Psychological Measurement	
	Applied Psychology	
	Applied Psycholinguistics	
news	APS Observer [professional issues, employment ads]	
	Archives of Sexual Behavior	
**	Australian Journal of Psychology	
**	Behavior Genetics	Behav Genet
	Behavior Modification	
**	Behavior Research Methods and Instrumentation	
**	Behavior Research Methods, Instruments, and Computers	
**	Behavior Therapy	
****	Behavioral and Brain Sciences	
***	Behavioral and Neural Biology	Behav Neural Biol
**½	Behavioral Biology	Behav Biol
***	Behavioral Brain Research	Behav Brain Res
**½	Behavioral Medicine	Behav Med
***	Behavioral Neuroscience	Behav Neurosci
**	Behavioral Science	Behav Sci
	Behavioral Processes	
**	Biofeedback and Self-Regulation	
	Biological Cybernetics	Biol Cybern
	Biological Psychiatry	Biol Psychiatry
**½	Biological Psychology	Biol Psychol
***	Brain	Brain
	Brain, Behavior and Evolution	Brain Behav Evol
***	Brain and Cognition	

***	Brain and Language	Brain Lang
***	Brain Research	Brain Res
***	Brain Research Bulletin	Brain Res Bull
***	Brain Research: Cognitive Brain Research	
	British Journal of Clinical Pharmacology	Br J Clin
	British Journal of Clinical Psychology	
	British Journal of Developmental Psychology	
	British Journal of Educational Psychology	Br J Educ Psychol
***	British Journal of Mathematical and Statistical Psychology	
	British Journal of Medical Psychology	Br J Med Psychol
	British Journal of Social Psychology	
	British Journal of Psychiatry	Br J Psychiatry
***½	British Journal of Psychology	Br J Psychol
	British Journal of Social and Clinical Psychology	
***½	British Medical Journal	Br Med J
*	Bulletin of the Psychonomic Society	
**½	Cahiers de Psychologie Cognitive	
	Canadian Journal of Experimental Psychology	
**	Canadian Journal of Psychology	Can J Psychol
**	Canadian Psychology/Psychologie Canadienne	
**	Child Development	Child Dev
	Child Study Journal	
	Clinical Neuropharmacology	
	Clinical Pharmacology and Therapeutics	
	Clinical Psychology Review	
***½	Cognition	Cognition
	Cognition and Emotion	
	Cognitive Development	
***½	Cognitive Neuropsychology	Cog Neuropsy
****	Cognitive Psychology	Cognit Psychol
***½	Cognitive Science	
	Cognitive Therapy and Research	
**½	Consciousness and Cognition	
****	Contemporary Psychology [invited book reviews only]	
***	Cortex	Cortex
**	Counseling Psychologist	
**½	Current Directions in Psychological Science	
	Developmental Psychobiology	
***	Developmental Psychology	
	Developmental Neuropsychology	
	Diseases of the Nervous System	Dis Nerv Syst
*	Dissertation Abstracts International	
	Drug and Alcohol Dependency	
**	Educational and Psychological Measurement	
**	Electroencephalography and Clinical Neurophysiology	
**½	Environment and Behavior	
	Epilepsy Research	Epilepsy Res
**	Ergonomics	Ergo
**	European Journal of Cognitive Psychology	
**	European Journal of Social Psychology	
***	Experimental Brain Research	Exp Brain Res
	Family Process	
	Family Therapy	

145

**	Genetic Psychology Monographs	
	Genetic, Social, and General Psychology Monographs	
	Hospital and Community Psychiatry	
**	Human Factors	Hum Factors
**	Human Learning	
**	Human Neurobiology	Hum Neurobiol
	Human Physiology	Hum Physiol
**½	Imagination, Cognition and Personality	
*½	Indian Journal of Psychology	
***	Intelligence	
**	International Journal of Aging and Human Development	
	International Journal of Neuropsychiatry	
**	International Journal of Neuroscience	Int J Neurosci
	International Journal of Psycho-Analysis	IJP-A
**	International Journal of Psychology	IJPsychol
**	International Journal of Psychophysiology	Int J Psychophysiol
	International Journal of the Addictions	Int J Addict
***	Investigative Ophthalmology and Visual Science	
	Japanese Journal of Physiology	Jpn J Physiol
*½	Japanese Journal of Psychology	Jpn J Psychol
	Journal de Psychologie Normale et Pathologique	
***½	Journal of Abnormal and Social Psychology	
***	Journal of Abnormal Psychology	J Abnorm Psychol
	Journal of Abnormal Child Psychology	
	Journal of Advances in Nursing	J Adv Nurs
	Journal of Affective Disorders	J Affect Disord
	Journal of Aging and Health	
**	Journal of Altered States of Consciousness	
***	Journal of Applied Behavior Analysis	J Appl Behav Anal
	Journal of Applied Behavioral Science	
	Journal of Applied Physiology	J Appl Physiol
****	Journal of Applied Psychology	J Appl Psychol
	Journal of Applied Social Psychology	
	Journal of Auditory Research	J Aud Res
***	Journal of Behavioral Decision Making	
	Journal of Behavioral Medicine	J Behav Med
	Journal of Child Psychology and Psychiatry	
	Journal of Clinical and Experimental Neuropsychology	
	Journal of Clinical Psychiatry	J Clin Psychiatry
**	Journal of Clinical Psychology	J Clin Psychol
***½	Journal of Cognitive Neuroscience	
	Journal of Communication	
***½	Journal of Comparative Psychology	
***	Journal of Comparative and Physiological Psychology	
***	Journal of Consulting and Clinical Psychology	
***	Journal of Counseling Psychology	
***	Journal of Cross-Cultural Psychology	
***	Journal of Educational Psychology	
**½	Journal of Environmental Psychology	
**	Journal of Experimental Child Psychology	J Exp Child Psychol
****	Journal of Experimental Psychology	J Exp Psychol
****	Journal of Experimental Psychology: Animal Behavior Proc.	
****	Journal of Experimental Psychology: General	J Exp Psychol Gen

****	Journal of Experimental Psychology: Human Learning and MemoryJ	
****	Journal of Experimental Psychology: Human Perception and Perfor...	
****	Journal of Experimental Psychology: Learning, Memory, and Cogn...	
**	Journal of General Psychology	J Gen Psychol
*½	Journal of Genetic Psychology	J Genet Psychol
	Journal of Geriatric Psychiatry	J Geriatr Psychiatry
**	Journal of Gerontology	J Gerontol
**	Journal of Gerontology: Psychological Sciences	
**	Journal of Humanistic Psychology	
	Journal of Human Movement Studies	
	Journal of Individual Psychology	J Individ Psychol
	Journal of Learning Disabilities	J Learn Disabil
***	Journal of Mathematical Psychology	
***½	Journal of Memory and Language	
	Journal of Mental Deficiency Research	J Ment Defic Res
	Journal of Mental Health Counseling	
	Journal of Mental Sciences	
**	Journal of Mind and Behavior	
**½	Journal of Motor Behavior	
***	Journal of Nervous and Mental Disease	J Nerv Ment Dis
	Journal of Neurology, Neurosurgery and Psychiatry	
	Journal of Neurophysiology	J Neurophysiol
***	Journal of Neuroscience	J Neurosci
	Journal of Nonverbal Behavior	
	Journal of Occupational Psychology	
	Journal of Organizational Behavior Management	
*	Journal of Personality	J Pers
****	Journal of Personality and Social Psychology	J Pers Soc Psychol
**	Journal of Personality Assessment	J Pers Assess
	Journal of Pharmacology and Experimental Therapeutics	
	Journal of Projective Techniques and Personality Assessment	
*½	Journal of Psychedelic Drugs	
	Journal of Psychiatric Research	
*½	Journal of Psychoactive Drugs	
	Journal of Psychohistory	
**	Journal of Psychology	J Psychol
	Journal of Psychosomatic Research	J Psychosom Res
*	Journal of Research in Personality	
	Journal of School Psychology	
	Journal of Social Issues	
**	Journal of Social Psychology	
	Journal of Social and Clinical Psychology	
	Journal of Speech and Hearing Research	J Speech Hear Res
	Journal of Sport and Exercise Psychology	
	Journal of Studies on Alcohol	J Stud Alcohol
	Journal of the Acoustical Society of America	J Acoust Soc Am
	Journal of the American Academy of Child Psychiatry	
	Journal of the American Geriatrics Society	J Am Geriatr Soc
	Journal of the American Psychoanalytic Association	
***	Journal of the Experimental Analysis of Behavior	J Exp Anal Behav
	Journal of the History of the Behavioral Sciences	
	Journal of the Optical Society of America	J Opt Soc Am
***	Journal of the Royal Society of Medicine	J R Soc Med

****	Journal of Verbal Learning and Verbal Behavior	
	Language and Speech	**Lang Speech**
new	Learning and Memory	
***	Learning and Motivation	
***	Life Sciences	**Life Sci**
	Life-Threatening Behavior	
new	Memory	
****	Memory and Cognition	**Mem Cognit**
	Mental Retardation	
	Motivation and Emotion	
	Monographs of the Society for Research in Child Development	
***	Multivariate Behavioral Research	
****	Nature	**Nature**
**½	Nature New Biology	**Nature New Biol**
***	Neuropsychobiology	*******
	Neuropsychologia	**Neuropsychologia**
	Neuropsychology	
	Neuroreport	**Neuroreport**
	Neuroscience and Behavioral Physiology	
	Neuroscience Letters	**Neurosci Lett**
****	Organizational Behavior and Human Decision Processes	
****	Organizational Behavior and Human Performance	
	Operational Research Quarterly	
	Pavlovian Journal of Biological Science	**Pavlov J Biol Sci**
***	Perception	**Perception**
****	Perception and Psychophysics	**Percept Psychophys**
*	Perceptual and Motor Skills	**Percept Mot Skills**
***	Personality and Individual Differences	
***	Personality and Social Psychology Bulletin	
***	Pharmacology, Biochemistry and Behavior	
***	Physiological Psychology	
**	Physiology and Behavior	**Physiol Behav**
**	Proceedings of the Annual Convention of the American Psych. Assoc.	
**	Proceedings of the National Academy of Sciences	**Proc Natl Acad Sci**
***	Professional Psychology	
**	Progress in Brain Research	**Prog Brain Res**
	Psychiatric Quarterly	**Psychiatr Q**
	Psychiatry	**Psychiatry**
	Psychiatry Research	**Psychiatry Res**
	Psychoanalytic Quarterly	**Psychoanal Q**
	Psychoanalytic Review	**Psychoanal Rev**
	Psychoanalytic Study of the Child	
***	Psychobiology	**Psychobio**
*	Psychologia	**Psycholog**
***	Psychological Assessment	
****	Psychological Bulletin	**Psychol Bull**
	Psychological Medicine	**Psychol Med**
***	Psychological Monographs	**Psychol Monogr**
*½	Psychological Record	
*	Psychological Reports	**Psychol Rep**
**	Psychological Research	**Psychol Res**
****	Psychological Review	**Psychol Rev**
***½	Psychological Science	

**	Psychologische Forschung	Psychol Forsch
*	Psychology	
***½	Psychology and Aging	Psychol Aging
	Psychology and Marketing	
	Psychology in the Schools	
***½	Psychology of Learning and Motivation	
	Psychology of Women Quarterly	
mag	Psychology Today [popular pseudo-hip magazine]	
**½	Psychometrica	
****	Psychonomic Bulletin and Review	
*	Psychonomic Science	
	Psychopathology	Psychopathology
	Psychopharmacology	
**	Psychophysiology	Psychophys
	Psychosomatic Medicine	Psychosomat Med
***	Quarterly Journal of Experimental Psychology	Q J Exp Psychol
***	Quarterly Journal of Experimental Psychology - Human Experiml...	
***	Quarterly Journal of Experimental Psychology - Compar. and Phys..	
	Quarterly Journal of Studies on Alcohol	Q J Stud Alcohol
**	Scandanavian Journal of Psychology	Scand J Psychol
	Schizophrenia Bulletin	Schizophr Bull
****	Science	Science
mag	Scientific American [excellent review articles]	
	Sex Roles	
	Small Group Behavior	
	Social Cognition	
	Social Science and Medicine	Soc Sci Med
**	Teaching of Psychology	
***½	Vision Research	Vision Res
**	Zeitschrift für Experimentelle und Angewandte Psychologie	Z Exp Angew
**	Zeitschrift für Gerontologie	Z Gerontol
**	Zeitschrift für Psychologie	Z Psychol
**	Zeitschrift für Tierpsychologie	Z Psychol

Appendix G

Glossary for Psychology

Abnormal behavior Behavior may be so labeled when it is unusual, causes distress to others, and makes it difficult for a person to adjust to his or her environment.

Absolute refractory period Period after a cell has fired, during which it will not fire again. Usually lasts for about 1 millisecond.

Absolute Threshold The weakest level of stimulus intensity that is capable of producing a sensation 50 percent of the time.

Abstraction In reasoning and thinking, the ability to go beyond surface appearances and understand the core of a problem.

Accommodation The process of revising a person's cognitive structure to meet environmental demands and make it more congruent with experience. (See also Assimilation)

Acetylcholine (aCh) Chemical transmitter in neurons that tends to transmit fast-acting, excitatory messages.

Achievement motive (nAch) Motive to do things as rapidly and/or as well as possible.

Achievement test An instrument designed to measure a person's present abilities.

Acquisition The classical conditioning process by which a conditioned stimulus comes to elicit a conditioned response.

Action potential The rapid change in electrical charge that flows along a neuron, caused by a change in the permeability of the cell membrane.

Adaptation The process of changing behavior to fit environmental conditions.

Adaptation level A person's frame of reference for judgment, based on previous sensory stimulation.

Adaptation level theory A theory that shows how prior stimulation can influence present sensory experience. Sensory adaptation provides a frame of reference so that changes in stimulation are more noticeable than unchanging inputs.

151

Addiction Physical dependence on a substance so that the body builds up a tolerance for a dose of the drug and needs ever-increasing amounts. If the drug is not taken, people experience painful symptoms of withdrawal, which may include headaches, cramps, nausea, uncontrollable trembling, and restlessness.

Addicts People who continue to use drugs despite the ill-effects of the drugs on their physical and social well-being.

Additive color mixture When lights of different wavelengths simultaneously stimulate the eye, their combined or additive effect is a new color determined by the positions of the wavelengths on the color circle. (See also Subtractive color mixture)

Adolescence The transitional period between puberty and adulthood, roughly ages 13 to 20.

Adolescent growth spurt Rapid increase in a person's height and weight during the early teenage years.

Adoption studies Research comparing children adopted at birth with those raised by natural parents to determine the relative impact of genes and the environment on development.

Adrenal glands Two glands located above the kidney that secrete hormones that influence our mood and our ability to cope with stress.

Affective disorders Group of disorders involving problems with emotions and mood. People are said to be suffering from an affective disorder when their moods, such as depression, take over and they have trouble functioning.

Affiliation motive Motive or desire to associate with and be around other people.

Afterimage The sensory experience that occurs following the withdrawal of prolonged stimulation. Staring at the color red, for example, will produce an afterimage of green when the red is replaced by a blank white field. Opponent-process theory provides an explanation of afterimages.

Aggression Behaviors that are intended to do harm.

Aggression cues Any stimuli that an individual has learned to associate with aggressive behavior.

Aggression motive Motive, whether innate or learned, to attack objects or other organisms.

Air pollution syndrome (APS) Physical reactions to pollution characterized by headache, insomnia, gastrointestinal problems, irritated eyes, and depression.

Alcohol The most commonly used depressant often mistaken for a stimulant because it affects the brain regions that normally inhibit behavior.

Alcohol-aversion therapy A treatment for alcoholism that involves the simultaneous ingestion of alcohol with the administration of antabuse, a drug that induces vomiting. The alcoholic gradually develops an aversion to alcohol as an association is formed between the sight, smell, and taste of alcohol and the unpleasant sensation of nausea.

Alcoholics People who are addicted to alcohol; they have an uncontrollable urge to drink and because of increasing tolerance, must continue to increase their consumption.

Algorithm A step-by-step procedure that produces a solution to a problem because it considers all possible solutions.

All-or-none law The principle that a neuron responds completely (that is, fires its action potential) or not at all. Thus, the impulse in a single neuron is independent of the strength of the stimulation.

Allele A single gene may occur in one of several different forms called alleles; alleles may be dominant or recessive.

Altered state of consciousness A change in mental experience from that of normal waking consciousness. (See also Consciousness.)

Altruism Behaviors that are intended to be helpful to others.

Alzheimer's disease A neurological disorder that attacks the brain and causes severe cognitive impairment.

American Sign Language (ASL) A method of communication used by deaf people, which utilizes hand gestures to represent units of speech.

Amnesia A form of memory loss that can be caused by physical trauma or psychological distress. Memory loss for events after a traumatic event is called anterograde amnesia; memory loss for events before a traumatic event is called retrograde amnesia.

Amniocentesis Process in which fluid is taken from a mother's womb to test for Down syndrome and other genetic disorders.

Amplitude The magnitude of a sound or light wave; the main determinants of loudness or brilliance.

Amygdala A small limbic structure that plays an important role in regulating emotions and storing memories.

Anal stage The second stage in Freud's theory of personality development, when a child's erotic feelings according to the theory, center on the anus and elimination.

Analogy A heuristic strategy in which the solution to one problem is used to guide solutions to another.

Analytic introspection Method used in structuralism; a way of isolating the elementary sensations of which experiences are made.

Analytical psychology Jung's complex, almost mystical theory of personality; includes his belief that the libido was a force resulting from the desire to be creative.

Androgens Male hormones secreted by the testes that increase male sex drive and influence the development of secondary sex characteristics.

Androgynous Possessing a balanced combination of characteristics formerly thought to be appropriate for only one gender or the other.

Animal cognition A term that refers to the animal's use of an internal representation as the basis for action.

Anorexia nervosa An eating disorder characterized by chronic self-starvation.

Anterograde Amnesia Following the onset of amnesia, the inability to learn or retain new information. (See also Amnesia; Retrograde amnesia)

Antianxiety drugs minor tranquilizers that reduce anxiety and tension without causing drowsiness or a loss of mental alertness. Most popular are Valium, Librium, and Miltown.

Antianxiety medications Psychoactive drugs that are prescribed to combat anxiety.

Antidepressants Psychoactive drugs designed to combat depression.

Antiobessional drugs Psychoactive drugs designed to combat obsessive-compulsive disorder.

Antipsychotic medications Drugs that reduce psychotic symptoms such as hallucinations and delusions of grandeur.

Antisocial personality A person who goes through life without anxiety or guilt, despite the fact that he or she exploits others to a degree that would shame a normal person.

Antrograde amnesia Difficulty in remembering events that happen after an injury

Anvil One of three small bones in the middle ear, it transmits sounds from the ear-drum to the inner ear.

Anxiety The term used for fearful emotional responses that occur in situations that do not seem to pose threat to life or limb.

Anxiety disorders Disorders in which anxiety is a characteristic feature or the avoidance of anxiety seems to motivate abnormal behavior.

Apgar scoring system Scale used to assess the condition of newborns; low scores show possible neurological damage.

Apparent movement The perception of movement where there is none.

Applied research Research that is directed toward solving specific individual or social problems (See also Basic Research).

Appraisal theory Automatic evaluation of a situation as threatening or nonthreatening. Appraisal influences both arousal (emotions) and behavior (response).

Aptitude tests Tests designed to predict what a person could potentially accomplish.

Aqueous humor Clear fluid that carries nourishment to the cornea of the eye.

Archetypes According to Carl Jung, inherited tendencies to perceive and feel in certain ways about certain objects.

Articulation Process of altering the shape of the pharynx, oral cavity, and nasal cavity in order to change speech sounds.

Artificial intelligence The use of computer programs to perform tasks normally done by the human mind.

Ascending nerves Nerves that carry sensory information up the spinal cord to specific areas of the brain.

Assimilation According to Piaget, the process by which a person perceives and modifies information from the external world in accordance with his or her cognitive structure. (See also Accommodation)

Association areas The areas of the cerebral cortex that integrate sensory information and appear to be involved in learning and thinking.

Associative bias A form of preparedness in which a learner is biologically predisposed to learn relationships between certain stimuli more easily than others.

Associative learning Learning of a relation or contingency between events in the world.

Atmospheric perspective A monocular depth cue based on the fact that the farther away an object is from an observer, the less sharp its retinal image and the less clearly the object is seen.

Attachment The development of specific behaviors whereby infants seek to be close to certain people, usually their parents or primary caregivers.

Attention The focusing of perception on a limited number of stimuli, resulting in heightened awareness.

Attention deficit disorder Inability of a child to concentrate on a task for the same length of time as another child of the same age.

Attitude change Accepting a new position or new information while giving up an old position.

Attitude system The interconnected feelings, thoughts, intentions, and behaviors that are the components of an attitude.

Attitudes The tendency to respond in a particular way toward certain issues, people, objects or events.

Attraction Liking between people.

Attribution Process of inferring characteristics of people from their observable behavior; a way of explaining the behavior of others.

Attribution theory A theory concerned with rules people use to infer the causes of behavior they observe in others.

Auditory canal One of two structures that make up the outer ear (see also Pinna).

Authoritarian personality Individuals who are extremely conventional in their behavior, rigid in their moral views, concerned with the propriety of others' behavior, and preoccupied with power and toughness.

Autism A form of abnormal behavior that primarily affects young children, thought to be caused by some type of neurological disorder. It is characterized by unresponsiveness, repetitive movements, and self-mutilation.

Autobiographical memory A record of the past that is filtered by one's personality and current beliefs.

Autokinetic effect Tendency for a stationary light viewed against darkness to look as if it is moving; the light seems to glide, jerk, and swoop through space.

Autokinetic movement An illusion of movement when a stationary point of light is perceived to move when viewed against a dark homogeneous background.

Automaticity The ability to perform a task with little or no demand on attentional capacity. Reduced attentional demand is achieved after considerable practice.

Autonomic nervous system A division of the peripheral nervous system that connects the brain and spinal cord to vital organs such as the stomach and heart. This system consists of the sympathetic and parasympathetic division. (See also Parasympathetic division; Peripheral nervous system; Sympathetic division)

Autoshaping In instrumental conditioning, the self-shaping of a conditioned response through the process of classical conditioning. (See also Shaping)

Availability heuristic A rule of thumb by which we estimate the frequency or likelihood of an event on the basis of how easily such examples come to mind.

Aversive conditioning A classical conditioning procedure that establishes a connection between an unpleasant stimulus and an undesired response.

Aversive counterconditioning (See Aversive conditioning)

Aversive punishment A form of punishment that takes the form of an unpleasant stimulus.

Avoidance conditioning A process through which an appropriate response avoids exposure to an aversive stimulus. (See also Escape conditioning)

Avoidance training Occurs when a subject learns to make a response to avoid a negative reinforcer.

Axon The single strand or fiber that emerges from the cell body of a neuron that is used to transmit neural impulses to other cells. (See also Dendrite; Neuron)

Axon terminal Tiny knob at the end of an axon's terminal branch.

Baby biographies Day-to-day accounts of individual development, first used by Darwin to record his son's perceptual and motor development.

Backward conditioning The classical conditioning procedure in which the unconditioned stimulus briefly precedes the presentation of the conditioned stimulus. (See also Delayed, Trace, and Simultaneous conditioning)

Backward masking Ability of a stimulus to wipe out the sensory memory of a preceding stimulus.

Balance theory A theory of social relations that postulates a need to have consistency between one's different attitudes.

Barbiturates A class of depressant drugs.

Basal ganglia Four masses of gray matter in the brain that control background muscle tone and large, general muscle movements - part of the motor system.

Base-rate fallacy A type of decision-making error that occurs when people ignore the frequency with which specific events normally occur.

Basic anxiety According to Karen Horney, the childhood feeling of being isolated and helpless in a potentially hostile world.

Basic research Studies of psychological phenomena aimed at establishing fundamental principles of behavior without regard to the immediate application of the results. (See also Applied research)

Basilar membrane Vibrating membrane in the cochlea of the inner ear that contains sense receptors for sound.

Behavior genetics A field that poses questions about the extent to which the differences between people are affected by the genes they inherit from their parents, their environments, and the interaction of genes and environmental factors.

Behavior modification The application of the principles of classical and operant conditioning to changing problem behaviors.

Behavior therapies Therapies based on the assumption that maladaptive behavior is learned through the same process as other behaviors and can be unlearned by substituting a more adaptive behavior in its place.

Behavioral assessment Assessment that consists of examining a person's present behavior to predict future actions. Can also be used to assign traits to people.

Behavioral medicine A new field in psychology that seeks to integrate knowledge and techniques from psychology and medical science.

Behavioral neuroscience The field of study that examines the biological roots of behavior. This interdisciplinary approach includes the study of genetic factors, hormonal factors, neuroanatomy, drugs, developmental factors, and environmental factors, to learn about brain-behavior relations.

Behavioral perspective The idea that psychology should focus only on observable behaviors and their relationship to events that can be objectively measured.

Behavioral sink A pattern of antisocial behaviors in animals associated with high-density living.

Behaviorism Approach to psychology based on the premise that human behavior can be described by focusing only on the observable stimulus and response.

Binocular cues Cues to depth perception that we use when we are looking with both eyes.

Binocular disparity A binocular depth cue based on the fact that an object projects slightly different images to each retina due to the slightly different positions of the two eyes.

Biofeedback The use of instrumental conditioning procedures with electronic equipment to allow people to monitor and change physiological responses formerly thought to be involuntary.

Biofeedback therapy Type of therapy designed to help people control their physiological functions without the use of drugs or other biotherapy techniques. Helps people reduce tension and stress, reduce phobic reactions, and control headaches. Has also been combined with other psychotherapies. (See also biofeedback)

Biomedical model Assumes that abnormal behavior is like other forms of illness, caused by bodily disturbances from outside infections or internal malfunctions.

Biomedical therapy Use of drugs, surgery, or electric shock, with or without accompanying psychotherapy, to induce behavior change.

Biopsychological perspective A modern general approach to understanding behavior, which emphasizes the examination of how behavior and mental processes are related to physiological states and neural structures.

Biopsychology The field of psychology that seeks to understand the role of the nervous and endocrine systems.

Bipolar cells Cells in the retina, connected to rods and cones, that actively participate in the process of coding or interpreting the information contained in light. One-to-one connections to cones; one-to-many connections to rods.

Bipolar disorder Disorder in which the person alternates between manic and depressive stages. Often the extremes of each mood state appear for only a short time and the person generally behaves normally when between states.

Blind spot The point where blood vessels and neurons enter and exit the eye.

Blocking The failure to learn about a second stimulus that has been presented in compound with a conditioned stimulus.

Bodily feedback theory The idea that bodily changes come before our conscious experience of an emotion and help us to decide which emotion we are feeling.

Body language communication through body movement.

Boilermaker's deafness Partial hearing loss caused by spending long periods of time a. round loud noises (above 85 decibels).

Bone conduction Another way that sound is transmitted; when a person speaks, the jaw bones conduct vibrations to the cochlea. We hear our own voice through bone-conducted and air-conducted sounds; we hear others' voices only through air-conducted sounds.

Bottom-up processing The view that perception is guided by the passage of information from the sensory receptors to the different areas of the brain. (See also Top-Down processing)

Brainstem The central core structure of the brain that provides a transition from the end of the spinal cord to the base of the brain. This structure controls the most fundamental aspects of behavior.

Brief sensory store A large capacity memory register that holds unprocessed sensory signals to allow time for pattern recognition processes to translate the information into a more meaningful form.

Brightness The amplitude or height of a color wavelength. The higher the amplitude, the brighter the color.

Brightness constancy Objects seem to stay the same brightness regardless of changes in illumination.

Broca's area A portion of the frontal lobe of the left hemisphere of the brain that is involved in the production of speech. People with brain damage in this area have difficulty enunciating words and speak in a halting, labored manner. (See also Wernicke's area)

Bulimia nervosa An eating disorder characterized by persistent binge-eating and purging (through self-induced vomiting, use of laxatives, or strict fasting).

Burnout Job-related emotional exhaustion that includes a depersonalized feeling and a reduced sense of accomplishment.

Bystander intervention Help for an emergency victim provided by onlookers.

Calories Units of energy produced when food is oxidized or burned by the body.

Case history Method used in psychology that looks in depth at a few individuals or at the effects of a single event.

Case study A narrative description of a person's life or a detailed description of a particular person or group.

Cataracts Widespread disease affecting vision that is characterized by cloudy lenses and can result in blindness if lenses are not removed surgically.

Catatonic schizophrenia A type of schizophrenia in which disturbed motor behaviors (including long periods of complete immobility) are prominent.

Catecholamines Chemical transmitters in neurones that tend to transmit slow-acting, inhibitory messages.

Catharsis The purging of aggressive impulses. Freud theorized that aggressive urges build up over time and get worse if they are not purged.

Causal attribution The process of developing an explanation about the causes of behavior.

Cell body The membrane body of a neuron that surrounds the nucleus and contents of the cells.

Central fissure The large convolution that runs from the top of the brain down each side and separates the frontal and parietal lobes.

Central nervous system The portion of the nervous system that receives sensory information and guides coordinated movement.

Cerebellum The lobed portion at the rear of the brain that receives sensory information and guides coordinated movement.

Cerebral cortex The outer surface of the brain that is responsible for intelligent behavior.

Cerebral hemispheres Two large halves of the brain, separated by a deep fissure, but connected by a thick bundle of nerve fibers called the corpus callosum. (See also Left hemisphere; Right hemisphere)

Cerebral lateralization The varying degrees of left or right hemisphere involvement shown by different cognitive functions.

Cerebral organization The organization of different abilities according to the involvement of the left and right cerebral hemispheres.

Chemical transmitters (neurotransmitters) Chemicals that carry messages between neurons; some are excitatory, some inhibitory.

Chemotherapy Treatment of disorders through the use of drugs; a form of bio-therapy.

Chromosomes Thread-like molecules that carry the genes, the fundamental units of heredity.

Chronological age A person's age in years and months.

Chunk A unit of information that functions as a single stimulus.

Cilia Hairlike receptors for the sense of smell that are located in the olfactory mucosa.

Circadian rhythm The daily pattern of changes in waking and sleeping, body temperature, and blood pressure that are tied to the 24 hour cycle of light and dark.

City size The total population of a city (See also Density)

Clairvoyance Perception of an object, action, or event by means of ESP.

161

Classical conditioning An elementary form of associative learning that enables us to make connections between events in the environment. In Pavlovian terms, the repeated pairing of a previously neutral conditioned stimulus with an unconditioned stimulus so that the conditioned stimulus comes to produce a conditioned response. (See also Instrumental conditioning)

Client-centered therapy Developed by Carl Rogers, the goal of this technique is to help the client get in touch with his or her inner feelings and to pull together all the parts of the self the person had learned to suppress.

Clinical psychology Sub-field of psychology dedicated to the diagnosis and treatment of emotional and behavioral disorders.

Clinical social worker Someone who has an M.A. in social work and has served an internship.

Cochlea Part of the inner ear; a tube coiled in on itself about three turns, like a spiral around a central core. Contains the basilar membrane inside it.

Codes Memory representations of the appearance, sound, and meaning of stimuli.

Cognition The mental operations involved in the acquisition and use of knowledge. These mental operations include perception, memory, language, and thought.

Cognitive approach The intelligence-testing approach that seeks to determine the mental processes that underlie intelligent behavior.

Cognitive bias The tendency to use inappropriate information or an inappropriate strategy in making a decision.

Cognitive consistency The motivation to maintain congruence between what one does and what one believes.

Cognitive development The changes in cognitive abilities that occur over the lifespan.

Cognitive dissonance According to Festinger's theory, an unpleasant state of arousal that occurs when our beliefs and our behaviors are not in line with one another.

Cognitive heuristics Rules of thumb that have usually worked to solve a problem in the past.

Cognitive learning A form of learning that involves forming internal representations of events in the world.

Cognitive maps A mental representation of a spatial layout that an animal or person stores in memory.

Cognitive model of depression The view that maladaptive ways of thinking contribute to depression.

Cognitive needs According to Maslow, those needs that involve the use of higher intelligence.

Cognitive neuroscience The field of study that focuses on the neural basis of cognition.

Cognitive overload An inability to respond to stimuli because there are too many events occurring in the environment.

Cognitive perspective The study of mental processes such as perceiving, remembering, and thinking.

Cognitive psychology The study of how people acquire and use knowledge.

Cognitive science The field of study concerned with how knowledge is acquired, represented, and transmitted.

Cognitive structure A set of behavior patterns or rules that determines how a child comes to understand the world.

Cognitive style A characteristic way in which a person approaches a cognitive task and the manner of thinking that constitutes a part of an individual's personality. (See also Field dependence; Field independence)

Cognitive-social learning perspective An extension of the behavioral perspective which adds an emphasis on such cognitive factors as expectancies in human learning.

Cohabitation Relationship between two unmarried people who live together.

Cold spots Areas of the skin where only cold is felt, even if stimulated by a warm object (when this occurs it is called paradoxical cold)

Collective unconscious According to Jung, a universal set of ideas inherited from our ancestors.

Color agnosia The inability to distinguish different colors or name colors that are associated with particular objects.

Color blindness Partial or total inability to perceive variations in color.

Color constancy The tendency to see objects as having the same color, even under very different conditions of illumination.

Color mixture The color produced when two or more different wavelengths of light combine.

Communal relationship A situation in which partners share rewards and costs rather than emphasize their own individual welfare.

Communication network Billions of individual neurons in the nervous system link widely separated parts of the body.

Community mental health An approach to treatment of disorder that focuses on leaving the patient to his or her environment, prevention of social problems, and the use of paraprofessionals.

Community psychology Sub-field of psychology dedicated to promoting mental health at the community level; seeks to prevent and treat psychological problems by working to evaluate and to improve community organizations.

Community therapy Treatment outside of hospitals in the patient's natural surroundings.

Comparative psychologists Psychologists who compare behavior across different species.

Complementary color Colors opposite each other on the color circle that when mixed together produce a neutral gray.

Complex tones Sounds containing many frequencies.

Compliance Changes in behavior that are instigated by requests from another person or a group.

Compulsion Irrational behavior or ritual that people cannot control; often they do not know why they need to do this. See also Obsession, which involves thought rather than behavior.

Computer simulation The use of a computer program to simulate human performance on some task.

Concepts Mental rules that organize knowledge. A concept is a property or relation that is common to a set of items.

Concordance rate The degree of similarity between two individuals on a measure of a psychological variable, usually indicated by a correlation coefficient.

Concrete operation period In Piaget's third period of cognitive development, children between the ages of 7 and 12 become capable of logical thought and achieve understanding of the general principles of conservation. (See also Conservation)

Concurrent validity The degree of agreement between different types of measures given at the same time.

Conditioned reinforcers In instrumental conditioning, stimuli that become reinforcing through their association with a primary reinforcer. (See also Primary reinforcers)

Conditioned response In classical conditioning, the response that is elicited by a conditioned stimulus by virtue of its prior pairing with an unconditioned stimulus. (See also Conditioned stimulus, Unconditioned response; Unconditioned stimulus)

Conditioned stimulus In classical conditioning, a previously neutral stimulus that, after being paired with an unconditioned stimulus, elicits a conditioned response. (See also Conditioned response; Unconditioned response; Unconditioned stimulus)

Conditioning The process by which conditioned responses are learned (See also Classical conditioning; Instrumental conditioning)

Conduction deafness Hearing loss caused by problems in the middle ear. Typically, the stapes becomes calcified and less able to transmit vibrations to the inner ear. Hearing aids can often correct the problem by amplifying the vibrations and forcing the stapes to transfer them to the inner ear. (See also Nerve deafness)

Cones Light sensitive cells in the retina of the eye that provide a high degree of visual acuity and the ability to distinguish different colors. (See also Rods)

Confabulation The term for the type of memory loss associated with patients with Korsakoff's syndrome, who sometimes fabricate stories of past events to conceal their memory loss.

Confirmation bias A tendency to seek information that is consistent with our existing beliefs.

Conflict State that occurs when a person is motivated to choose between two or more mutually exclusive goals or courses of action.

Conflict spiral A competitive situation that feeds itself, so that what begins as a fairly mild difference grows more and more intense.

Conformity A person's tendency to pattern his or her behavior after that of a larger social group to which he or she belongs.

Connectionism An approach used to study memory that uses the neural processes of the brain as a model for memory processes.

Conscientiousness One of the major clusters of traits emerging from factor analytic studies of personality, consisting of characteristics such as orderliness, promptness, and neatness.

Conscious mind According to Freud, this includes whatever the person is perceiving or thinking at the moment.

Consciousness Our awareness of body sensations, perception, emotions, thoughts, and recollections at a particular moment in time.

Conservation Piaget's term for the ability to recognize that certain properties of objects, such as their volume or mass, do not change despite changes in an object's appearance. (See also Preoperational period)

Constancies Aspects of perception such as an apparent size or shape that remain constant when visual information changes.

Construct validity The extent to which a test measures the particular psychological process it is designed to measure.

Content-addressable memory In the connectionist model of memory, retrieving partial information about an object or event will often lead to the recall of related information.

Contiguity The formation of mental associations between ideas.

Continuous reinforcement schedule A conditioning reinforcement schedule in which reinforcement follows a correct response each time that particular response is made.

Contrast effect A shift in the judgment of one stimulus away from a previously judged extreme along the same dimension. For instance, an average-looking face will be judged more attractive following a series of unattractive faces.

Contrast threshold The just-barely detectable difference in brightness between light and dark stripes in gratings. Gratings show how the visual system is designed to detect spatial and temporal changes in stimulation.

Control group A group that is treated identically to an experimental group, except that it is not exposed to the crucial experimental manipulation.

Controlled drinking The belief that former alcoholics can resume drinking following new learning experiences that attempt to teach them how to control their drinking.

Convergent thinking A type of thinking that proceeds toward a single solution to a problem.

Conversion disorder A disorder characterized by an apparent physical ailment, but believed to be rooted in psychological distress.

Convolutions The characteristic wrinkles of the brain that results from the vast evolutionary development of the cortex.

Coping Cognitive and behavioral attempts to bring stress under control.

Cornea The transparent covering at the front of the eye that provides protection and support.

Corpus callosum A thick bundle of nerve fibers that connect the left and right cerebral hemispheres.

Correlation A measure of the extent to which variables change together. If two variables increase and decrease at the same time, they are positively correlated; if one increases while the other decreases, they are negatively correlated. This does not necessarily indicate a cause-and-effect relationship between the variables, however.

Correlation coefficient A mathematical index of the direction and extent of a relationship between two sets of data. Correlations can be positive, negative, or zero, and range in value from -1.00 to +1.00.

Correlational method A means of looking for a relationship between two observed variables by examining the extent to which the variables occur together.

Cortical lobes The major areas of the cortex, including the frontal (front), parietal (top), temporal (sides), and occipital (back) lobes.

Counseling and school psychology Sub-field of psychology that helps people with social, educational, and job or career adjustments.

Countertransference The inappropriate transfer of a therapist's feelings onto his or her client.

Covert sensitization A form of therapy in which the client is instructed to think of something unpleasant every time he or she feels an undesirable impulse.

Creative thinking Capacity to think up new and useful ways of solving problems.

Creativity The ability to produce original and appropriate ides.

Crisis According to Jung, a period of time that can involve a psychological transformation in a person's life.

Critical period Stage of development during which the organism must have certain experiences or it will not develop normally.

Cross-cultural research A research technique that compares subjects from different cultural groups. For example, a comparison of children from the United States and China.

Cross-sectional research A research technique that compares the performance of subjects of different age groups at the same time. For example, a study of three groups of children, aged 6, 8, and 10.

Crowding The psychological experience of spatial restrictions.

Crystallized intelligence The factual knowledge that a person has acquired which increases over the age span. (See also Fluid intelligence)

CT scan A series of X-ray measurements made from different orientations around a person's head.

Cue-dependent forgetting A type of forgetting in which information that may be available is inaccessible without the right cue to guide the search for the information.

Cultural-familial retardation Impaired mental development associated with poor health, poor diet, and inadequate parenting.

Culture The common set of social norms, ideas, traditions, artifacts, and life experiences likely to be confronted by a person belonging to a given social group.

Cumulative recorder A device for measuring an animal's rate of response in an operant chamber.

Cycle The distance between wave crests in a sound wave.

Dancing reflex Causes infants to prance with their legs in a "tip-toe" stepping motion when they are held upright with feet touching a surface.

Dark adaptation An increase in sensitivity when illumination is considerably reduced.

Date rape Coercive sex that occurs in dating relationships.

Daydreaming A shift of attention away from an ongoing physical or mental task toward a response to an internally generated stimulus.

Daydreams Thoughts that divert attention away from an immediately demanding task.

Decay For memory the process of forgetting when information that is not rehearsed fades away with the passage of time.

Decibel Unit for measuring loudness; each tenfold increase in sound level adds 10 decibels.

Deductive reasoning The use of general rules to draw conclusions about particular instances. (See also Inductive reasoning)

Defense mechanism cognitive strategies that people use to cope with anxiety-provoking thoughts and impulses.

Deficiency needs In Maslow's scheme of motivation, physiological needs, safety needs, and needs for belongingness, love, and esteem; presumed to operate according to drive-reduction principles.

Deindividuation Refers to the feeling that one will not be held responsible for his or her behavior.

Deinstitutionalization The release of patients from mental hospitals.

Delayed conditioning The classical conditioning procedure in which the conditioned stimulus comes on briefly before the unconditioned stimulus and remains on until a response is made. (See also Backward, Simultaneous, and Trace conditioning)

Delirium tremens (DT's) A dangerous withdrawal syndrome that occurs when a person who has been drinking excessively for a long time suddenly stops. Symptoms include tremors, disorientation hallucinations, and acute sense of panic.

Delusions Faulty beliefs that have no basis in reality.

Demand characteristics Elements in a questionnaire or experiment that communicate what behavior is expected from the subjects.

Demographics The statistical study of the size and distribution of human populations.

Dendrite The neuron's major receptive surface (together with the cell body), this tree-like structure receives neural impulses from other neurons. (See also Axon; Neuron)

Density the number of people in a given spatial area.

Density-dependent mortality factors Mechanisms that act to kill more animals when population is high and less when it is low.

Deoxyribonucleic acid (DNA) Controls the way in which protein chains are built, and, thus, contains the basic blueprints for life; genes are made up of DNA.

Dependent variable In an experiment, the behavior that is measured. Changes in this variable are attributed to the influence of the independent variable. (See also Independent variable)

Depolarization Occurs when a neuron is sending or receiving a neural impulse.

Depressants A class of drugs that calm the user by slowing the heartbeat and relaxing the muscles or that induce sleep. Common depressants are sedatives, tranquilizers, and narcotics such as heroin, morphine, and opium.

Depression A mood disorder whose symptoms include an unhappy mood and the loss of interest and pleasure in life. This state is commonly associated with insomnia, loss of appetite, fatigue, feelings of guilt, and thoughts of suicide and death.

Deprivation theory According to this theory, any activity can function as a reinforcer if the subject is restricted from performing this activity as often as it would otherwise be performed.

Descending nerves Carry commands down the spinal cord to move muscles.

Descriptive methods Research techniques that provide different ways to describe behavior, without any attempt to interfere with the behavior under study. These methods provide useful information about how different events and behaviors are related to each other.

Descriptive statistics Tools for summarizing data taken of a group of objects, people, or events.

Deterministic A philosophical viewpoint that assumes that events are totally determined by prior events. When applied to behavior, it is contrary to the notion of "free will."

Development Process whereby the genes that an organism inherits from its parents come to be expressed as specific physical and behavioral characteristics.

Developmental behavioral genetics The field of study within biology and psychology that seeks to relate changes in behavioral characteristics that occur over the life span to changes in heredity.

Developmental psychology The field of psychology that seeks to describe and explain changes in physical, cognitive, and social development that occur over the life span.

Dichotic listening The subject hears different messages in each ear and is asked to repeat only one of them.

Difference threshold The smallest change in stimulus intensity that is capable of being detected 50 percent of the time. (See also Just-noticeable difference (JND))

Differentiation The process through which infants learn to differentiate people from inanimate objects, familiar people from strangers, and themselves from others.

Diffusion of responsibility Refers to the assumption that duty and accountability can be divided among the members of a group. When there are a number of potential helpers around, each may assume that the others will help.

Discrimination Differential responding to stimuli on the basis of prior association. (See also Generalization)

Discrimination training In instrumental conditioning, the process of learning that reinforcers are related to some stimuli but not to others.

Discriminative stimulus In instrumental conditioning, the stimulus that signals that reinforcement is available.

Dishabituation An increase in responsiveness to new stimulation. (See also Habituation)

Disorganized schizophrenia This syndrome is characterized by very bizarre symptoms, including extreme delusions, hallucinations, and completely inappropriate patterns of speech, mood, and movements.

Displaced aggression Taking out one's anger and/or frustration on someone or something other than the actual cause of one's anger.

Displacement Defense mechanism that involves redirecting an emotion from the person who caused it to another, safer or more available, target.

Dissociative amnesia A dramatic loss of personal memory that cannot be attributed to physical injury such as head injury.

Dissociative disorders Behavioral problems involving distinct splits in waking consciousness including dissociative amnesia and multiple personalities.

Dissociative identity disorder (See Multiple personality)

Distal stimuli Objects in the physical environment that produce proximal stimulation that can be received by the sense organs. (See also Proximal stimuli)

Divergent thinking A type of thinking that involves moving outward from a problem in many different directions.

Dizygotic twins Twins developed from separate eggs. They are no more genetically alike than ordinary brothers and sisters. (See also Monozygotic twins)

Dominant gene Member of a gene pair that controls the appearance of a certain trait.

Door-in-the-face approach Persuasive technique based on the fact that people who at first refuse a large request will be more likely after that to comply with a smaller request.

Doppler shift Occurs as cars zoom by on a racetrack; as they go by, the engine sound drops sharply to a lower pitch. Sound waves bunch up as cars approach on a racetrack and spread out as cars speed away. The bunched-up waves have a shorter distance between their wave crests (higher frequency); the spread-out waves have a longer distance between their wave crests (lower frequency).

Double helix Model of the structure of DNA molecules, similar to a spiral staircase, the steps of which contain a genetic code.

Double-bind conflict Results when children receive contradictory messages from their parents, messages that create a "no-win" situation for them - no matter what they do, they are wrong.

Double-bind control Procedure used in an experiment in which neither subject nor experiment is aware of how the independent variable is being manipulated.

Down's syndrome A form of chromosomal abnormality associated with various physical defects and moderate to severe mental retardation. In the most common form of this disorder, children have an extra or third chromosome in their twenty-first pair. (See also Chromosomes)

Dream interpretation Part of Freud's technique of psychoanalysis; involves helping clients to understand the latent content of their dreams, which represents the repressed feelings that are being expressed.

Dreaming An altered state of consciousness that occurs during sleep, appears to be real and immediate, and transcends rational thoughts.

Drive Tension or state that results when a need is not met; it compels the organism to satisfy the need.

Drive reduction The assumption that humans are motivated by a desire to turn off the physiological states associated with hunger, thirst, and other drives.

Drug Any substance other than food that when ingested can stimulate or depress mental and/or physical functioning by acting on the nervous system.

Drug dependence Continued use of a drug with or without addiction. Physical dependence is an addiction; psychological dependence, while not an addiction, results in a strong craving when the drug is not available. (See also Drug tolerance)

Drug therapy Use of medications to treat both mild and severe psychological disturbances.

Drug tolerance With continued use of a drug, larger doses become necessary to produce the desired effect. (See also Drug dependence)

DSM-IV Stands for Diagnostic and Statistical Manual, which was published in 1994. It is one of the most commonly used systems for classifying abnormal behavior, and was developed by the American Psychiatric Association.

Dual coding theory This theory says that pictures are remembered better than words because our probability of recalling either a pictorial or verbal code is higher than our probability of recalling only a verbal code.

Dualism Theory that the mind and brain are separate entities. See also monism.

Dyspareunia Sexual disorder in which females experience pain during intercourse.

Eardrum Transmits sound through its auditory passage by vibrating.

Echo A brief auditory memory trace that occurs following the presentation of an auditory stimulus. (See also Sensory memory stores)

Ectomorphs According to William Sheldon, one of three body types, characterized as thin and delicate, with the largest brains in proportion to their body size. Ectomorphs were hypothesized to be sensitive, self-conscious, private, and intellectual.

Effector cells A neural structure in our muscles or glands that generates movements or chemical secretions.

Ego According to Freud's theory of personality, the more sensible part of our personality that acts to get things done in an efficient and socially acceptable manner.

Egocentrism According to Piaget, the inability of a person to take the perspective of someone else during early childhood. During adolescence, it is a form of self-preoccupation that reflects a person's search for identity, according to Erikson.

Eidetic imagery The ability to retain visual information in an accurate and highly detailed visual image. Only a minority of people tested suggest evidence of eidetic imagery. (See also Mental imagery)

Elaborative rehearsal A form of thinking about information in short-term storage that, through alterations or additions, results in the establishment of strong traces in long-term storage. (See also Long-term memory store; Maintenance rehearsal)

Electrical stimulation A procedure for studying the effects of brain stimulation on an animal's behavior. Electrical current is passed directly to a particular brain structure by a thin wire called a micro-electrode inserted into the brain.

Electroconvulsive therapy (ECT) A treatment for severe depression in which an electrical current is passed through the brain, producing convulsions equivalent to an epileptic seizure.

Electroencephalogram (EEG) A brain wave record produced by a machine called an electroencephalograph.

Embryo The developing organism during its early differentiation of physical structures, a period lasting six to eight weeks after conception. (See also Fetus; Zygote)

Emotion-focused coping strategies Used in situations seen as unchangeable, these strategies are aimed at regulating distressing emotional responses.

Emotional development The changes in emotional reactions that occur over the lifespan.

Emotional stability One of the major clusters of traits emerging from factor analytic studies of personality, consisting of characteristics such as good adjustment, calmness under crisis, and lack of psychological disorder.

Encoding One of three memory processes in which we transform information into a representation that can be placed in memory. (See also Retrieval and Storage)

Encounter groups A technique used extensively by humanistic psychologists, in which group members share feelings and experiences with one another.

Endocrine glands Glands of the endocrine system that release hormones into the bloodstream.

Endocrine system A set of glands such as the pituitary and kidneys that influence behavior and internal states by secreting hormones directly into the bloodstream. The hormones serve to integrate bodily activity. (See also Hormones)

Endomorphs According to William Sheldon, one of three body types, characterized by a heavy-set build, and a tendency to love physical comfort, socializing, and eating.

Environmental psychology The study of person-environment interactions, including the effects of crowding, noise, and air pollution.

Epilepsy A neurological disorder of the brain produced by the uncontrolled firing of neurons. Two of the most common types of epilepsy are petit mal and grand mal epilepsy.

Epinephrine Hormone secreted by the adrenal gland during stressful situations. It constricts the blood vessels in the stomach and intestines and increases the heart rate.

Episodic memory A form of memory that represents knowledge of personally experienced events and their order of occurrence. (See also Procedural memory; Semantic memory)

Equipotentiality theory According to this view, there are few, if any, specialized regions of the brain. Instead, different areas of the brain are seen as equivalent to one another.

Equity The perception that the benefits of a relationship, minus the costs of being in the relationship, are balanced with one's partner's costs and benefits.

Escape conditioning A process through which an appropriate response terminates an aversive stimulus. (See also Avoidance conditioning)

Estrogen A hormone that is related to the development of secondary sex characteristics in women, and which is related to sexual receptivity in female mammals.

Ethnocentric A term used to describe people who see their own ethnic group as superior to others.

Ethological approach The study of animal behavior in its natural habitat with a focus on how innate behaviors are used to adapt to the environment.

Ethologist A researcher at the interface of psychology and zoology who studies animal behavior, often (but not always) using naturalistic observation.

Evolutionary perspective An approach to behavior that emphasizes the differences and similarities in behavior across different animal species, with a focus on the adaptive significance of inherited behavioral tendencies.

Excitatory influences Stimulation of the neuron that increases the likelihood of firing.

Expectancy The anticipation of a future stimulus based on past experience and current stimuli.

Experiment A research method involving the systematic manipulation of one or more independent variables in order to observe an effect on one or more dependent variables. (See also Dependent variables; Independent variables).

Experimental group A group for whom the experimenter alters some feature of the environment.

Experimental method (See Experiment)

Experimental psychology The study of psychological phenomena by means of the experimental method. (See also Experiment)

Expert systems Specialized problem-solving computer programs that are used to facilitate human decision making.

Expertise The ability to use a broad and highly organized body of knowledge systematically.

Explicit memory Conscious recollection of a past episode or event.

Expressive aphasia An inability to use speech normally. People suffering from expressive aphasia can understand speech, but have difficulty pronouncing words correctly.

Extinction In classical conditioning, the elimination of a conditioned response due to the withholding of the unconditioned stimulus. In instrumental conditioning, the elimination of a response due to the removal of the reinforcement.

Extrasensory perception (ESP) The belief that sensory information can be acquired in ways that are not dependent on any known form of sensory stimulation. Telepathy and Clairvoyance are two types of extrasensory perception.

Extraversion A major factor emerging in trait research; composed of characteristics such as talkative, sociable, and adventurous.

Extrinsic motives Instigations of behavior that stem from outside forces, such as the desire for reward, rather than internal forces such as curiosity.

Factitious disorder A physical complaint that is purposefully fabricated or greatly exaggerated by a patient.

Factor analysis A sophisticated method of data analysis used in test construction and in the interpretation of test scores. The method computes the least number of factors needed to account for the correlations of test scores in a battery of tests.

False consensus effect The tendency to overestimate the number of people who make the same inferences and hold the same opinions we do.

Family resemblances The condition in concept identification where no two stimuli are identical, but all have at least one feature in common.

Family systems therapy Based on the belief that behavioral problems stem from dysfunctional family interactions, family therapists treat the disturbed individual and his or her family environment.

Family therapy Type of psychotherapy that involves the whole family, rather than just one member of it, since it is often the family system as a whole that can create stress and contribute to the development of psychological disorders. Couples working on a relationship also participate in family therapy.

Farsighted An improper functioning of the lens. A farsighted person can only focus clearly on objects that are far away.

Fear Reaction to a specific danger in the environment.

Feature analysis In pattern recognition, analysis consists of features extraction, specifying the features that make up a stimulus, and features interpretation, matching those features to feature sets that define particular stimuli.

Feature detection The translation of different patterns of retinal stimulation into particular types of brain stimulation that enables us to see different features.

Feature extraction An aspect of pattern recognition that involves specifying the particular details that make up a stimulus.

Feature interpretation An aspect of pattern recognition that consists of matching details that make up a stimulus to feature sets that define different possible stimuli.

Fechner's law A psychophysical relationship in which ever-greater increases in stimulus intensity are needed to produce a constant increase in sensory experience.

Fetal alcohol syndrome A developmental malformation that affects infants born to alcoholic mothers.

Fetus The name of the developing organism in the womb from about two months after conception until birth. (See also Embryo; Zygote)

Field dependence A type of cognitive style that has difficulty ignoring extraneous cues from a surrounding perceptual field.

Field experiment Experiment performed in a natural setting rather than in the controlled setting of the laboratory.

Field independence A type of cognitive style that involves maintaining spatial orientation and ignoring irrelevant perceptual cues.

Fight-or-flight response Response of the sympathetic division of the autonomic nervous system that involves increased oxygen consumption, respiratory heart rate, blood pressure, and muscle tension.

Figure Object standing out against a background or against its surroundings

Figure-ground The perception of a form or pattern as the foreground (figure) against a background (ground). The figure is perceived as closer than the surroundings.

Figure-ground reversal (or multistable perception) Occurs when figure and ground in a picture suddenly reverse; what was seen as figure is seen as background, and vice versa.

Fissure of Rolando (central fissure) One of three fissures of the cerebral cortex.

Fissure of sylvius (lateral fissure) One of three fissures in the cerebral cortex.

Fixed action patterns Behavioral configurations that appear in the same form in all members of a species, such as tail-wagging in a dog.

Fixed interval schedule In instrumental conditioning, reinforcement follows the first response made after a specified period of time. (See also Fixed ratio, Variable interval, and Variable ratio schedule)

Fixed ratio schedule In instrumental conditioning, an animal is reinforced after it emits a fixed number of responses. (See also Fixed interval, Variable interval, and Variable ratio schedule)

Fluid intelligence The ability, which declines with age, to deal with new problems. (See also Crystallized intelligence)

Focal colors Eleven colors that are seen as being more distinct than other colors.

Foot-in-the-door approach Persuasive technique that gets people to agree first to a small request and then later be more willing to agree to a second request.

Forebrain The part of the brain that develops from the top core of the embryo brain; contains the hypothalamus, thalamus, and cerebrum.

Forensic psychology Sub-field of psychology concerned with behaviors that relate to our legal system. Forensic psychologists work with judges and lawyers who are trying to improve the reliability of witnesses and jury decisions and are also consulted on the mental competency of accused people.

Forgetting Inability to remember or retrieve information from memory.

Forgetting curve According to Ebbinghaus, the relation between savings number of trials needed to relearn information-and the time between learning and relearning.

Formal operational stage One of Piaget's stages of cognitive development; lasts from about 13 years of age through adulthood. Main theme is the ability to consider many possible solutions to a problem and the ability to systematically test those possibilities

Formal operations thinking The level of cognitive development in which a person can form hypotheses, reason abstractly, and think in a systematic way. Although not found in all people and not used all the time, formal operations thinking occurs during adolescence and adulthood. It is the highest level of cognitive development, according to Piaget.

Fovea A small indentation in the retina that is the center of the visual field.

Fraternal twins (See Dizygotic twins)

Free association A method developed for psychoanalysis in which a person says whatever comes to mind.

Free association test Procedure in which a person looks at or listens to, a target word, and then reports other words that come to mind.

Free recall task A procedure in which a subject studies a list of words and then recalls the words in any order possible.

Frequency The number of expansion and compression cycles per second in a sound wave; the primary determinant of pitch.

Frequency distribution A list of the number of scores that occur in each equal size interval over the entire range of scores.

Frequency histogram Way to show frequency distribution in graph form; intervals are placed along the horizontal axis, frequencies along the vertical axis.

Frequency of sound waves Number of wave crests that occur in a second. Changes in pitch correspond to changes in frequency.

Frequency polygon Way to show frequency distribution in graph form; line graph connects a series of points representing the frequency of scores in each interval.

Frequency theory Theory that pitch is determined by the rate of the brain cell's response.

Frontal lobes The largest of the association areas that make an important contribution to intelligent behavior.

Frostbite Result of ice forming in the skin cells; these frozen cells die, and if the affected area is large enough, a finger, toe, or large patch of skin may literally die.

Frustration Basically, the result of being blocked from getting what you want when you want it.

Frustration-aggression hypothesis The idea that aggression occurs when an obstacle prevents a person from reaching a goal.

Frustration-aggression theory Theory that aggression is always a consequence of frustration and that frustration always leads to some form of aggression.

Fugue Involves loss of memory and also physical flight in which the person wanders away from his or her home for a matter of an hour or, in some cases, for years.

Fugue state A condition in which a person runs away from a traumatic situation and suffers a memory loss for all personally identifying information.

Functional fixedness The inability to see a new or unique use for a common object.

Functionalism Approach to psychology that emphasizes the function of thought; led to important applications in education and the founding of educational psychology, a sub-field of psychology.

Fundamental attribution error The tendency to base attributions solely on behavior without considering the possible influence of the situation.

Fuzzy sets In concept learning, certain stimuli go together to form a concept even though there are no specific features that decisively define that concept. A game is an example of a fuzzy concept.

Galvanic skin response (GSR) Changes in the electrical conductivity of the skin, detected by a galvanometer. The GSR is commonly used as a physiological indicator of emotionality.

Gametes Sex cells; female gamete is an ovum, male gamete is a sperm. Each gamete has 23 chromosomes; ovum and sperm combine to form a zygote.

Gate control theory A theory of pain that holds that the brain or spinal cord can cut off receptivity to pain if there is stimulation in other areas

Gender conservation A child's realization, between ages five and seven, that he or she will always be male or female.

Gender identity disorder Disorder that can occur in childhood, when a child rigidly adopts the role and outlook of the opposite sex.

Gender roles Behavior that is considered culturally appropriate for a person because of the person's sex. Also called sex roles, these differences in characteristic ways of acting masculine and feminine are the result of differences in biology and socialization. (See also Sex roles; Socialization)

General adaptation syndrome According to Hans Selye, physiological response to any stressor follows a three-stage pattern: alarm, resistance, and exhaustion.

General intelligence (g) That aspect of intelligence, according to Spearman, that is constant across a variety of intelligence tests. (See also Intelligence)

General paresis a form of mental illness caused by syphilis. Symptoms include irritability, depression, and impaired judgment.

Generalization When a conditioned response has been acquired, stimuli that are similar to the conditioned stimulus will also evoke that response.

Generalized anxiety disorder Disorder in which people experience overwhelming anxiety, but cannot identify its source.

Genes The fundamental units of heredity, located in the chromosomes. Typically occurring in pairs, genes have one member of the pair provided by the father and the other member provided by the mother. Each chromosome contains numerous genes. (See also chromosome)

Genetics The study of how traits are inherited.

Genital stage The final stage in Freud's theory of psychosexual development, during which sexual feelings presumably re-emerge in the adolescent.

Genotype The genetic characteristics that a person has inherited and will transmit to descendants, whether or not the person manifests these different characteristics. (See also Genes; Phenotype)

Gerontology The study of aging and the problems of the aged.

Gestalt laws of organization Describes how we group stimulus elements according to their characteristics.

Gestalt psychology A psychological theory of perception that is concerned with the organization of stimulus elements into perceptual forms.

Gestalt therapy Therapy developed by Fritz Perls, proposing that unconscious thoughts and emotions (background) may lead to behaviors (figure) that are inappropriate to the situation. Encourages people to take responsibility for their actions in the present, while understanding the emotions that are influencing them.

Gifted retardates Term used to describe the very small minority of intellectually handicapped people who display skills that would be extraordinary even for people of normal intelligence.

Glaucoma Eye disease that causes pressure to build up inside the eye; most common cause of blindness.

Glial cells Nerve cells that support and protect the neurons.

Global therapies Therapies that focus on the individual as a whole and aim to help the person gain insight into his or her problems and life.

Glove anesthesia People with this symptom report losing all sensation in a hand, although they have normal sensation in the arm. This is physically impossible given the system of nerves in the hand and arm; glove anesthesia is a conversion disorder.

Glucoreceptors Cells in the hypothalamus that monitor the glucose content of the blood. If the blood is low in glucose, the glucoreceptors send out signals that cause hunger and motivate us to eat.

Gonadotropins Hormones that produce a series of changes in other endocrine glands. They stimulate the production of sex hormones, which eventually make a person capable of sexual reproduction.

Gonads The reproductive glands, testes in the male and ovaries in the female.

Graceful degradation The process by which the brain loses large numbers of neurons and their interconnections in the normal course of ageing, but leaving the memory still functional.

Grammar Set of rules for combining language symbols to form sentences.

Grasp reflex Causes infants to close their fingers tightly around an object that touches the palm.

GRIT strategy A strategy suggested for resolving international conflict that calls one side of the conflict to begin with some small step toward increased cooperation, followed by gradually increasing and reciprocal reductions of tensions.

Ground Background or surroundings against which an object stands out.

Group Two or more persons who are interacting with one another in such a manner that each person influences and is influenced by each other person.

Group hysteria (See Mass psychogenic illness)

Group polarization effect Groups tend to polarize people and move them to believe more strongly in the position that they first held.

Group therapy Involves 1 (sometimes 2) therapists and from 6 to 12 clients; clients receive feedback from others in the group as well as from the therapist. Many different therapeutic techniques may be used.

Groupthink Occurs when group members become so concerned with reaching agreement of all members of the group that they fail to critically evaluate their ideas.

GSR (See Galvanic skin response)

Habituation A decrease in responsiveness to unchanging stimulation. (See also Dishabituation).

Halfway houses Treatment facilities that allow former addicts or mental patients to live partly in the community and partly in a treatment environment.

Hallucinations Sensory experiences that have no basis in the external world.

Hallucinogenic A class of drugs that modify personal consciousness by affecting a person's sensation, perception, thinking, self-awareness, and emotion.

Hammer One of three small bones in the middle ear, transmits sounds from the eardrum to the inner ear.

Haptic perception The perception of objects by touch.

Hardiness A set of personal characteristics that relate to stress resistance.

Hassles Minor, but daily annoying events.

Health psychology That field of psychology concerned with the role of psychological factors in preventing illness and maintaining good health.

Heat exhaustion Reaction to heat which involves fainting, nausea, vomiting, and headaches.

Heatstroke Serious disorder that results when the body's sweating mechanism completely breaks down; it is accompanied by headache, staggering, coma, and possibly death.

Hedonic relevance Refers to the degree to which an actor's behavior is rewarding or costly to the observer.

Helping behavior Coming to the aid of another person.

Heritability A statistical estimate of the relative influence of genes on a trait, given a particular range of environmental stimulation.

Hertz One cycle per second of a sound wave.

Heuristics Mental short-cuts or rules of thumb that suggest possible solutions to a problem.

Hierarchy An organization that arranges information into levels of categories and subordinate categories.

Higher-order conditioning A variation of classical conditioning in which a new stimulus precedes a conditioned stimulus to elicit a conditioned response. (See also Classical conditioning).

Hindbrain Part of the brain that develops from the bottom core in the embryonic neural tube; contains the medulla, pons, and cerebellum.

Hippocampus A part of the limbic system that has an important role in normal memory functioning.

Histogram A bar graph representation of a frequency distribution.

Holonomic brain theory Theory proposed by Karl Pribram that learning alters information that is lawfully distributed throughout the brain.

Holophrastic speech Use of single words to express phrases. For example, "out" might mean "I want to go out."

Homeostasis An ideal balanced state in the body's internal environment.

Homosexuality Sexual desire for those of the same sex as oneself.

Hormonal effects The influence of hormones from the endocrine system on behavior and thought.

Hormones The chemical secretions of the endocrine glands that are distributed by the bloodstream throughout the body. (See also Endocrine system)

Hue The perception of color that is determined by the light's wavelength.

Human development Process by which the genes inherited from parents come to be expressed as specific physical and behavioral characteristics.

Human language Systematic means of communicating verbally, with the written word, or with a sign language.

Humanistic approach A view of behavior that stresses individuals' own interpretation of events in their lives and their free will to change themselves and their relationship to their environment.

Humanistic psychology Movement formed by Carl Rogers, Abraham Maslow, and Rollo May which rejects Freudian view of people; argues that people are basically good and worthy of respect; stresses the creative aspect of people in reaching their true potential.

Hypermnesia Improved recall of previously forgotten events with the passage of time.

Hypersomnia A sleeping disorder characterized by excessive sleepiness and many periods of microsleep at inappropriate times during the day. (See also Insomnias)

Hyperstimulation The relief of pain in one area of the body by irritation of another area.

Hypnagogic images Hallucinations that occur during the drowsy interval before sleep.

Hypnosis A state of consciousness characterized by increased suggestibility and imagination, along with reduced initiative and reality-testing. Some psychologists consider hypnosis an altered state, while others believe it to be a form of role-enactment.

Hypnotic age regression The idea that hypnotized subjects are able to relive earlier episodes of their lives.

Hypnotic susceptibility tests Tests that are used to predict the extent to which people are willing to yield to hypnotic suggestions.

Hypochondriasis A disorder characterized by exaggerated concerns about physical illness.

Hypothalamus Located under the thalamus, this small structure is involved in many different aspects of behavior, including eating, sleeping, sexual behavior, and maintaining the proper balance of essential bodily conditions.

Hypothermia Occurs when the internal body temperature drops below a normal level; heart rate and blood pressure increase dramatically and death due to heart attack can result if temperature does not increase.

Hypothesis A tentative and testable assumption, an "educated guess."

Hypothetico-deductive reasoning A manner of thinking or problem-solving in which hypotheses are formed and tested by logical systematic procedures. This form of thinking is first manifested during adolescence.

Icon A brief visual memory trace that occurs following the presentation of a visual stimulus. (See also Sensory memory

Iconic memory A momentary visual image that remains apparent after a stimulus is withdrawn.

Id According to Freud's theory of personality, the basic structural foundation for personality, composed of a common set of drives for self-preservation and reproduction. (See also Pleasure principle)

Identical twins (See Monozygotic twins)

Identification The process by which children copy, partly unconsciously, the social roles of important adults in their lives. (See also Gender roles)

Identity A unified, consistent personality embodying diverse values and beliefs. A sense of identity emerges during adolescence as a person changes from a child to an adult.

Identity crisis Term used by Erikson to describe the search for an identity during adolescence that involves trying out and testing different roles.

Identity foreclosure Selection of identity too early in adolescence before other alternatives have been considered. (See also Psychosocial moratorium)

Illusion A perceptual experiences that does not correspond to reality. Visual illusions are studied in perception to learning about accurate perception.

Illusory correlation The mistaken perception that two features go together.

Imaginal thought The conscious or unconscious manipulation of "mental images.""

Imaginative thinking The ability to see things in new ways, to recognize relations, and to make new connections.

Imitation Acquisition of knowledge and behavior by watching other people act and then doing the same thing ourselves.

Immune system The body's wall of defense against illness, including cells in the skin and bloodstream that detect and destroy potentially harmful bacteria and viruses.

Implicit memory Enhanced performance on a task without deliberate or conscious remembering.

Implicit theory A set of beliefs that we use to form opinions, for example, about the intelligence of the people we know.

Impossible figure Representation of three-dimensional figures that could not possibly exist in the world.

Impotence Sexual disorder in which males are unable to have an erection or maintain one long enough for ejaculation.

Imprinting Process whereby a young fowl or bird attaches itself to the first object it sees.

Incentives External stimuli, such as the smell of a pie baking, that excites drive.

Incubation effect The process through which the passage of time and a refocusing of attention reduce an inappropriate mental set and allow us to consider new strategies to solve a problem.

Incus One of three small bones, which, together with the malleus and the stapes, make up the middle ear and through which vibration from the eardrum is transmitted.

Indefensible spaces Areas in an apartment complex that are not open to observation, such as enclosed stairways and alleys; such areas invite intruders and breed crime.

Independent variable In an experiment, the factor that is manipulated to observe its effect on behavior. (See also Dependent variable)

Individual differences The study of psychological differences between individuals.

Individual psychology Adler's approach to personality development, based on his belief that each person is unique and adjusts differently to social influences.

Induced movement An illusion in which a small, stationary object appears to move when viewed against a larger, moving background.

Inductive reasoning The discovery of general rules from specific experiences. (See also Deductive reasoning)

Industrial-organizational psychology Sub-field of psychology concerned with selecting, training, and managing employees.

Infancy A period that extends through the second year of life.

Infantile autism Infants who from a very early age are withdrawn, do not react to others, and become attached to inanimate objects rather than to people.

Inferential statistics Used to test hypotheses made by psychologists.

Information processing A conceptual approach to memory that is concerned with the mental operations that intervene between a stimulus and a response.

Informational pressure A type of influence a group has, based on the group's value as a source of information.

Informational social influence Conforming to popular opinions about reality.

Inhibitory influences Stimulations of the neuron that slow it down.

Initiation rite During adolescent development, a ceremony that typically marks the passage of a child into the adult world.

Insanity Legal classification for a person who has been judged to have a mental disease or defect which renders that person unable to understand inappropriate or illegal conduct.

Insight In psychoanalysis, a cognitive and emotional understanding of the roots of a conflict.

Insight therapies Based on the assumption that many pathological behaviors would disappear if clients confronted unacceptable parts of themselves, these treatments usually involve a conversation between therapist and client, with the ultimate goal being personal understanding by the client.

Insomnia A sleep disorder characterized by an inability to get sufficient sleep. (See also Hypersomnia)

Instinct An inherited tendency to act in a certain way in response to a particular set of environmental and internal cues.

Instrumental conditioning A form of learning, first studied by Thorndike, that allows us to learn the consequences of our behavior. In instrumental conditioning, reinforcement is contingent upon a particular response being made. (See also Classical conditioning; Reinforcement)

Integrative network A function of the nervous system to organize information it receives from both inside and outside of the body.

Intelligence The ability to learn from experience, to think effectively, and adapt to changing environmental conditions. (See also Intelligence quotient)

Intelligence quotient (IQ) A scale unit that is used for reporting intelligence test scores, determined by dividing a person's mental age by chronological age and multiplying by 100. (See also Mental age)

Interaction distance Amount of space between people in various situations; differs with the relationship between people and the kind of interaction they're engaged in.

Interactionist perspective A modern view of psychology that links the various theoretical perspectives to understand the whole human being. According to this view, ongoing cognitive and behavioral responses to environmental inputs are constrained by past learning, which is in turn constrained by individual differences and evolved genetic constraints.

Interference The process of forgetting when information is dislodged from memory by the arrival of new information.

Interference theory Theory that we forget information because other information gets in the way. See also Proactive Inhibition; Retroactive Inhibition.

Intermittent reinforcement schedule A schedule of reinforcement in which only some of the responses are reinforced by reinforcement is available for only specified periods of time. (See also Schedules of reinforcement).

Internal representation The form in which information is held in memory.

Internalization Process of bringing behavior under the control of inner, personal standards that make people obey rules even if there are not external restraints.

Interneurons Nerve cells that transmit stimulation back and forth between different parts of the brain and the spinal cord. (See also Motor neurons; Sensory neurons)

Interposition (See Overlap)

Interpretation A psychoanalytic technique in which the analyst attempts to piece together the unconscious logic underlying a patient's conflicts.

Interview Assessment technique that involves direct questioning of a person. Unstructured interview consists of planned questions to start, but interviewer is free to develop the conversation as he or she wishes. Structured interview consists of a set of specific questions asked according to a set plan.

Intrinsic motivation The inclination to perform some behavior for the pure joy of it rather than for some external reward.

Introspection A process of analyzing a conscious experience by reporting the sensory qualities of the stimuli that are experienced, without the intrusion of meanings or interpretations.

Ions Electrically charged molecules located in the cell's protoplasm and in the liquid surrounding the cell.

Iris A richly pigmented, muscular structure that determines the size of the pupil and gives the eyes their color.

Irreversibility The inability demonstrated by young children to rearrange objects mentally.

Just-barely-sufficient threat Aspect of dissonance theory that suggests that we will derogate attractive objects or activities that we choose to forgo without strong external constraints.

Just-noticeable difference (JND) The smallest change in stimulus intensity that is capable of being detected 50 percent of the time. Each JND produces a new sensory experience. (See also Difference threshold)

Key-word method Mnemonic system of using imagery to learn foreign vocabulary; consists of forming an image that will act as a link between the key word and the other word we want to remember.

Kidneys The glandular organs responsible for separating waste products from the blood.

Kinesis Study of body language, or communication through body movement.

Kinesthesis A proprioceptive sense in which sensory reception in the muscles, tendons, and joints provides information about body position and limb movements.

Kinetic depth effect Detection of depth through movement.

Knowledge base In problem solving, a background of information about the problem area under study.

Korsakoff's syndrome A disorder that is characterized by profound memory impairment due to extensive brain damage associated with chronic alcohol consumption.

Laboratory experiment Experiment performed in a controlled environment created for the experiment.

Language A system of gestures, sounds, or written symbols that is used for communication.

Latency stage The fourth hypothesized stage of Freud's theory of personality development, during which a child's sexual urges are presumably suppressed until puberty.

Latent content According to Freud, the hidden content of dreams, which contains the underlying motives that would disturb a sleeping person if they were consciously expressed. (See also Manifest content)

Latent learning Learning that is not immediately shown in performance. Latent learning is demonstrated when motivation to perform is enhanced by the availability of reinforcement.

Lateral fissure A major brain convolution that separates the frontal and temporal lobes.

Lateralization A difference or asymmetry of function for each of the cerebral hemispheres.

Law of brightness constancy Law stating that we see an object's brightness as constant when the amount of light striking it changes.

Law of connectedness We group connected elements.

Law of effect A principle of learning, stated by Thorndike, that responses followed by satisfaction (reinforcement) will tend to increase in strength or frequency. (See also Instrumental conditioning; Reinforcement)

Law of enclosure We group elements in the same perceived enclosed region.

Law of nearness or proximity One of the Gestalt laws of organization; states that we group elements that are close together.

Law of psychology Examines factors that influence jury verdicts, the way in which people determine what is just, and how procedural aspects of a trial affect its outcome.

Law of shape constancy Law stating that we see an object's shape as constant when the object's slant changes, or when we view it from a different angle.

Law of similarity One of the Gestalt laws or organizations; states that we group elements that are similar or look alike.

Law of size constancy Law stating that we see an object's size as constant even if the object's distance from us changes.

Laws of organization According to Gestalt psychologists, patterns of perceptual grouping--proximity, similarity, good continuation, closure, and common fate--that capture various elements and determine how we see them.

Leader The person in a group who has the most amount of influence.

Learned helplessness The tendency to give up without trying to overcome a stressor, presumably acquired as a result of failed attempts to control stressors in the past; believed to be a component of depression.

Learning A relatively permanent change in behavior or behavior potentiality that results from experience.

Learning set Occurs when one's previous experience makes one ready to solve a particular problem.

Left hemisphere The left cerebral hemisphere is specialized for language, analyzing information, and sequential tasks. It controls the right side of the body. (See also Right hemisphere)

Lens A transparent structure in the eye that focuses light. (See also Retina)

Lesbians Female homosexuals.

Lesion procedure A brain operation to determine how damage to a particular area or structure affects an animal's behavior.

Letters The smallest meaningful units of written language.

Level of processing The progression of stimulus analysis from analysis of physical features to the analysis of meaning.

Libido Energy force that propels people to satisfy the drive for survival (includes eating, drinking and sexual activity)

Life transition Events or nonevents that alter our roles, relationships, and beliefs.

Lifespan psychology The study of the description, explanation, and optimalization of developmental processes that occur during human life between conception and death. Much life-span research focuses on developmental changes during adulthood and ageing.

Light adaptation A reduction in sensitivity when illumination changes from dim to very bright.

Limbic system A set of interrelated structures between the brain-stem and the cerebral cortex of the brain that coordinates information transmission, regulates emotional responses, and monitors motivated behaviors essential for survival.

Linear perspective A monocular depth cue based on the fact that as objects become more distant they appear to recede and converge on a distant point.

Linguistic relativity hypothesis Holds that the language of any culture determines how the people in that culture perceive and understand their world.

Linguistics The study of natural languages and their grammatical rules.

Lithium carbonate A drug used in the treatment of manic behavior.

Localization theory The view that specific psychological functions are associated with specific areas or locations of the brain.

Locus of control A scale that measures individual differences in beliefs about whether we can control the rewards and punishments we receive.

Long-term memory store The relatively permanent component of the memory system that is the repository of all the things we know. (See also Sensory memory stores; Short-term memory store)

Long-term potentiation(LTP) The increase in synaptic response strength when a neural pathway is stimulated. LTP also occurs when two converging neural pathways are stimulated at the same time. LTP is believed to be an important memory mechanism.

Longitudinal fissure One of three fissures in the cerebral cortex; separates the two cerebral hemispheres.

Longitudinal research A research technique that examines the performance of the same subjects at different periods of development; for example, a comparison of the performance of the same people at ages 12, 20, and 40.

Loudness Measurement of sound based on the amplitude of sound waves.

Lungs Organs of respiration lying within the chest cavity. Supply the blood with oxygen and are the source of energy for the production of speech sounds.

Maintenance rehearsal A form of mental repetition that serves mainly to hold information in short-term storage. (See also Elaborative rehearsal; Short-term memory store)

Major life events Stressful occurrences that involve some change in a person's life.

Malleus One of three small bones, which, together with the incus and the stapes, make up the middle ear and through which vibration from the eardrum is transmitted.

Mania A mood disorder characterized by extreme upswings of mood. Individuals in a manic state often lose control of themselves in their excitement and begin to act in inappropriate and self-destructive ways.

Manifest content According to Freud, the obvious content of dreams, which comes from a person's memory, daily events, and bodily sensations during the night. (See also Latent content)

Mantra Secret world, sound, or phrase used in Transcendental Meditation.

Masochism Becoming sexually aroused by having pain inflicted on oneself.

Mass psychogenic illness A phenomenon in which a group of people suddenly come down with symptoms that seem to have no organic basis.

Masturbation Self-manipulation of one's genitals.

Maturation Growth processes that result in orderly changes in behavior. The timing and pattern of these processes are independent of experience given a normal environment.

Mean The numerical average of a frequency distribution of scores obtained by adding the scores together and dividing the sum by the total number of scores.

Means-end analysis A type of heuristic in which a problem is divided into a number of subproblems or components to reduce the difference between the original state and the goal state.

Measure of central tendency Score value that represents the mathematical center of a group of scores.

Median The middle score in a frequency distribution. The median is used when the distribution is skewed. (See also Skewness)

Meditation A set of primarily mental exercises designed to produce concentration, awareness, and a sense of tranquility and equilibrium.

Medulla The lowest part of the brain, the medulla regulates vital body functions such as heart rate, blood pressure, respiration, and digestion (See also Pons)

Meiosis The process through which mature sex cells of each parent split to form separate cells.

Membrane potential An electric tension that exists in a neuron between the cell's inside and outside environment. Also called polarization.

Memoirists People who demonstrate superior memory.

Memory The ability to acquire, retain, and use information or knowledge.

Memory span The maximum number of stimuli that can be recalled in perfect order 50 percent of the time. The memory span has an upper limit of seven plus or minus two chunks. (See also Chunk)

Memory structures The parts of the memory system that are permanent. These include the sensory memory store, the short-term memory store, and the long-term memory store.

Memory trace A physical change in the nervous system that is produced by all of our experiences.

Menarche The first menstrual period, a sign of sexual maturity in a girl.

Menopause Cessation of menstruation, marking the end of a woman's ability to bear children; accompanied by physical and hormonal changes.

Mental age In a test such as the Stanford-Binet, the age level associated with the last task (or series of tasks) a child could complete successfully.

Mental imagery The process of constructing mental pictures that bear a resemblance to physical reality. Mental imagery is used as an aid to memory. Note that mental imagery is different from eidetic imagery. (See also Eidetic imagery; Mnemonics)

Mental operations According to Piaget, a process children use to transform and manipulate what they see or hear according to logical rules.

Mental rehearsal A process for maintaining information placed in the short-term store by repeating the information over and over.

Mental retardation Subnormal mental functioning (IQ below 70) and impairment in adaptive behavior.

Mental set In pattern recognition, the context for how a stimulus should be received.

Mentally gifted People who score above 130 on an intelligence test.

Mesmerism The precursor of hypnosis developed by Fredrich Mesmer.

Mesomorphs According to William Sheldon, one of three body types, characterized as predominantly bone and muscle. Mesomorphs are hypothesized to love adventure, risk, and competition.

Meta-analysis Statistical technique used to organize findings in areas where there are many, often-contradictory, studies.

Meta-components of intelligence High-order process that we use to analyze a problem and to pick a strategy for solving it.

Metabolic rate Rate at which food is transformed by the body into energy.

Metamemory Awareness of one's own memory and mental ability.

Method of constant stimuli A procedure used for calculating the absolute threshold of a sensory stimulus. Stimuli of different intensities are presented in a random order until the absolute threshold is established. (See also Method of limits)

Method of limits A procedure used for calculating the absolute threshold of a sensory stimulus. The energy level is changed in an ascending to descending manner until the stimulus passes its absolute threshold (See also Method of constant stimuli).

Method of magnitude estimation A direct measure of sensitivity in which observers provide a psychophysical scale by making judgments of sensory stimuli of different magnitudes in comparison to a standard.

Method of successive approximation The procedure of shaping a desired behavior by carefully reinforcing and strengthening each small step toward a target response.

Mid-life crisis A term, originated by Jung, that describes developmental changes at mid-life.

Midbrain Part of the brain that develops from the middle core of the embryo brain; contains the reticular formation.

Minnesota Multiphasic Personality Inventory (MMPI) One of the most popular personality questionnaires used by clinicians. Designed to identify specific psychological disorders. Consists of 550 statements to which people can respond true, false or cannot say. Aimed at identifying 10 different disorders

Mnemonic systems Systems created to aid memory; examples are the key-word method and verbal mediation.

Mnemonics Techniques or strategies used to enhance memory. Mnemonics work because they organize information, ensure a deep level of processing, and provide a plan for remembering.

Mode The most frequently occurring score in a frequency distribution.

Modeling A process of learning in subjects who simply observe another person but do not themselves perform any overt behavior nor receive any direct reinforcement.

Modularity theory The belief that complex psychological functions are based on combinations of more fundamental, abilities, each relatively localized in a different brain area.

Monism Theory that the mind and brain are one organic whole. (See also Dualism).

Monocular depth cues The different types of sensory information available to perceivers to see a three-dimensional world from flat, two-dimensional retinal images.

Monozygotic twins Twins developed from the same egg. They are always of the same sex and often similar in appearance. (See also Dizygotic twins)

Mood General diffuse feelings states that are often long-lasting and low-intensity.

Mood disorders Group of general, non-specific disturbances that cause high or low feelings and affect a person's ability to function normally.

Moral reasoning The process by which children come to adopt their society's standards of right and wrong.

Morphemes The smallest language unit that possesses meaning.

Motherese Simplified speech characterized by a special tone of voice, slow rate of talking, high pitch, and exaggerated intonations, used by adults in talking to an infant.

Motion parallax Apparent motion seen when an observer moves past objects.

Motivation Why an organism acts in a certain way at a certain time.

Motive Condition that energizes and directs the behavior of an organism.

Motor cortex A thin strip of cortex, located directly in front of the central tissue in the frontal lobe, that governs motor movements. (See also Somatosensory cortex)

Motor neurons Nerve cells that transmit stimulation from the brain and spinal cord to the effector cells in the muscles and glands. (See also Interneurons; Sensory neurons)

Motor system Functional subdivision of the nervous system; includes basal ganglia, cerebellum, and the motor cortex. Controls voluntary muscle movements.

Movement aftereffect An illusion of movement that follows prolonged perception of movement in a particular direction. When a stationary field is viewed, movement in the direction opposite the initial perception is observed.

Movement parallax In perception, a depth cue in which nearby objects move across the field of vision faster than more distant objects.

MRI scan Provides an image of the brain's interior structure.

Multiple personality A form of dissociative disorder in which a person shifts back and forth between two or more distinct identities (now called "dissociative identity disorder").

Multistable perceptions (also called figure-ground reversal) Occurs when a picture shows alternating appearances; what was seen as figure becomes the background, and vice versa.

Mutation Abnormal chromosome structure, responsible for such diseases as Down syndrome.

Myelin sheath A fatty, insulating material that surrounds certain axons. Axons with myelin insulation transmit impulses faster than those without such insulation. (See also Axon)

Myelinization Development of myelin sheaths during infancy, childhood, and adolescence.

Mysticism View that alternate state experiences are a response to an external reality that exists beyond the visible and understandable universe.

Narcolepsy A disorder in which one is chronically sleepy and suffers irresistible attacks of sleepiness at inappropriate times of the day.

Narcotics A class of depressant drugs.

Nasal cavity Open space inside the nose.

Naturalistic observation A method of research that involves observing and recording the behavior of people or animals in their natural environments.

Near point of accommodation Nearest point at which print can be read distinctly.

Nearsightedness An improper functioning of the lens which only focuses clearly on objects that are near.

Need Internal or homeostatic imbalance that must be satisfied in order to keep the body performing at a consistent level.

Need for achievement The need to compete with some standard of excellence.

Negative contrast effect In instrumental conditioning, a decrease in the effectiveness of a reinforcer that occurs when the reinforcer is presented later than expected.

Negative identity According to Erikson, a form of acting out through delinquency, drug abuse, or suicide that results from a failure to achieve a positive sense of identity during adolescence.

Negative imprinting An aversion for forming a sexual attraction based on experience, occurs when social animals avoid other animals with whom they were raised.

Negative reinforcement In instrumental conditioning, stimuli whose termination or removal increases the likelihood of a response.

Negative set Mental set that reduces the chance of learning a new relationship.

Neonatal period The first month after birth.

Neorepinephrine Hormone secreted by the adrenal gland that causes blood pressure to rise. It can also function as a neurotransmitter when released by a presynaptic neuron.

Nerve A group of elongated axons composed of hundreds or even thousands of neurons. (See also Axon; Neuron)

Nerve cell (See Neuron)

Nerve deafness Hearing loss caused by problems with the inner ear. (See also Conduction deafness)

Nervous set Pervasive communication system in the body that monitors the outside world and manages the brain and behavior.

Neural impulse The wave of electrical activity that travels down the axon of a neuron when the cell's firing threshold is reached. Synonymous with action potential.

Neural noise Spontaneous neural activity that can make near-threshold sensory stimuli more difficult to detect. In signal detection theory, observers must distinguish sensory signals from background neural noise.

Neurofibrillary tangles Cell damage in the form of twisted filaments that fill brain cells in Alzheimer's patients.

Neurologists Physicians who treat patients with diseased or damaged nervous systems.

Neuron The nerve cell; the functional unit of the nervous system. Neurons receive and transmit signals to all parts of the body. (See also Neurotransmitter; Synapse)

Neuropsychology The field of psychology that seeks to understand the role of the nervous system in behavior.

Neurosis Broad pattern of psychological disorders characterized by anxiety, fear, and self-defeating behaviors.

Neurotic behaviors Attempts to cope with anxiety.

Neurotransmitter A chemical substance used in the transmission of neural impulses across a synaptic junction from one neuron to another. (See also Neuron; Synapse)

NMDA receptor A molecule that is believed to turn on certain biochemical reactions that lead to the encoding of memories.

Noise Psychological concept; unwanted sound, sound that is unpleasant, bothersome, or actually physiologically harmful.

Nonspecificity hypothesis The assumption that any type of stress will lead to a general pattern of physical deterioration.

Nonverbal communication Communication through facial expression, gesture, body movement, etc.

Nonverbal leakage Betrayal through non-verbal cues of emotions people are attempting to hide.

Norm The average or typical performance of individuals under specific conditions. Norms can provide standards of average growth and performance on intellectual tasks. In another sense, norms can be standards of conduct by which people are expected to act.

Normal curve The standard symmetrical bell-shaped frequency distribution.

Normal distribution A symmetrical, bell-shaped frequency distribution that describes scores on many different physical and psychological variables. In a normal distribution, the mean, median, and mode are identical. (See also Normal curve)

Normative social influence Compliance with arbitrary social rules and conventions.

Obedience A change of behavior in response to a command from another person, typically an authority figure.

Obesity In humans, being more than 15 percent over the "ideal" weight, given the person's height and overall body build.

Object permanence Piaget's term for the realization that objects continue to exist even if they are hidden from view. This reality is the principle achievement of the sensorimotor period of cognitive development. (See also Sensorimotor period)

Observational learning Learning that occurs from watching the behavior of others and observing the consequences of their actions.

Obsession Recurring, irrational thought that cannot be controlled or banished from one's mind. See also compulsion, which involves behavior rather than thought.

Obsessive-compulsive disorder A disorder that involves repetitious behaviors and thoughts a person cannot get out of his or her mind.

Occipital lobe Part of the cerebral cortex that is involved in integrating visual information.

Oedipus complex According to Freud, boy desires sexual relationship with mother, but is afraid father will find out and castrate him as punishment. In order to get rid of these fears, boy identifies with and tries to be like father. Identification with father helps form the super-ego because boy internalizes the father's values.

Olfaction The sense of smell, dependent on odor molecules stimulating the receptors at the top of the nose. Stimulation may result from chemical or physical stimuli.

Olfactory cells Odor-sensitive cells contained in the passageway between the nose and the throat.

Open-office design Office space or area that has no real closure rather than a traditional concept of an office with floor-to-ceiling walls and a door.

Operant conditioning The form of behavioral conditioning studied by B. F. Skinner. (See also Instrumental conditioning; Reinforcement)

Ophthalmoscope Uses mirrors or prisms to direct light through the pupil so that eye doctors can examine the eye's internal structures.

Opponent-process model of motivation The idea that every physiological state of arousal automatically leads to an opposing state, used to explain phenomena such as drug tolerance.

Opponent-process theory of vision Theory of color vision that proposes that three sets of color receptors respond in an either/or fashion to determine the color you experience.

Optic nerve Bundle of nerve fibers that carry neural signals to the brain.

Optical rearrangement The alteration of the normal relationship between distal stimuli and their retinal images by the use of special lenses worn over the eye.

Optimum level of arousal A theory of motivation that assumes that either too much or too little arousal is unpleasant, and that the individual seeks to maintain some moderate level of input.

Oral cavity Open space inside the mouth.

Oral stage According to Freud's theory of personality development, the first year of life, when breast feeding and weaning usually occur.

Oral-aggressive personality According to Freud, a syndrome of adult personality that may develop when a mother is too harsh when weaning a child from the breast. It is supposedly characterized by pessimism, suspiciousness, sarcasm, and argumentativeness.

Oral-receptive personality According to Freud, a syndrome of adult personality that may develop if a mother is too indulgent. It is supposedly characterized by dependency, gullibility, and a fondness for sweets and smoking, as well as an obsession with oral sex.

Organ of Corti Transmits neural impulse to nerve fibers in the auditory nerve.

Organic disorders Psychological disorders caused by physical illness. (See also General paresis; Senile dementia)

Organic retardation Mental retardation due to biological causes.

Organization In perception, the strong tendency to group stimulus elements on the basis of their similarity, proximity, continuation, and simplicity.

Organizational psychology Branch of psychology that studies how organizational structures and dynamics affect people's behavior in business and industrial settings.

Orthographic rules Law that specifies legal and illegal letter combinations in a word.

Oscillation theory The belief that when brain cells for different visual features fire at the same time they can form a cell network that serves as a basis for conscious awareness of a particular stimulus.

Oscilloscope Device for converting sound waves to visible waves.

Osmometric thirst Thirst motivated by osmoreceptors in the hypothalamus that detect the depletion of intercellular water cells.

Osmoreceptors Cells in the hypothalamus that are sensitive to intercellular water levels; they send "thirst" signals to other areas of the brain when they detect that water is being depleted from the cells.

Osteoporosis Condition of aging where the loss of bone calcium causes bones to become thinner and weaker. After menopause, the rate of loss is greater for women than men.

Otolith structures Organs that signal head orientation with respect to gravity.

Outcome research A method of comparing improvements in therapy clients with changes in other distressed people who have not been treated, or who have received alternative therapies.

Oval window Membrane stretched over the opening of the inner ear.

Ovaries Female reproductive glands that secrete estrogen into the bloodstream.

Overlap A monocular depth cue in which objects that are partially obscured by other objects are perceived as farther away.

Ovulation In women, the time when the egg is available to be fertilized and secretion of estrogen is at its highest; occurs once a month.

Ovum Mature female sex cell which after fertilization develops into an offspring. The first two-week period of development after fertilization is called the period of the ovum.

Pain Unpleasant sensory and emotional experience that accompanies actual or potential tissue damage.

Pancreas The endocrine system gland that regulates metabolism.

Panic disorder Sudden onset of anxiety, overcoming the person with physiological symptoms such as sweating, dizziness, and shortness of breath. This disorder disrupts normal daily functioning.

Papillae Small elevations on the tongue; contain our taste sensors, called taste buds.

Paradoxical cold Occurs when a cold object stimulates a cold spot on the skin-cold is felt.

Paradoxical intervention A technique used by family therapists in which the problem behavior is actually encouraged.

Paradoxical warmth Occurs when a cold object stimulates a warm spot on the skin-warmth is felt.

Paranoid People suffering from delusions of persecution are called paranoid; they believe that people are "out to get" them and interpret others' actions as plots against them.

Paranoid schizophrenia A behavioral disorder characterized by a belief that others are plotting against one and commonly by accompanying attributions about one's own religious or political importance.

Paraphilia Attraction to deviant objects or acts that interferes with the capacity for reciprocal and affectionate sexual activity.

Paraprofessional Someone without an advanced degree who can provide treatment. An important component of the community approach to treatment.

Parapsychologists Those who study ESP and PK

Parasympathetic division A division of the autonomic nervous system that is active during relaxed or quiescent states. (See also Sympathetic division)

Parathyroid glands Four tiny glands embedded in the thyroid that maintain the level of calcium in the blood.

Parietal lobes Part of the cerebral cortex that is particularly important for directing attention to changes in the environment and developing expectations of what is likely to happen next.

Partial reinforcement (See Intermittent reinforcement)

Pattern recognition In perception, the meaningful interpretation of form. Pattern recognition entails feature extraction and feature interpretation. (See also Feature analysis)

Peak experiences Fleeting moments in people's lives where they feel truly spontaneous and unconcerned with time or other physical constraints. A feeling of being totally absorbed in the situation, in the moment, without cares from the past or concern for the future.

Pegword mnemonic A type of mnemonic that relies on the use of visual imagery to form strong associations to organize information in memory.

Perception The processes of organizing and interpreting sensory information. (See also Distal stimulus; Proximal stimuli)

Perceptual constancy The unchanging perception of objects, despite changes in retinal stimulation.

Perceptual dilemma A situation that contributes to intergroup conflict, characterized by mistaken negative beliefs about what the other side wants, and exaggerated views of the innocence of motivation on one's own side.

Perceptual invariant An unchanging aspect of a stimulus that can be used as a cue for accurate perception. Texture gradients, for example, provide invariant information on depth. (See also Texture gradient)

Perceptual organization The manner in which elements are grouped together to perceive a pattern or form.

Perceptual release theory This theory holds that dreams and hallucinations are caused by actions and reactions in the brain.

Peripheral nervous system The portion of the nervous system, outside of the brain and spinal cord, that includes the autonomic and somatic nervous systems. (See also Autonomic nervous system; Somatic nervous system)

Peripheral vision Using the sides of one's eyes (and thus depending on the rods rather than the cones) to see something-usually occurs at night or in dim light.

Person-centered therapy Theory created by Carl Rogers aimed at providing the proper setting for the self-growth of the person. Since the person (rather than the therapist) determines what will be discussed during therapy, it is referred to as person-centered therapy.

Person-environment fit The physical and social conditions that best suit our living needs.

Personal constructs According to George Kelly, individuals' personal theories about themselves and their world.

Personal space The area around the body that people feel "belongs" to them. When interacting with others, people maintain a distance to protect their personal space.

Personality Unique set of enduring characteristics and patterns of behavior (including thoughts and emotions) that influence the way a person adjusts to his or her environment.

Personality assessment Description and measurement of individual characteristics.

Personality disorders Rigid and maladaptive ways of dealing with the environment, characterized by a general approach to dealing with events rather than by any one specific behavior. The example discussed in the text is the antisocial personality disorder, which is the type of personality disorder most often found in Western society.

Personality psychology Sub-field of psychology that focuses on individual differences and on explaining and predicting the unique ways that people respond to their environment.

Personality traits Recurring patterns of behavior such as friendliness, social dominance, conventionality, emotional adjustment, and aesthetic inclination.

PET Scan Measures the amount of glucose-a form of sugar that is the brain's primary source of energy-being consumed in numerous brain locations.

Phallic stage in Freud's theory of personality development, the stage occurring during the third to fifth years when a child often becomes obsessed with genitalia.

Phantom limb pain Pain in a part of the body that no longer exists. Phantom limb pain is fairly common in amputees.

Pharynx Open space inside the throat.

Phenomenological perspective A view of behavior that focuses on a person's subjective, conscious experience.

Phenotype The genetic characteristics that are displayed by a person such as eye color or height. (See also Genes; Genotype)

Pheromones Chemicals released by different organisms to elicit specific reactions by other members of the same species. Lower organisms use pheromones as a primitive method of communication.

Phobia A persistent fear reaction that is greatly out of proportion to the reality of danger.

Phonemes A limited number of distinct speech sounds which are used to distinguish one word from another.

Phonological rule Rule that specifies legal and illegal phoneme combinations.

Phosphenes Visual sensations arising from spontaneous discharges of light-sensitive neurons in the eyes.

Photographic memory The undocumented ability to remember information in a photo like manner.

Phrenology The nineteenth-century belief that character analysis could be determined by examining the bumps on a person's head.

Physical dependency The term for the condition when termination of use of drug results in severe withdrawal symptoms.

Physiological psychology Sub-field of psychology that examines the areas of learning, memory, perception, motivation, and emotion by studying the neurobiological events that underlie them.

Pineal An endocrine system gland that is involved in long-term circadian rhythms.

Pinna One of two structures that make up the outer ear. (See also Auditory canal)

Pitch Difference between low and high notes. Changes in pitch correspond to changes in frequency of sound waves.

Pituitary gland Located at the base of the brain, the pituitary gland produces many different hormones that exert control over the other endocrine glands.

Place theory States that sound waves of different frequencies cause different portions of the basilar membrane to vibrate.

Placebo In drug studies, a drug substitute made from inactive materials that is given to the control group in drug research.

Placebo effect An improvement in symptoms that follows any form of treatment that a person believes in, even if the treatment has no therapeutic substance, such as an inert sugar pill.

Placenta Special filter used to exchange food and wastes between an embryo and his or her mother.

Play Exploratory and pleasurable activity that may not aim toward specific goals.

Pleasure principle According to Freud, the way in which the id seeks immediate gratification for an impulse.

Polarization Electric tension that exists in a neuron between the cell's inside and outside environment. Also called membrane potential.

Polygenic traits Traits that are determined by the action of more than one gene pair. Most human traits are polygenic.

Polygraph Also called a lie detector. Machine that records changes in heart rate, blood pressure, respiration, and galvanic skin response. Lies are identified when there is a change from baseline responses to neutral questions to a heightened response to questions about critical events.

Pons The large bulge in the brainstem involved in alertness, attention, and movement. (See also Medulla)

Population All the members of a group from which a sample may be drawn. In survey research, a randomly drawn sample permits an investigator to draw conclusions about a population. (See also Sample)

Positive incentive theory of addiction The view that addicts take drugs to obtain their pleasurable effects, not to avoid unpleasant withdrawal symptoms.

Positive reinforcers Primary and secondary reinforcers in instrumental conditioning that serve to increase the frequency of the behavior they follow.

Positron emission tomography (PET scan) Computer-generated representation of brain activity.

Post-Traumatic Stress Disorder Reexperiencing a stressful event that can occur months or years after the event.

Posthypnotic amnesia Inability of a hypnotized subject to recall certain experiences until an appropriate cue is given.

Posthypnotic suggestions Suggestions made to a subject while hypnotized which are to be carried out after hypnosis has ended.

Postsynaptic neuron The cell that receives stimulation from the electrical impulses that travel through the presynaptic neuron. (See also Neurotransmitter; Presynaptic neuron)

Power Capacity to influence other people.

Practical intelligence Intelligence that operates in the real world and is shown by a person's ability to adapt to or change an environment. (See also Intelligence)

Precognition Perception of future thoughts, events or actions.

Preconscious mind According to Freud, the preconscious is essentially one's memory, including thoughts that people may not be aware of but that they can retrieve from memory.

Preconscious processes Underlying mental processes that precede conscious awareness.

Preconscious processing theory A theory of emotion developed by Cannon that presumes that both a cognitive label (such as fear) and a behavioral response (such as trembling) occur after an initial preconscious analysis of the potentially emotionally arousing event.

Predictive validity The extent to which a test score predicts future behaviors, as when an IQ test predicts later academic success.

Prefrontal lobotomy The surgical removal of an excitable or aggressive patient's frontal lobes from the rest of the brain.

Prejudice An unwarranted generalization about a group or a particular member of that group.

Premack principle A view that any behavior with a high frequency of occurrence could be used to reinforce any other behavior that has a lower frequency of occurrence.

Premature ejaculation Ejaculation which occurs too quickly, according to the definition of the male and the couple.

Preoperational period In Piaget's second period of cognitive development, children between the ages of two and seven can think symbolically, but their thinking is egocentric and dominated by their perceptual experience. They do not understand the principles of conservation. (See also Conservation; Egocentrism)

Preparedness (See Associative bias)

Presynaptic neuron The transmitting cell through which electrical impulses travel to stimulate another neuron across the synaptic junction. (See also Neurotransmitter)

Primacy effect The tendency for our first impression of a person to bias how we interpret what he or she does later.

Primary drives Unlearned physiologically-based motivations, such as hunger, that are not learned.

Primary motives Motives such as hunger, thirst, and the need for air and rest. These motives are usually unlearned, common to all animals, and vital for the survival of the organism or the species.

Primary reinforcers Stimuli in instrumental conditioning, such as food or warmth, that are essential for an animal's survival. (See also Conditioned reinforcers)

Primary sex characteristics The physiological characteristics that enable an organism to sexually reproduce. During puberty females show development of their ovaries, uterus and vagina and begin menstruation, while males show growth in their scrotum, testes, and penis and begin to produce sperm.

Primary territories Owned and controlled by people; these territories are central to their lives.

Priming The tendency for recent events to influence current interpretations.

Privacy Freedom to decide what we will communicate about ourselves to a person or group and when that communication will occur.

Proactive interference The forgetting of new material due to the disruptive effects of previously learned material.

Problem drinkers People who often drink too much and whose drinking has undesirable effects on their lives or on others. (See also Alcoholics.)

Problem solving The various strategies used to reach a goal that is not readily attainable.

Problem-focused coping strategies Used in situations seen as changeable, these strategies are aimed at doing something to change the problem causing distress.

Procedural memory A form of memory that enables people to remember how to perform various acts. (See also Episodic memory; Semantic memory)

Product-moment correlation Measure of the extent to which changes in two variables are related to each other.

Projection A defense mechanism in which a person deals with a threatening impulse by attributing it to others.

Projective test A test with ambiguous items for which there are no objectively "correct" answers. It is designed to allow subjects to "project" their own needs and desires into their responses.

Propositional thinking The ability during adolescence to reason about abstractions and verbal statements.

Proprioception The sense of bodily feedback.

Prosopagnosia A brain damage syndrome characterized by the inability to recognize faces.

Prototype Typical, or standard, example.

Prototypical instances In concept learning, some instances are better examples of a concept than others. For instance, a robin is better than a penguin to illustrate the concept bird.

Provocative motion A form of body motion in which there is a mismatch between sensory cues and information about gravity. The result is dizziness and nausea.

Proxemics Study of personal space

Proximal stimuli Patterns of physical energy that strike sensory receptors and cause them to generate neural impulses. (See also Distal stimuli)

Proximate Explanations that focus on the short-term or immediate causes of behavior.

Proximity Physical closeness.

Psychiatric nurse Registered nurse who has received special training in dealing with psychological disorders.

Psychiatrist Medical doctor who has received an M.D. degree and has taken part in a residency program in emotional disorders; the only type of therapist who can prescribe drugs or conduct psycho-surgery.

Psychoactive substances Drugs that affect sensation, perception, thinking, self-awareness, and emotion. They include such drugs as LSD, mescaline, PCP, and marijuana. (See also Drug dependence; Drug tolerance)

Psychoanalysis An approach to therapy, popularized by Freud, that seeks to reveal the unconscious motives that underlie behavior through intensive discussions between patient and therapist.

Psychoanalyst Psychiatrist who has had a great deal of training in psychoanalytic techniques and has often undergone psychoanalysis personally.

Psychoanalytic perspective The general viewpoint developed by Freud and his followers. According to this view, much of what we think and do is motivated by thoughts that may exist completely outside of our conscious awareness.

Psychodynamic model (See Psychoanalytic perspective)

Psychogenic amnesia Refers to a dramatic loss of memory that cannot be attributed to a physical trauma such as head injury (now called "dissociative amnesia").

Psychokinesis (PK) Direct mental influence over physical objects or processes.

Psycholinguistics A branch of psychology that examines language as an aspect of behavior.

Psychological dependency The condition in which drugs are used to manipulate consciousness and maintain a sense of well-being; physical dependence is absent.

Psychological test Test designed to identify individual differences among people; tests have been developed to measure attitudes, abilities, achievement, and personality traits.

Psychology The science of behavior and mental processes.

Psychology of minorities Sub-field of psychology that examines behavior of people in minority groups, including women who are minorities in some contexts.

Psychometric approach Involves analyzing the results of intelligence tests to determine the structure of human intelligence and whether intelligence consists of one general factor or a variety of factors.

Psychopath (See Antisocial personality)

Psychopathology Translated from its Greek roots into "mental illness," this term is used to describe disordered behavior.

Psychopharmacology Study of drugs to treat psychological disorders.

Psychophysical function The relationship between physical energies and psychological experiences over a wide range of physical magnitudes.

Psychophysical scale The relationship between a quantifiable physical stimulus and a subjective measure of its sensory experience.

Psychophysics The study of the relationship between physical stimulation and sensory experience.

Psychophysiological disorders Physical disorders (such as ulcers) that result, at least in part, from prolonged psychological conflict.

Psychosis Disturbance caused by unresolved conflicts that is so great that the person can no longer deal with reality.

Psychosocial moratorium During adolescence, a time for education and personal development before selecting an adult role and assuming the responsibilities of family and work. (See also Identity foreclosure)

Psychosomatic disorders Physical disorders that seem to result from prolonged psychological conflict.

Psychosurgery The destruction of brain tissue to alleviate emotional and behavioral disorders, usually reserved for severe and otherwise untreatable problems.

Psychotherapy Use of psychological interventions to treat disordered behaviors.

Puberty The sexual maturation of the child, demonstrated by menstruation in girls and the production of sperm in boys.

Public territories Territories that do not improve feelings of ownership, but people feel that they control them while they are occupying them; an example is a table at a restaurant.

Punishment In instrumental conditioning, the use of an aversive stimulus to decrease the likelihood of a particular response.

Pupil The opening or black spot that appears in the center of the iris. The size of the pupil controls the amount of light that enters the eye. (See also Iris; Lens; Retina)

Pure tones Sounds containing a single frequency.

Purity The number of different wave-lengths that make up a particular color. The fewer the number, the greater the purity.

Pyramidal cells Giant cells of the motor cortex that sends a long axon through the brain down to neurons in the spinal cord. Control precise physical movements and speech.

Questionnaire Standard set of questions used to assess behavior that can be given to many people at one time and usually can be scored quickly.

Randomization Procedure used in an experiment whereby subjects are randomly assigned to either the control group or the experimental group(s). It ensures that each person has an equal chance of being assigned to each group, thus making it highly probably that subject differences will be equally distributed between groups.

Range A crude measure of variability that is obtained by subtracting the lowest from the highest score in a frequency distribution.

Range of reaction The limits on development set by a person's genes.

Rape Coercive sexual assault on an individual.

Rapid eye movements (REM) Rapid movements of the eyes during sleep that are associated with periods of dreaming.

Rational Emotive Therapy (RET) Type of therapy developed by Albert Ellis; focuses on the present and on the client's irrational beliefs. Therapist plays a much more directive and even challenging role than in most other therapies

Rational-emotive therapy A form of psychotherapy in which the therapist persuades, teaches, and provides information, in an attempt to break down the client's irrational and self-defeating ideas.

Rationalist A philosophical position holding that our actions are grounded in free choices of the rational mind.

Rationalization A defense mechanism that involves making excuses for one's failures or transgressions.

Reactance Psychological state that motivates us to regain our freedom by resisting group pressure.

Reaction formation A psychological defense mechanism in which the person is presumed to convert an unacceptable impulse into its opposite.

Real difference A difference that could occur by chance less than 5 percent of the time.

Reality anxiety Response to a specific danger in the environment.

Reality principle According to Freud, the principle by which the ego operates-performing behaviors that are likely to result in pleasant outcomes, without negative consequences.

Reasoning The aspect of thought used to draw new conclusions from facts already known.

Recall tests Measure a person's ability to reproduce material. Cued recall is when part of the material is provided as a cue for the rest; free recall is when no cues are provided and any order of recall is allowed.

Receptive aphasia The inability to comprehend speech.

Receptive field The area in the visual field in which a stimulus will produce a response.

Receptor cell A neural structure in our sense organs-for example, the eyes or ears-that receives environmental stimulation.

Receptor sites Areas on the dendrite that receive the chemical transmitter.

Recessive gene Member of a gene pair that can control the appearance of a certain trait only if it is paired with another recessive gene.

Reciprocal socialization The belief that children influence their parents as much as parents influence their children.

Reciprocity norm The social convention that if someone does us a favor, we ought to return it.

Recognition tests Measure a person's ability to pick the correct answer when several answers are given; often occur in the form of multiple-choice questions on tests.

Reconstruction Organization and recording (often done unconsciously) of memory over time; may lead to distortions of memory.

Reflected appraisal Basing self-image on the image we believe others have of us.

Reflexes Involuntary responses to particular stimuli that are based on existing connections in the nervous system.

Regressions Backward eye movements during reading.

Rehearsal Process of repeating information in order to retain it in short-term memory or transfer it to long-term memory.

Reinforcement A stimulus in instrumental conditioning that increases the likelihood of the behavior it follows.

Relative height A monocular cue for depth. For objects above the visual horizon, the higher the object, the closer it appears; for objects below the horizon, the higher the object, the farther away the object appears.

Relative refractory period Period during which a cell will only fire in response to an extra-strong impulse; lasts for a few milliseconds.

Relative size A monocular depth cue based on the fact that as objects become more distant, their retinal image grows smaller in size.

Relaxation response Phrase used by Benson to refer to the physiological patterns observed during meditation; a decrease in oxygen consumption, respiratory rate, heart rate, blood pressure, and muscle tension.

Releasing stimulus In animals, an event that causes a predetermined response. For example, some female mammals release pheromones, a chemical substance signaling the male that the female is sexually receptive.

Reliability The consistency with which a test measures whatever it is intended to measure.

Reliability of a test Means that you get the same results on the test every time you administer it.

REM rebound Sharp increase of REM sleep after going through a period of sleep deprivation.

REM sleep Stage of sleep marked by rapid eye movements (REMs) and dreams.

Replication The ability to reproduce the results of any given study in a different setting and under the same or slightly different conditions.

Representativeness heuristic A decision-making process in which the likelihood of an event is determined by noting the similarity between the evidence and the possible outcomes.

Repression An unconscious defense mechanism designed to protect a person by preventing unpleasant memories from reaching conscious awareness.

Resistance A point in therapy at which the person presumably begins to approach a repressed conflict and tries to escape the confrontation.

Response chaining Chains of behavior in which the responses of one animal are linked to the responses of another.

Response cost In punishment, the removal of positive reinforcement.

Response generalization Means giving different, but similar, responses to the same stimulus.

Response sequences In instrumental conditioning, linking or tying together a series of instrumentally-conditioned responses.

Resting potential The relatively constant electrical charge that exists when a neuron is left undisturbed.

Resting state Occurs whenever a neuron is not sending or receiving neural impulses.

Retention Process of holding information in memory.

Reticular activating system (RAS) Functional subdivision of the nervous system; activates all regions of the brain for incoming sensory impulses, plays an important part in alertness and selective attention.

Reticular formation A network of neural pathways in the brainstem that relays sensory information and controls arousal and sleep.

Retina A paper-thin lining at the rear of the eye that is composed of millions of light-sensitive receptors.

Retinal image The image that the object projects on to the back wall of the eye.

Retrieval One of three memory processes in which the representation of information is recovered through the act of remembering. (See also Encoding; Storage)

Retrieval cues Aids to retrieval that are often encoded with the information to be remembered; an example would be category names.

Retroactive inhibition Interference of new learning with memory for previous learning.

Retroactive interference The forgetting of previously learned material due to the disruptive effect of new learning.

Retrograde amnesia The inability to remember events that were immediately followed by a traumatic event. (See also Amnesia; Anterograde amnesia)

Reversibility The process of changing an object in some fashion and then returning that object to its original state. Piaget used reversible objects to study reasoning in children.

Ribonucleic acid (RNA) Messenger molecules sent out by DNA to control how specific kinds of protein chains are made.

Right Hemisphere The right cerebral hemisphere is specialized for spatial abilities and synthesizing information; it controls the left side of the body. (See also Left hemisphere)

Rods Light sensitive cells in the eye that distinguish black, white, and shades of gray. The rods provide for night vision and peripheral vision, the sensitivity to visual stimuli away from the center of focus. (See also Cones)

Role confusion Uncertainty over one's role in life brought on by a failure to develop a sense of identity during adolescence.

Role models The use of other people to observe how to act in particular situations.

Role-taking Child's ability to comprehend what another person sees, feels, and thinks.

Roles Group rules that apply only to people in certain positions; roles define the obligations and expectations of that specific position.

Rooting reflex A reflex in newborn infants that causes them to turn their heads and mouths in the direction of stimulation to their cheeks.

Rorschach inkblot test Projective test that measures personality by having subjects describe what they see in ten different inkblots.

Saccades Voluntary eye movements that occur between one and five times a second.

Salience effect The human tendency to devote extra attention to noticeable or striking people.

Sample In survey research, a subset that is randomly drawn from a population. (See also Population)

Sampling error The discrepancy between the true values of a population and the estimates of those values obtained from a sample.

Saturation The apparent purity of a color.

Scattergram A graph that shows how two different data sets are related. The shape of the cluster of data points indicates the type and degree of relationship.

Schedules of reinforcement In instrumental conditioning, a relationship or contingency that exists between a response and a reinforcer. (See also Fixed interval, Fixed ration, Variable interval, and Variable ratio schedules).

Schema A memory structure that is an abstract representation of objects or events in the real world.

Schizophrenia A disorder characterized by delusions, hallucinations, incoherent thinking, social isolation or withdrawal, inappropriate emotions, and strange motor behaviors.

Script A generalized sequence of actions that describes a well-learned routine.

Seasonal affective disorder A form of depression occurring during the winter.

Secondary drives Specific preferences that are learned through classical conditioning.

Secondary reinforcers (See also Conditioned reinforcers)

Secondary sex characteristics The physical characteristics that distinguish a sexually mature male from a sexually mature female.

Sedatives A class of depressant drugs.

Selection biases Tendencies to pay attention to certain types of information and to ignore others.

Self-actualized personalities People who develop to the highest reaches of their potential.

Self-awareness The state of becoming conscious of ourselves as distinct from the environment.

Self-concept One's knowledge of, and beliefs about, oneself.

Self-efficacy beliefs The belief that one will succeed in the future. (See also Learned helplessness)

Self-esteem How we evaluate ourselves.

Self-fulfilling prophecy A belief that was originally false but leads to behavior that makes it come true.

Self-monitoring The tendency to look to the social environment to determine one's course of behavior.

Self-perception A theory of attitudes that assumes that we infer our attitudes from observing our past behaviors.

Self-reinforcement Rewarding oneself with actual reinforcers, such as a movie, or with cognitive reinforcers such as self-praise.

Self-serving bias A tendency to compare ourselves to others in such a way that we flatter ourselves.

Semantic memory A form of memory that represents knowledge of words, symbols and concepts, including their meaning and rules for manipulation. (See also Episodic memory; Procedural memory)

Semicircular canals Three ring-like structures that extend from the cochlea and help provide our sense of balance.

Senile dementia Commonly called senility, this disorder affecting older people is characterized by signs of disorganized thinking, loss of recent memory, and shifts of mood.

Senile plaques Degenerated neural axon terminals in the brain cells of patients with Alzheimer's disease.

Sensation The process of obtaining environmental information from the sensory channels and the conscious experience associated with that stimulation.

Sensation seeking A personality scale related to the tendency to seek (or avoid) stimulating and exciting experiences.

Sensorimotor period Piaget's first period of cognitive development in which an infant learns through its senses and motor behavior. (See also Object permanence)

Sensory adaptation The reduction in sensitivity that occurs as a result of prolonged, continuous stimulation.

Sensory memory store The part of the memory system that maintains sensory information very briefly after a stimulus is presented. (See also Long-term and Short-term memory store)

Sensory neurons Nerve cells that receive stimulation from the receptor cells in the sense organs and transmit it to the brain and spinal cord. (See also Motor neurons).

Sensory physiology The field of study concerned with how sensory cells translate physical energy into electrochemical messages that the brain can decipher.

Sensory preconditioning A procedure through which one stimulus becomes associated with another stimulus before either is related to an unconditioned stimulus.

Serial position effect In a free recall task, people remember the beginning (primacy effect) and ending (recency effect) items in a list better than the middle items.

Set point A body's target weight maintained by increases or decreases in metabolism and hunger.

Sex roles Characteristic ways of acting masculine or feminine. (See also Gender roles).

Sex-typed behavior Behavior that is held to be appropriate for only members of one sex. (See also Gender roles; Socialization)

Sexual imprinting A process in which some animals are attracted to potential mates whose features are similar to those to which they were exposed early on in life.

Sexual selection A form of evolution in which a trait increases in prevalence when it assists in competing with the same sex or attracting the opposite sex.

Shape constancy The tendency to see a familiar object as the same shape regardless of the change in retinal image caused by changes in viewing angle or distance.

Shaping In instrumental conditioning, the process of reinforcing behaviors that are increasingly similar to the desired behavior until that behavior is produced. (See also Reinforcement)

Short-term memory store A limited capacity component of the memory system that can retain information in conscious awareness for a brief period of time. (See also Long-term memory; Sensory memory store)

Sign stimuli Physical characteristics in one animal that elicit certain reactions in other animals.

Signal detection theory A theory of sensitivity that separates an observer's sensitivity from factors such as motivation and expectations that can influence sensory judgments.

Simultaneous conditioning The classical conditioning procedure in which the conditioned and unconditioned stimuli are presented at the same time. (See also Backward, Delayed, and Trace conditioning)

Size constancy The tendency to see a familiar object according to its actual size regardless of the changes in the retinal image due to changes in object distance.

Skewness A term used to describe an asymmetrical frequency distribution where the majority of scores are either high (negatively skewed) or low (positively skewed).

Skilled memory theory The belief that memoirists have learned to use special strategies to memorize information at a fast rate.

Sleep apnea Difficulty in breathing while asleep.

Social cognition A field of psychology that examines how we pay attention to, interpret, and remember social events.

Social expectation Perceptions of how others expect us to behave.

Social facilitation A change in performance due to the presence of observers.

Social influence Changes people make in their behavior in response to real or imagined pressures from others.

Social motives Motivations related to interactions with other people, such as the need to affiliate with others and the need to achieve.

Social perception The processes by which we organize and interpret information about other people.

Social support Consists of emotional, informational, and material aid from others that assists in coping with stress.

Social traps Situations in which the pursuit of short-term benefits leads to disastrous long-run consequences.

Socialization The process by which children acquire the attitudes, beliefs, and customs of their family and culture. (See also Identification)

Sociological perspective on disorder A model in which disordered behavior is viewed as being rooted in the wider society rather than in the individual.

Somatic nervous system A division of the peripheral nervous system that connects the brain and spinal cord to the muscles and sensory receptors. (See also Peripheral nervous system)

Somatoform disorders Disorders involving symptoms of chronic physical complaints for which medical professionals are unable to find any actual physical cause.

Somatosensory cortex A narrow strip of the parietal lobe, just behind the central fissure, where the sense of touch is localized on the surface of the brain. (See also Motor cortex)

Sound localization The ability to locate the source of a sound.

Sound waves Air pressure fluctuations that stimulate the receptor cells of the ear. People are normally sensitive to sound waves with frequencies between 20 and 20,000 Hz.

Span of attention The number of stimuli that can simultaneously be perceived and reported.

Spatial neglect A disorder in which patients with parietal lobe lesions do not pay attention to areas of space that are opposite the side of their lesions.

Specificity hypothesis The hypothesis that assumes that specific conflicts are associated with specific illness.

Speech perception The identification of auditory linguistic stimuli.

Speech spectrogram A visual representation of the different auditory frequencies in an utterance.

Spontaneous improvements Beneficial changes in disordered behavior over time, independent of receiving therapy.

Spontaneous recovery The return of a classically or instrumentally conditioned response after extinction, following a period of rest. (See also Extinction)

Standard deviation The most frequently used measure of variability, it is the average distance of each score in a frequency distribution from the mean of the distribution.

Standardization The requirement that tests be given according to standard instructions, be scored objectively, and that a representative sample of people be used to interpret relative test performance.

Stapes One of three small bones that make up the middle ear and through which vibration from the eardrum is transmitted.

Statistical data A group of numbers that represents measurements of some property or phenomenon.

Statistical inference The process of making judgments about population values based on observations of samples.

Statistics The branch of mathematics that deals with the collection and interpretation of numerical data. Psychologists use both descriptive and inferential statistics.

Stimulants A class of drugs that reduce fatigue when administered in small amounts, and increase energy and excitement when given in large amounts.

Storage One of three memory processes in which the representation of information is retained in the memory system. (See also Encoding; Retrieval)

Stress The physical and psychological response to perceived environmental threat.

Striving for superiority According to Adler, a basic human motivation to become socially dominant over other people.

Stroboscopic movement An illusion of movement that results from the successive presentation of individual stimuli arranged in a sequence.

Stroop effect An example of a failure of selective attention. Perceivers cannot ignore color words when they are trying to name the colors that form the words.

Structuralism An early approach to the study of consciousness that sought to understand how basic elements were structured by the mind to produce different conscious experiences.

Subjective contour A type of illusion in which there is a perception of a well-defined form where there really is none.

Subliminal perception The perception of objects and events below the threshold of awareness.

Subtractive color mixture Mixing paints together causes certain wavelengths to be absorbed or subtracted from a painted surface so that a new color is reflected when light shines on the surface. (See also Additive color mixture)

Superego According to Freudian theory, an internalized representation of parents' value system.

Supernatural model The historical view that disordered behavior is caused by supernatural forces (such as demonic possession)

Superordinate tasks Tasks that require competing groups to join together to accomplish mutual benefits.

Suppression A defense mechanism which involves a person becoming aware of an unpleasant memory of impulse, but consciously trying not to think about it.

Survey A large-scale questionnaire or interview method of research which yields summaries of the opinions, beliefs, and behaviors of a group of people.

Syllogism Used to study deductive reasoning, it is an argument that consists of two statements called premises and a conclusion that logically follows from them.

Sympathetic division A division of the autonomic nervous system that is active during excitement and stress. (See also Parasympathetic division)

Synapse The tiny gap that separates an axon from one neuron from the receiving portion of another cell. (See also Neuron; Neurotransmitter)

Syntax Grammatical rules for combining words into phrases and sentences.

Systematic desensitization A classical conditioning therapy for anxiety which involves a patient gradually confronting threatening stimuli under non-threatening circumstances.

T-maze A t-shaped runway used to study instrumental conditioning of choice behavior.

Taste The sensory experience resulting from the stimulation of the taste buds.

Taste aversion The association of food and physical illness, which results in avoidance of the particular food in the future.

Taste buds Receptors for the sense of taste, located primarily on the tongue and responsive to the qualities of sweet, sour, salty, and bitter.

Templates In perception, forms or memory representations used to produce pattern recognition through the matching of stimulus features.

Temporal lobes Part of the cerebral cortex that is important for the processing of auditory and, to a lesser extent, visual information.

Terminals Small structures at the end of the axon that transmit neural signals to the dendrites or cell body of an adjacent cell.

Testosterone The hormone produced in adrenal glands and the male's testes that appears to be a primary determinant of the sex drive in men and women, and which has also been found to lead to increases in aggressive behavior in animals.

Texture gradient The gradual change in the apparent size of objects as the eyes scan a visual field.

Thalamus Located above the brainstem, the thalamus relays sensory information from the different sensory systems, including eyes, ears, and skin, to higher centers in the brain.

Thematic apperception Test (TAT) A projective test used to uncover motivations such as the need for achievement.

Theory A set of assumptions that helps us organize a complicated set of findings and that helps a scientist decide where to look for new evidence.

Thought The mental manipulation of symbols that stand for objects, events, or ideas in memory.

Threshold level The level of stimulation a neuron must receive to generate an impulse.

Thyroid gland Endocrine gland located below the voice box.

Token economy The use of tokens (usually poker chips or play money) that patients, inmates, or students can earn by doing something desirable or by refraining from doing something undesirable. The tokens can then be exchanged for actual rewards.

Tolerance After extended use of a drug, continued use requires larger doses to achieve the same effect.

Top-down processing The view that perception is guided by mental processes such as set or expectancy. (See also Bottom-up processing)

Trace conditioning The classical conditioning procedure in which the conditioned stimulus comes on and goes off briefly before the unconditioned stimulus is presented. (See also Backward, Delayed, and Simultaneous conditioning)

Trait approach A systematic effort to describe and classify the behavior characteristics that differentiate people from one another.

Tranquilizers Sedatives that calm the user.

Transduction The conversion of physical energy, by sensory receptors, into neural impulses that are transmitted to the different sensory areas of the brain.

Transference In psychoanalysis, the idea that patients view the therapist as the symbolic equivalent of the important figures in their lives, especially their parents.

Trephining The ancient practice of chipping a hole in the skull of a disturbed person to rid the brain of the evil forces believed to cause abnormal behavior.

Trial-and-error learning The use of one problem-solving strategy after another until one is successful.

Triangulation The process of observing a phenomenon using two (or more) different methods to determine whether similar findings appear from different vantage points.

Triarchic theory A theory of intelligence involving componential, experiential, and contextual aspects of intelligence.

Trichromatic theory The view that perceived color is based on the output of three color receptors in the retina (usually red, green, and blue receptors).

Twin studies Research carried out with fraternal and identical twins who have been separated at birth and raised in separate environments to determine the relative impact of genes and the environment on behavior and development.

Type A syndrome A pattern of behavior characterized by hostility and time urgency and believed to increase susceptibility to stress-related illness.

Ultimate explanations Explanations of behavior that take a relatively long-range view, focusing on previous learning history, genes, or the evolutionary history of the human species.

Unconditioned response A response in classical conditioning that is elicited automatically by an unconditioned stimulus. (See also Conditioned response; Conditioned stimulus; Unconditioned response)

Unconscious inference The belief that people unconsciously interpret sensory information in order to perceive accurately.

Unconscious processes Underlying mental process that cannot be brought into conscious awareness.

Validity The requirement that a test measures what it purports to measure.

Variable interval schedule In instrumental conditioning, reinforcement occurs after the first response that is made after a specified period of time that varies from one reinforcement to the next. (See also Fixed interval, Fixed ratio, and Variable ratio schedule)

Variable ratio schedule In instrumental conditioning, an animal is reinforced after a specified number of responses have been emitted, but this number varies from one reinforcement to the next. (See also Fixed interval, Fixed ratio, and Variable interval schedule)

Variables Any changes in the environment or behavior that can be measured or controlled by a researcher.

Ventricles The fluid-filled cavities of the brain.

Vestibular sacs Sacs in the inner ear that are filled with a jelly-like substance and that serve as a mechanism of balance.

Vestibular sense Our sense of balance is achieved by receptors located in the inner ear.

Visual acuity The ability to see fine detail clearly.

Visual object agnosia The inability to name a familiar object, show how it is used, or recall ever having seen it before. (See also Color agnosia; Prosopagnosia)

Visual object imagery The ability to visualize objects in the absence of external visual stimulation.

Visual spatial imagery The ability to visualize objects in three-dimensional space.

Visual spectrum The portion of the electromagnetic energy spectrum that is visible to the eye, the visual spectrum consists of a narrow band of wavelengths from 390 to 760 nanometers.

Wavelength Because electromagnetic energy travels in waves, this energy spectrum is scaled in terms of wavelengths which are the distance from the crest of one wave to the crest of the next.

Weber's Law A psychophysical relationship that states a just-noticeable difference is always proportional to the magnitude or intensity of a stimulus. (See also Just-noticeable difference (JND))

Wechsler Adult Intelligence Scale (WAIS) An intelligence test used to measure IQ in children aged seven to 16.

Wernicke's area The portion of the temporal lobe of the left hemisphere of the brain that is involved in understanding language. People with brain damage in this area have difficulty comprehending speech. (See also Broca's area)

Working backward A heuristic strategy in which we begin knowing the desired outcome or goal state and work back to the original state.

Working memory A form of short-term memory storage that is used to manipulate information available to consciousness.

Yerkes-Dodson Law The hypothesized principle that arousal, whether due to stress, exercise, or a cup of coffee, will lead to an improvement in performance up to a point but hurt performance beyond that point.

Zener Cards Special cards used to test for ESP.

Zygote A fertilized ovum or egg. (See also Embryo; Fetus)

(Adapted from Worchel and Shebliske 5th edition and Seamon and Kenrick 2nd edition)

Appendix H

General Teaching References

These references are intended as historical references for classic materials in the field of teaching (some texts may be in newer editions). For a listing of current references see Appendix C.

Adams, A., Carnine, D., & Gersten, R. (1982). Instructional strategies for studying content area texts in the intermediate grades. *Reading Research Quarterly, 18,* 27-53.

Aiken, W. M. (1942). *Story of the eight-year study.* New York: Harper.

Akin, J.N. (1985). Teacher Supply/Demand 1985. Madison, WI: *Association for School, College, and University Staffing.*

Alderman, D.L., Appel, L.R., & Murphy, R.T. (1978). PLATO and TICCIT: An evaluation of CAI in the community college. *Educational Technology,* 18, 40-45.

Alderman, D.L., & Powers, D.E. (1980). The effects of special preparation on SAT-verbal scores. *American Educational Research Journal,* 17, 239-253.

Alderman, M.K. (1985). Achievement motivation and the preservice teacher. In M. Alderman & M. Cohen (Eds.), *Motivation theory and practice for preservice teachers* (pp. 37-49). Washington, DC: Eric Clearinghouse on Teacher Education.

Alessi, S.M., & Trollip, S.R. (1985). *Computer-based instruction: Methods and development.* Englewood Cliffs, NJ: Prentice Hall.

Alwain, D., & Thornton, A. (1984). Family origins and schooling processes: Early versus late influence of prenatal characteristics. *American Sociological Review,* 49, 484-802.

American Educational Research Association, Committee on the Criteria of Teaching Effectiveness. (1953). *Journal of Educational Research* (2nd Rep.), 46, 641-658.

American Psychological Association. (1976). *Preliminary report of the commission on behavior modification: Case study issues raised by behavior modification in the schools.* Washington, DC: American Psychological Association.

Ames, C. (1985). Attributions and cognition in motivation theory. In M. Alderman & M. Cohen (Eds.), *Motivation theory and practice for preservice teachers (pp. 16-21)*. Washington, DC: Eric Clearinghouse on Teacher Education.

Ames, R. & Lau, S. (1982). An attributional analysis of student help-seeking in academic settings. *Journal of Educational Psychology*, 74, 414-423.

Anand, P., & Ross, S.M. (1987). Using computer-assisted instruction to personalize math learning materials for elementary school children. *Journal of Educational Psychology*, 79, 72-80.

Anastasi, A. (1988). *Psychological testing* (6th ed.). New York: Macmillan.

Anderson, C. (1989). The role of education in the academic disciplines in teacher education. In A. Woolfolk (Ed.), *Research bases for the graduate preparation of teachers (pp. 88-107)*. Englewood Cliffs, NJ: Prentice Hall.

Anderson, J.R. (1985). *Cognitive psychology and its implications* (2nd ed.). San Francisco: W. H. Freeman.

Anderson, L.M. (1985). What are students doing when they do all that seatwork? In C. Fisher & D. Berliner (Eds.:), *Perspectives on instructional time*. New York: Longman.

Anderson, R.E., Klassen, D.L., & Johnson, D.C. (1986). In defense of a comprehensive view of computer literacy--A reply to Luehrmann. In T. R. Cannings & S.W. Brown (Eds.), *The information-age classroom: Using the computer as a tool*. Irvine, CA: Franklin, Beedle & Associates.

Arlin, M. (1984). Time, equality, and mastery learning. *Review of Educational Research*, 54, 65-86.

Armbruster, B.B., & Anderson, T.H. (1981). Research synthesis on study skills. *Educational Leadership*, 39, 154-156.

Ashton-Warner, S. (1963). *Teacher*, New York: Simon & Schuster.

Atkinson, R.C. (1975). Mnemotechnics in second-language learning. *American Psychologist, 30*, 821-828.

Atkinson, J.W. (1964).. *An introduction to motivation*. Princeton, NJ: Van Nostrand.

Atkinson, R.C., & Shifferin, R.M. (1968). Human memory: A proposed system and its control processes. In K. Spence & J. Spence (Eds.), *The psychology of learning and motivation* (Vol. 2). New York: Academic Press.

Atkinson, R.C., & Raugh, M.R. (1975). An application of the mnemonic keyword method to the acquisition of Russian vocabulary. Journal of Experimental Psychology: *Human Learning and Memory*, 104, 126-133.

Ausubel, D.P. (1963). *The psychology of meaningful verbal learning*. New York: Grune and Stratton.

Ausubel, D.P. (1977). The facilitation of meaningful verbal meaning in the classroom. *Educational Psychologist, 12*, 162-178.

Babad, E.Y., Inbar, J., & Rosenthal, R. (1982). Pygmalion, Galatea, and the Golem: Investigations of biased and unbiased teachers. *Journal of Educational Psychology, 74*, 459-574.

Backman, M. (1972, Winter). Patterns of mental abilities: Ethnic, socioeconomic, and sex differences. *American Educational Research Journal, 9(1),*

Baker, L., & Brown, A.L. (1984). Metacognitive skills and reading. In P. D. Pearson, M. Kamil, R. Barr, & P. Mosenthal (Eds.), *Handbook of reading research* (pp. 353-394). New York: Longman. (a)

Baker, L., & Brown, A. L. (1984). Cognitive monitoring in reading. In J. Flood (Ed.), *Understanding reading comprehension* (pp. 21-44). Newark, DE: International Reading Association. (b)

Baldwin, J.D., & Baldwin, J.I. (1986). *Behavioral principles in everyday life (2nd ed.:).* Englewood Cliffs, NJ: Prentice Hall.

Bandura, A. (1973). *Aggression: A social learning analysis.* Englewood Cliffs, NJ: Prentice Hall.

Bandura, A. (1977). *Social learning theory.* Englewood Cliffs, NJ: Prentice Hall.

Bandura, A. (1978). The self-system in reciprocal determinism. *American Psychologist, 33,* 344-358.

Bandura, A. (1986). *Social foundations of thought and action.* Englewood Cliffs, NJ: Prentice Hall.

Bandura, A., Ross, D., & Ross, S.A. (1963). Vicarious reinforcement and imitative learning. *Journal of Abnormal and Social Psychology, 67,* 601-607.

Barger, R. (1984). Computer literacy: Toward a clearer definition. In J. H. Tashner (Ed.), *Computer literacy for teachers: Issues, questions and concerns.* Phoenix, AZ: The Oryz Press.

Barron, F., & Harrington, D.M. (1981). Creativity, intelligence, and personality. In M. Rosenzweig & L. W. Porter (Eds.), *Annual Review of Psychology.* Palo Alto, CA: Annual Reviews, Inc.

Bartlett, F. C. (1932). *Remembering: A study in experimental and social psychology.* New York: Macmillan.

Barton, E.J. (1981). Developing sharing: An analysis of modeling and other behavioral techniques. *Behavior Modification, 5,* 386-398.

Becker, W.C., Engelman, S., & Thomas, D.R. (1975). *Teaching 1: Classroom management.* Chicago: Science Research Associates.

227

Benbow, C.P., & Stanley, J.C. (1980). Sex differences in mathematical ability: Fact or artifact? *Science, 210,* 1262-1264.

Benbow, C.P., & Stanley, J.C. (1983). Differential course-taking hypothesis revisited. *American Educational Researach Journal, 20,* 469-473.

Berger, K.S. (1983). *The developing person through the life span.* New York: Worth.

Berliner, D. (1983). Developing concepts of classroom environments: Some light on the T in studies of ATI. *Educational Psychologist, 18,* 1-13.

Berliner, D. (1987). But do they understand? In V. Richardson-Koehler (Ed.), *Educators' handbook: A research perspective.* (pp. 259-293). New York: Longman.

Berliner, D. (1988). Simple views of effective teaching and a simple theory of classroom instruction. In D. Berliner & B. Rosenshine (Eds.), *Talks to teachers* (pp. 93-110). New York: Random House.

Beyer, B.K. (1984). Improving thinking skills: Practical approaches. *Phi Delta Kappan, 65,* 556-560.

Beyer, B.K. (1985). Practical strategies for the direct teaching of thinking skills. In A. Costa (Ed.), *Developing minds: A resource book for teaching thinking* (pp. 145-150). Alexandria, VA: Association for Supervision and Curriculum Development.

Blackman, S., & Goldstein, K. (1982). Cognitive styles and learning disabilities. *Journal of Learning Disabilities, 15,* 106-115.

Bloom, B.S. (1968). *Learning for mastery.* Evaluation Comment, 1(2). Los Angeles: University of California, Center for the Study of Evaluation of Instructional Programs.

Bloom, B.S. (1973). Individual differences in achievement. In L. J. Rubin (Ed.), *Facts and feelings in the classroom.* New York: Viking.

Bloom, B.S. (1976). *Human characteristics and school learning.* New York: McGraw-Hill.

Bloom, B.S., Engelhart, M.D., Frost, E.J., Hill, W.H., & Krathwohl, D.R. (1956). *Taxonomy of educational objectives. Handbook I:* Cognitive domain. New York: McGraw-Hill.

Bloom, B.S., Hastings, J.T., & Madaus, G.F. (1971). *Handbook on formative and summarized evaluation of student learning.* New York: McGraw-Hill.

Bloom, R., & Bourdon, L. (1980). Types and frequencies of teachers' written instructional feedback. *Journal of Educational Research, 74,* 13-15.

Bork, A. (1978). Machines for computer-assisted learning. *Educational Technology, 18,* 17-20.

228

Bork, A. (1984). Computers in education today--and some possible futures. *Phi Delta Kappan, 66,* 239-243.

Bork, A., & Franklin, S. (1979). Personal computers in learning. *Educational Technology, 19,* 7-12.

Borko, H. (1989). Research on learning to teach: Implications for graduate teacher preparation. In A. Woolfolk (Ed.), *Research perspectives on the graduate preparation of teachers* (pp. 69-87). Englewood Cliffs, NJ: Prentice Hall.

Borkowski, J.G., Johnston, M.B., & Reid, M.K. (1986). *Metacognition, motivation, and the transfer of control processes.* In S. J. Ceci (Ed.), Handbook of cognition: Social and neurological aspects of learning disabilities. Hillsdale, NJ: Erlbaum.

Bornstein, P.H. (1985). Self-instructional training: A commentary and state-of-the-art. *Journal of Applied Behavior Analysis, 18,* 69-72.

Bourne, L.E., Dominowski, R.L., Loftus, E.F., & Healy, A. (1986). *Cognitive processes (2nd ed.).* Englewood Cliffs, NJ: Prentice Hall.

Bower, G.H., & Hilgard, E.L. (1981). *Theories of learning.* Englewood Cliffs, NJ: Prentice Hall.

Bozeman, W., & House, J. (1988). Microcomputers in education: The second decade. *T. H. E. Journal,* 15(6), 82-86.

Bransford, J.D., Stein, B.S., Vye, N.J., Franks, J.J., Auble, P.M., Mezynski, K.J., & Perfetto, G.A. (1982). Differences in approaches to learning: An overview. *Journal of Experimental Psychology: General, 111,* 390-398.

Braun, C. (1976). Teacher expectation: Sociopsychological dynamics. *Review of Educational Research, 46(2),* 185-212.

Brenner, L.P., & Agee, C.C. (1979). The symbiosis of PLATO and microcomputers. *Educational Technology, 19,* 45-52.

Brewer, W.F. (1974). There is no convincing evidence for operant and classical conditioning in humans. In W. B. Weimer & D. S. Permo (Eds.), *Cognition and symbolic processes.* Hillsdale, NJ: Erlbaum.

Brophy, J.E. (1973). Stability of teacher effectiveness. *American Educational Research Journal, 10,* 245-252.

Brophy, J.E. (1981). Teacher praise: A functional analysis. *Review of Educational Research, 51,* 5-21.

Brophy, J.E. (1988). On motivating students. In D. Berliner & B. Rosenshine (Eds.), *Talks to teachers* (pp. 201-245). New York: Random House.

Brophy, J.E., & Evertson, C. (1976). *Learning from teaching: A developmental perspective.* Boston: Allyn & Bacon.

Brophy, J.E., & Evertson, C. (1978). Context variables in teaching. *Educational Psychologist, 12,* 310-316.

Brophy, J.E., & Good, T. (1986). Teacher behavior and student achievement. In M. Wittrock (Ed.):, *Handbook of research on teaching (3rd ed., pp. 328-375).* New York: Macmillan.

Brophy, J.E., & Kher, N. (1986). Teacher socialization as a mechanism for developing student motivation to learn. In R. Feldman (Ed.), *Social psychology applied to education* (pp. 256-288). New York: Cambridge University Press.

Brown, A.L., Bransford, J.D., Ferrara, R.A., & Campione, J.C. (1983). Learning, remembering, and understanding. In P. Mussen (Ed.), *Carmichael's manual of child psychology. Vol. 3: Cognitive development* (E. Markman & J. Flavell, Volume Eds.). New York: Wiley.

Brown, A.L., Compione, J.C., & Day, J.D. (1981). Learning to learn: On training students to learn from tests. *Educational Researcher, 9,* 14-21.

Brown, J.S., & Burton, R.R. (1979). Diagnostic models for procedural bugs in basic mathematical skills. *Cognitive Science, 2,* 155-192.

Brown, R., & McNeill, D. (1966). The "tip-of-the-tongue" phenomenon. *Journal of Verbal Learning and Verbal Behavior, 5,* 325-337.

Bruner, J.S. (1960). *The process of education* New York: Vintage Books.

Bruner, J.S. (1962). *The process of education.* Cambridge: Harvard University Press.

Bruner, J.S. (1966). *Toward a theory of instruction.* New York: Norton.

Bruner, J.S. (1973). *Beyond the information given: Studies in the psychology of knowing.* New York: Norton.

Burbach, H.J. (1981). The labeling process: A sociological analysis. In J. Kauffman & D. Hallahan (Eds.), *Handbook of special education.* Englewood Cliffs, NJ: Prentice Hall.

Burton, R.V. (1963). The generality of honesty reconsidered. *Psychological Review, 70,* 481-499.

Butler, R., & Nisan, M. (1986). Effects of no feedback, task-related comments, and grades on intrinsic motivation and performance. *Journal of Educational Psychology, 78,* 210-224.

Canter, L., & Canter, M. (1976). *Assertive discipline: A take-charge approach for today's educator.* Los Angeles: Lee Canter and Associates.

Cantrell, R.P., Stenner, A.J., & Katzenmeyer, W.G. (1977). Teacher knowledge, attitudes, and classroom teaching correlates of student achievement. *Journal of Educational Psychology, 69,* 180-190.

Carter, K. (1984). Do teachers understand principles of writing tests? *Journal of Teacher Education, 35,* 57-60.

Casanova, U. (1987). Ethnic and cultural differences. In V. Richardson-Koehler (Ed.), *Educators' handbook: A researach perspective.* New York: Longman.

Case, R. (1978). Piaget and beyond: Toward a developmentally-based theory and technology of instruction. In R. Glaser (Ed.)., *Advances in instructional psychology (Vol. 1).* Hillsdale, NJ: Erlbaum. (a).

Case, R. (1978). Developmentally-based theory and technology of instruction. *Review of Educational research, 48,* 439-463. (b)

Case, R. (1980). Intellectual development: A systematic reinterpretation. In F. Farley & N. J. Gordon (Eds.), *Psychology and education: The state of the union.* Berkeley, CA: McCutchan.

Case, R. (1985). A developmentally-based approach to the problem of instructional design. In R. Glaser, S. Chipman, & J. Segal (Eds.), *Teaching thinking skills* (Vol. 2, pp. 545-562). Hillsdale, NJ: Erlbaum. (b).

Cattell, R.B. (1963). The fluid and crytalized intelligence: A critical experiment. *Journal of Educational Psychology, 54,* 1-22.

Cazden, C.B. (1988). *Classroom discourse: The language of teaching and learning.* Portsmouth, NH: Heinemann.

Chapman, D.W., & Hutcheson, S.M. (1982). Attrition from teaching careers: A discriminant analysis. *American Educationnal Research Journl, 19,* 93-106.

Charles, C.M. (1981). *Building classroom discipline: From models to practice (2nd ed.).* New York: Longman.

Chase, C.I. (1978). *Measurement for eductional evaluation (2nd ed.).* Reading, MA: Addison-Wesley.

Chomsky, N. (1965). *Aspects of a theory of syntax.* Cambridge, MA: MIT Press.

Clairborn, W.L. (1969). Expectancy effects in the classroom: A failure to replicate. *Journal of Eduction Psychology, 60,* 377-383.

Clarizio, H.F. (1971). *Toward positive classroom discipline.* New York: Wiley.

Clark, C.M., Gage, N.L., Marx, R.W., Petersonn, P.L., Staybrook, N.G., & Winnie, P.H. (1979). A factorial experiment on teacher structuring, soliciting, and reacting. *Journal of Educational Psychology, 71,* 534-550.

Clark, C., & Yinger, R. (1988). Teacher planning. In D. Berliner & B. Rosenshine (Eds.), *Talks to teachers* (pp. 342-365). New York: Random Houe.

Clark, C.M. & Peterson, P.L. (1986). Teachers' thought processes. In M. Wittrock (Ed.), *Handbook of research on teaching (3rd ed.)* (pp. 255-296). New York: Macmillan.

Clark, R.E. (1983). Reconsidering research on learning from media. *Review of educational Research, 53*, 445-459.

Clark, R.E. (1984). Research on student thought processes during computer-based instruction. *Journal of Instructional Development, 7,* 2-5.

Clark, R.E. (1985). Evidence for confounding in computer-based instruction studies: Analyzing the meta-analyses. Educational Communication and *Technology Journal, 33,* 249-262.

Clements, D.H., & Gullo, D.F. (1984). Effects of computer programming on young children's cognition. *Journal of Educational Psychology, 76,* 1051-1058.

Clifford, M.M. (1979). Effects of failure: Alternative explanations and possible implications. *Educational Psychologist, 14,* 44-52.

Clifford, M.M. (1984). *Educational psychology.* In Encyclopedia of Education (pp. 413-416). New York: Macmillan.

Clifford, M.M. (1984). Thoughts on a theory of constructive failure. *Educational Psychologist, 19,* 108-120.

Coates, J.F. (1978). Population and education: How demographic trends will shape the U.S. *The Futurist, 12,* 35-42.

Coates, T.J., & Thoresen, C.E. (1979). *Behavioral self-control and educational practice or do we really need self-control?* In D. C. Berliner (Ed.), Review of research in education, (Vol. 7). Itasca, IL: F. E. Peacock.

Coburn, P., Kelman, P., Roberts, N., Snyder, T.F.F., Watt, D.H., & Weiner, C. (1985). *Practical guide to computers in education.* Reading, MA: Addison-Wesley.

Cole, N.S. (1981). *Bias in testing.* American Psychologist, 36, 1067-1077.

Coleman, J.S., Campbell, J., Wood, A.M., Weinfeld, F.D., & York, R.L. (1966). *Equality of educational opportunity.* Washington, DC: United States Department of Health, Education and Welfare, Office of Education.

Collins, A., & Smith, E. (1980). *Teaching the process of reading comprehension* (Tech. Rep. No. 182). Urbana-Champaign: University of Illinois, Center for the Study of Reading.

Collins, A., & Smith, E. (1982). Teaching the process of reading. In D. K. Detterman & R. J. Sternberg (Eds.), *How and how much can intelligence be increased* (Table 1, p. 175). Norwood, NJ: Ablex.

Cooper, G., & Sweller, J. (1987). Effects of schema acquisition and rule automation on mathematical problem-solving transfer. *Journal of Educational Psychology*, 79, 347-362.

Cooper, H. (1979). Pygmalion grows up: A model for teacher expectation communication and performance influence. *Review of Educational Research, 49,* 389-410.

Cooper, H.M., & Good, T. (1983). Pygmalion grows up: Studies in the expectation communication process. New York: Longman.

Copi, I.M. (1961). *Introduction to logic.* New York: Macmillan.

Corno, L. (1988). Teaching and self-regulated learning. In D. Berliner & B. Rosenshine (Eds.:), *Talks to teachers* (pp. 249-266). New York: Random House.

Corno, L., & Snow, R.E. (1986). Adapting teaching to individual differences in learners. In M. Wittrock (Ed.), *Handbook of researach on teaching (3rd ed.).* New York: Macmillan.

Costa, A.L. (Ed.). (1985). *Developing minds: A resource book for teaching thinking.* Alexandria, VA: Association for Supervision and Curriculum Development.

Covington, M.V., & Omelich, C.L. (1984). An empirical examination of Weiner's critique of attribution research. *Journal of Educational Psychology, 76,* 1214-1225.

Covington, M. (1984). Strategic thinking and the fear of failure. In J. Segal, S. Chipman, & R. Glaser (Eds.), *Thinking and learning skills: Relating instruction to basic research.* Hillsdale, NJ: Erlbaum.

Covington, M., & Omelich, C. (1987). "I knew it cold before the exam": A test of the anxiety-blockage hypothesis. *Journal of Educational Psychology, 79,* 393-400.

Cox, C.C. (1926). The early mental traits of three hundred geniuses. In L. M. terman (Ed.), *Genetic studies of genius (Vol. 2).* Stanford, CA: Stanford University Press.

Cox, W.F., & Dunn, T.G. (1979). Mastery learning: A psychological trap? *Educational Psychologist, 14,* 24-29.

Craig, G. (1986). *Human development (4th ed.).* Englewood Cliffs, NJ: Prentice Hall.

Craik, F.I.M. (1979). Human memory. *Annual Review of Psychology, 30,* 63-102.

Craik, F.I.M., & Lockhart, R.S. (1972). Levels of processing: A framework for memory research. *Journal of Verbal Learning and Verbal Behavior, 11,* 671-684.

Cronbach, L., & Snow, R. (1977). *Aptitudes and instuctional methods.* New York: Irvington.

Crouse, J.M. (1971). Retroactive interference in reading prose materials. *Journal of Educational Psychology, 62,* 39-44.

Daiute, C. (:1985). *Writing and computers.* The Harvard Education Letter, 1(4).

Dansereau, D.F. (1985). Learning strategy research. In J. Segal, S. Chipman, & R. Glaser (Eds.), *Thinking and learning skills. Vol. 1: Relating instruction to research.* Hillsdale, NJ: Erlbaum.

Darley, J., & Fazio, R. (1980). Expectancy confirmation processes arising in the social interaction sequence. *American Psychologist, 35,* 867-881.

Darling-Hammond, L. (1984). *Beyond the commission reports: The coming crisis in teaching.* Santa Monica, CA: Rand.

Daurio, S.P. (1979). Educational enrichment versus acceleration: A review of the literature. In W. George, S. Cohn, & J. Stanley (Eds.), *Educating the gifted: Acceleration and enrichment.* Baltimore: Johns Hopkins Press.

De Charms, R. (1968). *Personal causation.* New York: Academic Press.

De Charms, R. (1976). *Enhancing motivation: Change in the classroom.* New York: Irvington.

De Charms, R. (1983). Intrinsic motivation, peer tutoring, and cooperative learning: Practical maxims. In J. Levine & M. Wang (Eds.):, *Teacher and student perceptions: Implications for learning* (pp. 391-398). Hillsdale, NJ: Erlbaum.

Deci, E. (1975). *Intrinsic motivation.* New York: Plenum.

Deci, E., & Ryan, R.M. (1985). *Intrinsic motivation and self-determination in human behvior.* New York: Plenum.

Deiderich, P.B. (1973). *Short-cut statistics for teacher-made tests.* Princeton, NJ: Educational Testing Services.

De Lisi, R., & Staudt, J. (1980). Individual differences in college students' performances on formal operations tasks. *Journal of Applied Developmental Psychology, 1,* 201-208.

Dellow, D.A., & Ross, S.M. (1982-1983). Implications of personal computers for social science faculty. *Community College Social Science Journal, 4,* 72-75.

Dempster, F.N. (1981). Memory span: Sources of individual and devleopmental differences. *Psychological Bulletin, 89,* 63-100.

Denham, C., & Lieberman, A. (1980). *Time to learn.* Washington, DC: National Institute of Education.

Derry, S.J. (in press). Strategy and expertise in solving word problems. In C. McCormick, G. Mille, & M. Pressley (Eds.), *Cognitive strategies research: From basic research to educational applications.* New York: Springer-Verlag.

Derry, S.J., & Murphy, D.A. (1986). Designing systems that train learning ability: From theory to practice. *Review of Educational Research, 56,* 1-39.

Dinnel, D., & Glover, J.A. (1985). Advance organizers: Encoding manipulations. *Journal of Educational Psychology, 77,* 514-522.

Doctorow, M., Wittrock, M.C., & Marks, C. (1978). Generative processes in reading comprehension. *Journal of Educational Psychology, 70,* 109-118.

Doyle, W. (1977). The uses of nonverbal behaviors: Toward an ecological model of classrooms. *Merrill-Palmer Quarterly, 23,* 179-192.

Doyle, W. (1979). Making managerial decisions in classrooms. In D. Duke (Ed.), *Classroom management: 78th Yearbook of the National Society for the Study of Education* (Part 2). Chicago: University of Chicago Press.

Doyle, W. (1980). *Classroom management.* West Lafayette, IN: Kappa Delta Pi.

Doyle, W. (1983). Academic work. *Review of Educational Research, 53,* 287-312.

Doyle, W. (1985, May/June). Recent research on classroom management: Implications for teacher preparation. *Journal of Teacher Education, pp. 31-35.*

Doyle, W. (1986). Classroom organization and management. In M. Wittrock (Ed.), *Handbook of research on teaching* (3rd ed., pp. 392-431). New York: Macmillan.

Doyle, W., & Ponder, G. (1977-1978). The practicality ethic in teacher decision making. *Interchange, 8(3),* 1-12.

Dreikurs, R., Grunwald, B.B., & Pepper, F.C. (1971). *Maintaining santity in the classroom: Illustrated teaching techniques.* New York: Harper and Row.

Dressel, P.L. (1977). The nature and role of objectives in instruction. *Educational Technology, 17,* 7-15.

Duchastel, P. (1979). Learning objectives and the organization of prose. *Journal of Educational Psychology, 71*, 100-106.

Duffy, G., Roehler, L.R., Meloth, M.S., & Vavrus, L.G. (1986). Conceptualizing instructional explanation. *Teaching and Teacher Education, 2,* 197-214.

Duncker, K. (1945). On solving problems. *Psychological Monographs, 58,* (5, Whole No. 270).

Dunkin, M.J., & Biddle, B.J. (1974). *The study of teaching.* New York: Holt, Rinehart & Winston.

Dunn, K., & Dunn, R. (1978). *Teaching students through their individual learning styles.* Reston, VA: Reston.

Dunn, K., & Dunn, R. (1987). *Dispelling outmoded beliefs about student learning.* Educational Leadership, 44(6), 55-63.

Dunn, R., Dunn, K., & Price, G.E. (1984). *Learning Style Inventory.* Lawrence, KS: Price Systems.

Dush, D.M., Hirt, M.L., & Schroider, H. (1983). Self-management modification with adults: A meta-analysis. *Psychological Bulletin, 94,* 408-422.

Dweck, C.S. (1986). Motivational processes affecting learning. *American Psychologist, 41,* 1040-1047.

Dweck, C. (1983). Theories of intelligence and achievement motivation. In S. Paris, G. Olson, & H. Stevenson (Eds.), *Learning and motivation in the classroom.* Hillsdale, NJ: Erlbaum. Princeton, NJ: Educational Testing Service.

Eatonn, S., & Olson, J. (1986). "Doing computers?" The micro in the elementary curriculum. *Journal of Curriculum Studies, 18(3),* 342-344.

Eccles, J., & Wigfield, A. (1985). Teacher expectations and student motivation. In J. Dusek (Ed.), *Teacher expectancies* (pp. 185-226). Hillsdale, NJ: Erlbaum.

Eisner, E. (1983, January). The art and craft of teaching. *Educational Leadership, 40,* 4-13.

Eisner, E. (1986). A secretary in the classroom. *Teaching and Teacher Education, 2,* 325-328.

Elashoff, J.D., & Snow, R.E. (1971). *Pygmalion reconsidered.* Worthington, OH: Charles A. Jones.

Elawar, M.C., & Corno, L. (1985). A factorial experiment in teachers' written feedback on student homework: Changing teacher behavior a little rather than a lot. *Journal of Educational Psychology, 77,* 162-173.

Electronic Learning (1987). Educational technology 1987: A report on EL's seventh annual survey of the states. *Electronic Learning. 7(2),* 39-44, 53-57, 83.

Elkind, D. (1981). Obituary--Jean Piaget (1896-1980). American Psychologist, 36, 911-913.

Emmer, E.T., & Evertson, C.M. (1981). Synthesis of research on classroom management. Educational Leadership, 38, 342-345.

Emmer, E.T., & Millett, JG. (1970). Improving teaching through experimentation: A laboratory approach. Englewood Cliffs, NJ: Prentice Hall.

Erickson, JF., & Shultz, J. (1977). When is context? Some issues and methods in the analysis of social competence. Quarterly Newsletter for the Institute for Comparative Human Development, 1(2), 5-10.

Evans, E.D. (1976). Transition to teaching. New York: Holt, Rinehart & Winston.

Evertson, C.M. (1988). Managing classrooms: A framework for teachers. In D. Berliner & B. Rosenshine (Eds.), Talks to teachers (pp. 54-74). New York: Random House.

Evertson, C.M., & Green, J. (1986). Observation as inquiry and method. In M. Wittrock (Ed.), Handbook of researach on teaching (3rd ed., pp. 162-213). New York: Macmillan.

Faw, H.W., & Waller, T.G. (1976). Mathemagenic behaviors and efficiency in learning from prose. Review of Educational Research, 46, 691-720.

Feiman-Nemser, S. (1983). Learning to teach. In L. Shulman & G. Sykes (Eds.), Handbook of teaching and policy (pp. 150-170). New York: Longman.

Feitler, F., & Tokar, E. (1982). Getting a handle on teacher stress: How bad is the problem? Educational Leadership, 39, 456-458.

Fennema, E., & Sherman, J. (1977). Sex-related differences in mathematics achievement, spatial visualization and affective factors. American Educational Research Journal, 14(1), 51-71.

Ferguson, D.L., Ferguson, P.M., & Bogdan, R.C. (1987). If mainstreaming is the answer, what is the question? In V. Richardson-Koehler (Ed.), Educators' handbook: A research perspective. New York: Longman.

Ferster, C.B., & Skinner, B.F. (1957). Schedules of reinforcement. New York: Appleton Century Crofts

Feurerstein, R. (1979). The dynamic assessment of retarded performers: The Learning Potential Assessment Device, theory, instruments, and techniques. Baltimore: University Park Press.

Finn, J. (1972). Expectations and the educational environment. Review of Educational Research, 42, 387-410.

Fiske, E.B. (1981, October 27). Teachers reward muddy prose, study finds. The New York Times, p. C1.

Fiske, E.B. (1988, April 10),. America's test mania. *The New York Times* (Education Life Section), pp. 16-20.

Flavell, J.H. (1976). Metacognitive aspects of problem solving. In L. Resnick (Ed.), *The nature of intelligence.* Hillsdale, NJ: Erlbaum.

Flavell, J.H. (1985). *Cognitive development (2nd ed.).* Englewood Cliffs, NJ: Prentice Hall.

Flavell, J.H., Friedrichs, A.G., & Hoyt, J.D. (1970). Developmental changes in memorization processes. *Cognitive Psychology, 1,* 324-340.

Fox, L.H. (1979). Programs for the gifted and talented: An overview. In A. Passow (Ed.), *The gifted and talented: Their education and development.* Chicago: University of Chicago Press.

Fox, L.H. (1981). Identification of the academically gifted. *American Psychologist, 36,* 1103-1111.

Frederiksen, N. (1984). Implications of cognitive theory for instruction in problem solving. *Review of Educational Research, 54,* 363-407.

Frender, R., Brown, B., & Lambert, W. (1970). The role of speech characteristics in scholastic success. *Canadian Journal of Behavioral Science, 2,* 299-306.

Friedlander, B. (1985, November/December). Get your class in-line and on-line with a modem. *Electronic Education,* pp. 14-15.

Frostig, M., & Horne, D. (1964). *The Frostig program for the development of visual perception: Teacher's guide.* Chicago: Follett.

Fuller, F. G. (1969). Concerns of teachers: A developmental conceptualization. *American Educational Research Journal, 6,* 207-226.

Furst, E.J. (1981). Bloom's taxonomy of educational objectives for the cognitive domain: Philosophical and educational issues. *Review of Educational Research, 51,* 441-454.

Furth, H., & Wachs, H. (1974). *Thinking goes to school: Piaget's theory in practice.* New York: Oxford University Press.

Gagne, E.D. (1985). *The psychology of school learning.* Boston: Little, Brown.

Gagne, R.M. (1977). *The conditions of learning (3rd ed.).* New York: Holt, Rinehart & Winston.

Gagne, R.M. (1985). *The conditions of learning and theory of instruction (4th ed.).* New York: Holt, Rinehart & Winston.

Gagne, R.M., & Driscoll, M.P. (1988). *Essentials of learning for instruction (2nd ed.).* Englewood Cliffs, NJ: Prentice Hall.

Gagne, R.M., & Smith, E. (19;62). A study of the effects of verbalization on problem solving. *Journal of Experimental Psychology, 63,* 12-18.

Gall, M.D. (1970). The use of questions in teaching. *Review of Educational Research, 40,* 707-721.

Gall, M.D. (1984). Synthesis of research on teachers' questionning. *Educational Leadership, 41,* 40-47.

Gallini, J.K. (1989). Schema-based strategies and implications for instructional design in strategy training. In C. McCormick, G. Miller, & M. Pressley (Eds.), *Cognitive strategies research: From basic research to educational applications.* New York: Springer-Verlag.

Gardner, H. (1982). *Developmental psychology (2nd ed.).* Boston: Little, Brown.

Gardner, H. (1983). *Frames of mind: The theory of multiple intelligences.* New York: Basic Books.

Garrett, S.S., Sadker, M., & Sadker, D. (1986). Interpersonal communication skills. In J. Cooper (ed.), *Classroom teaching skills (3rd ed.).* Lexington, MA: D. C. Heath.

Gartner, A., & Lipsky, D.K. (1987). Beyond special education: Toward a quality sytem for all students. *Harvard Educational Review, 57,* 367-395.

Gentner, D. (1975). Evidence for the psychological reality of semantic components: The verbs of possession. In D. Norman & D. Rumelhart (Eds.), *Explorations in cognition.* San Francisco: W. H. Freeman.

Gibbs, J.W., & Luyben, P.D. (1985). Treatment of self-injurious behavior: Contingent versus noncontingent positive practice overcorrection. *Behavior Modification, 9,* 3-21.

Gick, M.L. (1986). *Problem-solving strategies. Educational Psychologist, 21,* 99-120.

Gilligan, C. (1977). In a different voice: Women's conceptions of self and of morality. *Harvard Educational Review, 47,* 481-517.

Gilstrap, R.L., & Martin, W.R. (:1975). *Current strategies for teachers: A resource for personalizing education.* Pacific Palisades, CA: Goodyear.

Ginsburg, H. (1985). Piaget and education. In N. Entwistle (Ed.), *New directions in educational psychology. Vol. 1: Learning and teaching.* Philadelphia: Falmer Press.

Ginsburg, H., & Opper, S. (1988). *Piaget's theory of intellectual development (3rd ed.).* Englewood Cliffs, NJ: Prentice Hall.

Glaser, R. (1981). The future of testing: A research agenda for cognitive psychology and psychometrics. *American Psychologist, 36,* 923-936.

Gleitman, H. (1988). *Psychology (3rd ed.).* New York: Norton.

Gleitman, H. (1987). *Basic psychology (2nd Ed.).* New York: Norton.

Goleman, D. (1988, April 10). An emerging theory on Blacks' I.Q. scores. *The New York Times* (Education Life Section), 22-24.

Good, T.L. (1983). Classroom research: A decade of progress. *Educational Psychologist, 18,* 127-144.

Good, T.L. (1983). Research on classroom teaching. In L. Shulman & G. Sykes (Eds.), *Handbook of teaching and policy* (pp. 42-80). New York: Longman.

Good, T.L. (1988). Teacher expectations. In D. Berliner & B. Rosenshine (Eds.), *Talks to teachers.* New York: Random House.

Good, T.L., Biddle, B., & Brophy, J.E. (1975). *Teachers make a difference.* New York: Holt, Rinehart & Winston.

Good, T.L., & Brophy, J.E. (1984). *Looking in classrooms (3rd ed.).* New York: Harper and Row.

Good, T.L., Grouws, D., & Ebmeier, H. (1983). *Active mathematics teaching.* New York: Longman.

Good, T.L., & Marshall, S. (1984). Do students learn more in heterogeneous or homogeneous groups? In P. Peterson, L.C. Wilkinson, & M. Hallinan (Eds.):, *The social context of instruction: Group organization and group processes* (pp. 15-38). Orlando, FL: Academic Press.

Good, T.L., & Stipek, D.J. (1983). Individual differences in the classroom: A psychological perspective. In G. Fenstermacher & J. Goodlad (Eds.):, *1983 National Society for the Study of Education Yearbook.* Chicago: University of Chicago Press.

Goodspeed, J. (1988). Two million microcomputers now used in U.S. schools. *Electronic Learning, 7(8),* 16.

Grabe, M., & Latta, R.M. (1981). Cumulative achievement in a mastery instructional system: The impact of differences in resultant achievement motivation and persistence. *American Educational Research Journal, 18,* 7-14.

Green, B.F. (1981). A primer of testing. *American Psychologist, 36,* 1001-1012.

Green, J., & Weade, R. (1985). Reading between the lines: Social cues to lesson participation. *Theory into Practice, 24,* 14-21.

Gregorc, A.F. (1982). *Gregorc Style Delineator: Development, technical, and administrative manual.* Maynard, MA: Gabriel Systems.

Griffin, G. (1984). Why use research in preservice teacher education? A Proposal. *Journal of Teacher Education, 35(4)*, 36-40.

Gronlund, N.E. (1977). *Constructing achievement tests (2nd ed.).* Englewood Cliffs, NJ: Prentice Hall.

Gronlund, N.E. (1978). *Stating behavioral objectives for classroom instruction (2nd ed.).* Toronto: Macmillan.

Gronlund, N.E. (1985). *Measurement and evaluation in teaching (5th ed.).* New York: Macmillan.

Gronlund, N.E. (1988). *How to construct achievement tests (4th ed.).* Englewood Cliffs, NJ: Prentice Hall.

Guilford, J.P. (1967). *The nature of human intelligence.* New York: McGraw-Hill.

Guskey, T.R., & Gates, S.L. (1986). Synthesis of research on mastery learning. *Education Leadership, 43,* 73-81.

Guttmacher (Alan) Institute (1984). *Issues in brief (Vol. 4, No. 2).* Washington, DC: Alan Guttmacher Institute.

Hamilton, R.J. (1985). A framework for the evaluation of the effectiveness of adjunct questions and objectives. *Review of Educational Research, 55,* 47-86.

Haney, W. (1981). Validity, vaudeville, and values: A short history of social concerns over standardized testing. *American Psychologist, 36,* 1021-1034.

Hansen, D.N., Ross, S.M., & Bowman, H.L. (1978, December). Cost effectiveness of navy computer-managed instruction. In T. A. Ryan (Ed.), *Systems research in Education.* Columbia, SC: University of South Carolina.

Hansen, R.A. (1977). Anxiety. In S.J. Ball (Ed.), *Motivation in education.* New York: Academic Press.

Hansford, B.C., & Hattie, J.A. (1982). The relationship between self and achievement/performance measures. *Review of Educational Research, 52,* 123-142.

Harris, V.W., & Sherman, J.A. (1973). Use and analysis of the "Good Behavior Game" to reduce disruptive classroom behavior. *Journal of Applied Behavior Analysis, 6,* 405-417.

Harrow, A.J. (1972). *A taxonomy of the psychomotor domain: A guide for developing behavioral objectives.* New York: David McKay.

Harvard University. (1986, March). When the student becomes the teacher. *Harvard Education Letter, 2(3)*, 5-6.

Harvard University. (1988, March). Cultural differences in the classroom. *The Harvard Education Letter, 4(2)*, 1-4.

Havighurst, R.J. (1981). Life-span development and educational psychology. In F. H. Farley & N. J. Gordon (Eds.), *Psychology and education: The state of the union*. Berkeley, CA: McCutchan.

Hayes, J.R., Waterman, D.A., & Robinson, C.S. (1977). Identifying relevant aspects of a problem text. *Cognitive Sciences, 1*, 297-313.

Hayes, S.C., Rosenfarb, I., Wulfert, E., Munt, E.D., Korn, Z., & Zettle, R.D. (1985). Self-reinnforcement effects: An artifact of social standard setting? *Journal of Applied Behavior Analysis, 18*, 201-214.

Hill, W.F. (1985). *Learning: A survey of psychological interpretations (4th ed.)*. New York: Harper and Row.

Hiller, J.H. (1971). Verbal response indicators of conceptual vagueness. *American Educational Research Journal, 8*, 151-16;1.

Hills, J.. (1976). *Measurement and evaluation in the classroom*. Columbus, OH: Charles E. Merrill.

Hines, C.V., Cruickshank, D.R., & Kennedy, J.J. (1985). Teacher clarity and its relation to student achievement and satisfaction. *American Educational Research Journal, 22*, 87-99.

Hinsley, D., Hayes, J.R., & Simon, H.A. (1977). From words to equations. In P. Carpenter & M. Just (Eds.), *Cognitive processes in comprehension*. Hillsdale, NJ: Erlbaum.

Hoffman, L.W. (1977). Changes in family roles, socialization, and sex differences. *American Psychologist, 32(8)*, 644-657.

Hoffman, M.L. (1978). Empathy: Its development and prosocial implications. In C. B. Keasey, (Ed.):, *Nebraska Symposium on Motivation, 1977*. Lincoln, NE: University of Nebraska Press.

Hoffman, M.L. (1979). Development of moral thought, feeling, and behavior. *American Psychologist, 34*, 958-966.

Hoffman, M.L. (1983). Affective and cognitive processes in moral internal moralization. In T. Higgins, D. Ruble, & W. Hartup (Eds.), *Social cognition and social development*. Cambridge: Cambridge University Press.

Hoffman, M.L. (1984). Empathy: its limitations and its role in a comprehensive moral theory. In W. Kurtines & J. Gewirtz (Eds.), *Morality, moral behavior, and moral devleopment*. New York: Wiley.

Horn, J.L., & Donaldson, G. (1980). Cognitive development in adulthood. In O. Brim & J. Kagan (Eds.), *Constancy and change in human development.* Cambridge, MA: Harvard University Press.

Howe, H. (1983, November). Education moves center stage: An overview of recent studies. *Phi Delta Kappan, 65,* 167-172.

Hudgins, B.B. (1977). *Learning and thinking: A primer for teachers.* Itasca, IL: F. E. Peacock.

Huessman, L.R., Lagarspetz, K., & Eron, L. (1984). Intervening variables in the TV violence-aggression relation: Evidence from two countries. *Developmental Psychology, 20,* 746-775.

Hunt, J. (1981). Comments on "The modification of intelligence through early experience" by Ramey and Haskins. *Intelligence, 5,* 21-27.

Hunt, J. MCV. (1961). *Intelligence and experience.* New York: Ronald.

Hunter, M. (1982). *Mastery teaching.* El Segundo, CA: TIP Publications.

Hyde, J. (1981). How large are cognitive gender differences? *American Psychologist, 36,* 292-301.

Irving, O., & Martin, J. (1982). Withitness: The confusing variable. *American Educational Research Jouranl, 19,* 313-319.

Irwin, J.W. (1986). *Teaching reading comprehension.* Englewood Cliffs, NJ: Prentice Hall.

Jencks, C., Smith, M., Acland, H., Bane, M., Cohen, D., Gintis, H., Heyns, B., & Michelson, S. (1972). *Inequality: A reassessment of the effect of family and schooling in America.* New Basic Books.

Jensen, A.R. (1980). *Bias in testing.* New York: Free Press.

Jensen, A.R. (1981). Raising the IQ: The Ramey and Haskins study. *Intelligence, 5,* 29-40.

Jensen, W.R., Sloane, H.N., & Young, K.R. (1988). *Applied behavior analysis in education: A structured teaching approach.* Englewood Cliffs, NJ: Prentice Hall.

Johnson, D.W. (1986). *Reaching out: Interpersonal effectiveness and self-actualization. (3rd ed.).* Englewood Cliffs, NJ: Prentice Hall.

Johnson, D., & Johnson, R. (1975). *Learning together and alone: Cooperation, competition, and individualization.* Englewood Cliffs, NJ: Prentice Hall.

Johnson, D., & Johnson, R. (1985). Motivational processes in cooperative, competitive, and individualistic learning situations. In C. Ames & R. Ames (Eds.), *Research on motivation in education. Vol. 2: The classroom milieu* (pp., 249-286). New York: Academic Press.

Jones, V.F., & Jones, L.S. (1986). *Comprehensive classroom management: Creating positive learning environments (2nd ed.)*. Boston: Allyn & Bacon.

Joshua, S., & Dupin, J.J. (1987). Taking into account student conceptions in instructional strategy: An example in physics. *Cognition and Instruction, 4*, 117-135.

Joyce, B., & Weil, M. (1986). *Models of teaching*. Englewood Cliffs, NJ: Prentice Hall.

Kanfer, F.H., & Gaelick, L. (1986). Self-management methods. In F. Kanfer & A. Goldstein (Eds.): *Helping people change: A textbook of methods (3rd ed.)*. New York: Pergamon.

Kaplan, B. (1984). *Development and growth*. Hillsdale, NJ: Erlbaum.

Karweit, N. (1981). Time in school. Research in *Sociology of Education and Socialization, 2,* 77-110.

Karweit, N., & Slavin, R. (1981). *Measurement and modeling choices in studies of time and learning*. American Educational Research Journal, 18, 157-171.

Kazdin, A.E. (1984). *Behavior modification in applied settings*. Homewood, IL: Dorsey Press.

Kearsley, G. (1984). Instructional design and authoring software. *Journal of Instructional Development, 7,* 11-16.

Keller, F.S. (1966). A personal course in psychology. In R. Urlich, T. Stachnik, & J. Mabry (Eds.), *Control of human behavior (Vol. 1)*. Glenview, IL: Scott, Foresman.

Kennedy, J.L., Cruickshank, D.C., Bush, A.J., & Myers, B. (1978). Additional investigations into the nature of teacher clarity. *Journal of Educational Research, 72,* 3-10.

Kiewra, K.A. (1988). Cognitive aspects of autonomous note taking: Control processes, learning strategies, and prior knowledge. *Educational Psychologist, 23,* 39-56.

King, G. (1979, June). *Personal communication*. University of Texas at Austin.

Kirby, B. (1984). *Sexuality. An evaluation of programs and their effects: An executive summary*. Santa Cruz, CA: Network Publications.

Klausmeier, H.J., & Sipple, T.S. (1982). Factor structure of the Piagetian stage of concrete operations. *Contemporary Educational Psychology, 7,* 161-180.

Kneedler, P. (1985). California assesses critical thinking. In A. Costa (Ed.), *Developing minds: A resource book for teaching thinking*. Alexandria, VA: Association for Supervision and Curriculum Development.

Kneedler, R. (1984). *Special education for today.* Englewood Cliffs, NJ: Prentice Hall.

Kohlberg, L. (1975). The cognitive-developmental approach to moral education. *Phi Delta Kappan, 56,* 670-677.

Kohlberg, L. (1981). *The philosophy of moral development.* New York: Harper and Row.

Kohn, A. (1988). Humanism's paradoxical champion. *Psychology Today, 22(9),* 70.

Kolesnik, W.B. (1978). *Motivation: Understanding and influencing human behavior.* Boston: Allyn & Bacon.

Kounin, J. (1970). *Discipline and group management in classrooms.* New York: Holt, Rinehart & Winston.

Krathwohl, D.R., Bloom, B.S., & Masia, B.B. (1956). *Taxonomy of educational objectives. Handbook II: Affective domain.* New York: David McKay.

Kulik, J.A., Kulik, C.C., & Bangert, R.L. (1984, April). Effects of practice on aptitude and achievement test scores. *American Educational Research Journal, 21,* 435-447.

Kulik, J.A., Kulik, C.C., & Cohen, P.A. (1979). A meta-analysis of outcome studies of Keller's Personalized System of Instruction. *American Psychologist, 34,* 307-318.

Kulik, J.A., Kulik, C.C., & Cohen, P.A. (1980). Effectiveness of computer-based college teaching: A meta-analysis of findings. *Review of Educational Research, 50,* 525-544.

Kurtz, J.J., & Swenson, E.J. (1951). Factors related to over-achievement and under-achievement in school. *School Review, 59,* 472-480.

Lamb, D.R. (1984). *Physiology of exercise: Response and adaptation (2nd ed.).* New York: Macmillan.

Land, M.L., & Smith, L.R. (1979). Effect of low inference teacher clarity inhibitors on student achievement. *Journal of Teacher Education, 31,* 55-57.

Langer, P.C. (1972). What's the score on programmed instruction? *Today's Education, 61,* 59.

Laosa, L. (1984). Ethnic, socioeconomic, and home language influences on early performance on measures of ability. *Journal of Educational Psychology, 76,* 1178-1198.

Larrivee, B. (1985). *Effective teaching behaviors for successful mainstreaming.* New York: Longman.

Lathrop, A., & Goodson, B. (1983). *Courseware in the classroom: Selecting, organizing, and using educational software.* Reading, MA: Addison-Wesley.

Lefcourt, H. (1966). Internal versus external control of reinforcement: A review. *Psychological Bulletin, 65,* 206-220.

Leinhardt, G. (1986). Expertise in mathematics teaching. *Educational Leadership, 43,* 28-33.

Leinhardt, G., & Greeno, J.D. (1986). The cognitive skill of teaching. *Journal of Educational Psychology, 78,* 75-95.

Leinhardt, G., & Smith, D. (1985). Expertise in mathematics instruction: Subject matter knowledge. *Journal of Educational Psychology, 77,* 247-271.

Lepper, M.R., & Greene, D. (1978). *The hidden costs of rewards: New perspectives on the psychology of human motivation.* Hillsdale, NJ: Erlbaum.

Lerner, B. (1981). The minimum competency testing movement: Social, scientific, and legal implications. *American Psychologist, 36,* 1057-1066.

Levin, J.R. (1985). Educational applications of mnemonic pictures: Possibilities beyond your wildest imagination. In A. A. Sheikh (Ed.), *Imagery in the educational process.* Farmingdale, NY: Baywood.

Levin, J.R., Dretzke, B.J., McCormick, C.B., Scruggs, T.E., McGivern, S., & Mastropieri, M. (1983). Learning via mnemonic pictures: Analysis of the presidential process. *Educational Communication and Technology Journal, 31,* 161-173.

Lewis, J., Jr. (1981). Do you encourage teacher absenteeism? *The American School Board Journal, 168,* 29-30.

Liebert, R.M., Wicks-Nelson, R., & Kail, R.V. (1986). *Developmental psychology (4th ed.).* Englewood Cliffs, NJ: Prentice Hall.

Lindsay, P.H., & Norman, D.A. (1977). *Human information processing: An introduction to psychology (2nd ed.).* New York: Academic Press.

Linn, R.L. (1986). Educational testing and assessment: Research needs and policy issues. *American Psychologist, 41,* 1153-1160.

Linn, R., Klein, S., & Hart, F. (1972). The nature and correlates of law school essay grades. *Educational and Psychological Measurement, 32,* 267-279.

Loehlin, J.C., Lindzey, G., & Spuhler, J.N. (1979). Cross-group comparisons of intellectual abilities. In L. Willerman & R. Turner (Eds.), *Readings about individuals and group differences.* San Francisco: W. H. Freeman

Luehrmann, A.L. (1981). Computer literacy--what should it be? *The Mathematics Teacher, 74(9).*

Luehrmann, A.L. 1984). Computer literacy: The what, why, and how. In D. Peterson (Ed.), Intelligent schoolhouse: *Readings on computers and learning* (pp. 53-58). Reston, VA: Reston.

Luehrmann, A.L. (1986). Don't feel bad teaching BASIC. In T. R. Cannings & S. W. Brown (Eds.). *The information-age classroom: Using the computer as a tool.* Irvine, CA: Franklin, Beedle & Associates.

Luiten, J., Ames, W., & Ackerson, G. (1980). A meta-analysis of the effects of advance organizers on learning and retention. *American Educational Research Journal, 17,* 211-218.

Lyman, H.B. (1986). *Test scores and what they mean (4th ed.).* Englewood Cliffs, NJ: Prentice Hall.

Maccoby, E.E., & Jacklin, C.N. (1974). *The psychology of sex differences.* Stanford, CA: Stanford University Press.

McClelland, D. (1973). Testing for competence rather than for intelligence. *American Psychologist, 28,* 1-14.

McClelland, D. (1985). *Human motivation.* Glenview, IL: Scott, Foresman.

McClelland, D., Atkinson, J.W., Clark, R.W., & Lowell, E.L. (1953). *The achievement motive.* New York: Appleton-Century-Crofts.

McCormick, C.B., & Levin, J.R. (1987). Mnemonic prose-learning strategies. In M. Pressley & M. McDaniel (Eds.), *Imaginery and related mnemonic processes.* New York: Springer-Verlag.

McDonald, F. (1976). *Teachers do make a difference.* Princeton, NJ: Eductional Testing Service. (b)

MacDonald-Ross, M. (1974). Behavioral objectives: A critical review. *Instructional Science, 2,* 1-51.

McGinley, P., & McGinley, H. (1970). Reading groups as psychological groups. *Journal of Experimental Education, 39,* 36-42.

McKenzie, T.L., & Rushall, B.S. (1974). Effects of self-recording on attendance and performancce in a competitive swimming training environment. *Journal of Applied Behavior Analysis, 7,* 199-206.

McNeill, D. (1966). Developmental psycholinguistics. In F. Smith & G. Miller (Eds.), *The genesis of language: A psycholinguistic approach.* Cambridge, MA: MIT Press.

McNemar, Q. (1964). Lost: Our intelligence? Why? *American Psychologist, 19,* 871-882.

Maehr, M.L. (1974). *Sociocultural origins of achievement.* Monterey, CA: Brooks/Cole.

Mager, R. (1975). *Preparing instructional objectives (2nd ed.).* Palo Alto, CA: Fearon.

Mahoney, K.B., & Hopkins, B.L. (1973). The modification of sentence structure and its relationship to subjective judgments of creativity in writing. *Journal of Applied Behavior Analysis, 6,* 425-434.

Mahoney, M.J., & Thoresen, C.E. (1974). *Self-control: Power to the person.* Monterey, CA: Brooks/Cole.

Maier, N.R.F. (1933). An aspect of human reasoning. *British Journal of Psychology, 24,* 144-155.

Maier, S.F., Seligman, M.E.P., & Solomon, R.L. (1969). Pavlovian fear conditioning and learned helplessness. In B. Campbell & R. Church (Eds.), *Punishment and aversive control.* New York: Appleton-Century-Crofts.

Maker, C.J. (1987). Gifted and talented. In V. Richardson-Koehler (Ed.), *Educators' handbook: A research perspective* (pp. 420-55). New York: Longman.

Marcia, J. (1987). The identity status approach to the study ego identity development. In T. Honess & K. Yardley (Eds.). *Self and identity: Perspectives across the life span.* London: Routledge & Kagan Paul.

Market Data Retrieval. (1982). *Annual report on school computer use.* Shelton, CT: Market Data Retrieval.

Market Data Retrieval. (1984). *Annual report on school computer use.* Shelton, CT: Market Data Retrieval.

Marsh, H.W. (1987). The big-fish-little-pond effect on academic self-concept. *Journal of Educational Psychology, 79,* 280-295.

Marsh, H.W., & Shavelson, R. (1985). Self-concept: Its multifaceted, hierarchical structure. *Educational Psychologist, 20,* 107-123.

Martin, G., & Pear, J. (1988). *Behavior modification: What it is and how to do it (3rd ed.).* Englewood Cliffs, NJ: Prentice Hall.

Martinson, R.A. (1961). *Educational programs for gifted pupils.* Sacramento: California Department of Education.

Maslow, A.H. (1968). *Toward a psychology of being (2nd ed.).* Princeton, NJ: Van Nostrand.

Maslow, A.H. (1970). *Motivation and personality (2nd ed.).* New York: Harper and Row.

Matarazzo, J.D. (1972). *Wechsler's measurement and appraisal of adult intelligence (5th ed.).* Fair Lawn, NJ: Oxford University Press.

Mayer, R.E. (1979). Can advance organizers influence meaningful learning? *Review of Educational Research, 49,* 371-383.

Mayer, R.E. (1983). Can you repeat that? Qualitative and quantitative effects of repetition and advance organizers on learning from science prose. *Journal of Educational Psychology, 75,* 40-49. (a)

Mayer, R.E. (1983). *Thinking, problem solving, cognition.* San Francisco, CA: W. H. Freeman. (b)

Mayer, R.E. (1984). Twenty-five years of research on advance organizers. *Instructional Science, 8,* 133-169.

Mayer, R.E., & Bromage, B. (1980). Different recall protocols for technical texts due to advance organizers. *Journal of Educational Psychology, 72,* 209-225.

Medley, D.M. (:1979). The effectiveness of teachers. In P. Peterson & H. Walberg (Eds.), *Research on teaching: Concepts, findings, and implications.* Berkeley, CA: McCutchan.

Mehan, H. (1979). *Learning lessons.* Cambridge, MA: Harvard University Press.

Meichenbaum, D. (1977). *Cognitive behavior modification: An integrative approach.* New York: Plenum.

Meichenbaum, D. (1986). Cognitive behavior modification. In F. Kanfer & A. Goldstein (Eds.), *Helping people change: A textbook of methods (3rd ed.,* (pp. 346-380). New York: Pergamon.

Merrill, M.C., Schneider, E.W., & Fletcher, K.A. (1980). *TICCIT.* Englewood Cliffs, NJ: Educational Technology Publications.

Messer, S. (1970). Reflection-impulsivity: Stability and school failure. *Journal of Educational Psychology, 61,* 487-490.

Metcalfe, B. (1981). Self-concept and attitude toward school. *British Journal of Educational Psychology, 51,* 66-76.

Miller, G.A. (1956). The magical number seven, plus or minus two: Some limits on our capacity for processing information. *Psychological Review, 63,* 81-97.

Miller, G.A., Galanter, E., & Pribram, K.H. (1960). *Plans and the structure of behavior.* New York: Holt, Rinehart & Winston.

Miller, R.B. (1962). Analysis and specification of behavior for training. In R. Glaser (Ed.), *Training research and education: Science edition.* New York: Wiley.

Mitchell, B.M. (1984). An update on gifted and talented education in the U.S. *Roeper Review, 6,* 161-163.

Moely, B.E., Hart, S.S., Santulli, K., Leal, L., Johnson, T., Rao, N., & Burney, L. (1986). How do teachers teach memory skills? In J. Levin & M. Pressley (Eds.), *Educational Psychologist, 21 (Special issue on learning strategies),* 55-72.

Morgan, M. (1984). Reward-induced decrements and increments in intrinsic motivation. *Review of Educational Research, 54,* 5-30.

Morgan, M. (1985). Self-monitoring of attained subgoals in private study. *Journal of Educational Psychology, 77*, 623-630.

Morris, C.G. (1988). *Psychology: An Introduction (6th ed.)*. Englewood Cliffs, NJ: Prentice Hall.

Morrow, L. (1983). Home and school correlates of early interest in literature. *Journal of Educational research, 76*, 221-230.

Morrow, L., & Weinstein, C. (1986). Encouraging voluntary reading: *The impact of a literature. Reading Research Quarterly, 21*, 330-346.

Moshman, D., Glover, J.A., & Bruning, R.H. (1987). *Developmental Psychology*. Boston: Little, Brown.

Moskowitz, B.A. (1978). The acquisition of language. *Scientific American, 239*, 92-108.

Moskowitz, G., & Hayman, M.L. (1976). Successful strategies of inner-city teachers: A year-long study. *Journal of Educational Research, 69*, 283-289.

Murray, H.G. (1983). Low inference classroom teaching behavior and student ratings of college teaching effectiveness. *Journal of Educational Psychology, 75*, 138-149.

Musgrave, G.R. (1975). Individualized instruction: *Teaching strategies focusing on the learner*. Boston, MA: Allyn & Bacon.

National Commission on Excellence in Education. (1983). *A nation at risk: The imperative for educational reform*. Washington, DC: U.S. Government Printing Office.

National Education Association. (1984). *Nationwide teacher opinion poll*. Washington, DC: Author.

National Education Association. (1985). *Estimates of School Statistics, 1984-85*. Washington, DC: Author.

National Task Force on Educational Technology. (1986). Transforming American education: Reducing the risk to the nation. *T. H. E. Journal*, August, 58-67.

Naveh-Benjamin, M., McKeachie, W.J., & Lin, Y. (1987). Two types of test-anxious students: Support for an information processing model. *Journal of Educational Psychology, 79*, 131-136.

Nicholls, J.G., & Miller, A. (1984). Conceptions of ability and achievement motivation. In R. Ames & C. Ames (Eds.), *Research on motivation in education. Vol. 1: Student Motivation* (pp. 39-73). New York: Academic Press.

Nelson, K. (1981). Individual differences in language development: Implications for development and language. *Developmental Psychology, 17*, 170-187.

Norman, D.P. (1982). *Learning and memory.* San Francisco: W. H. Freeman.

Nungester, R.J., & Duchastel, P.C. (1982). Testing versus review: Effects on retention. *Journal of Eductional Psychology, 74,* 18-22.

O'Connor, R.D. (1969). Modification of social withdrawal through symbolic modeling. *Journal of Applied Behavior Analysis, 2,* 15-22.

O'Day, E.F., Kulhavy, R.W., Anderson, W., & Malczynski, R.J. (1971). *Programmed instruction: Techniques and trends.* New York: Appleton-Century-Crofts.

O'Leary, K.D., & O'Leary, S. (Eds.). (1977). Classroom management: *The successful use of behavior modification (2nd ed.).* Elmsford, NY: Pergamon.

O'Leary, K.D., & Wilson, G.T. (1987). *Behavior therapy: Application and outcome.* Englewood Cliffs, NJ: Prentice Hall.

O'Leary, S.G., & O'Leary, K.D. (1976). Behavior modification in the schools. In H. Leitenberg (Ed.), *Handbook of behavior modification and behavior therapy.* Englewood Cliffs, NJ: Prentice Hall.

Ollendick, T.h., Dailey, D., & Shapiro, E.S. (1983). Vicarious reinforcement: Expected and unexpected effects. *Journal of Applied Behavior analysis, 16,* 485-491.

Ollendick, T.H., Matson, J.L., Esveldt-Dawson, K., & Shapiro, E.S. (1980). Increasing spelling achievement: An analysis of treatment procedures utilizing an alternating treatments design. *Journal of Applied Behavior Analysis, 13,* 645-654.

Olson, D.R. (1985). Computers as tools of the intellect. *Educational Researcher, 14,* 5-7.

Orlansky, J., & String, J. (1981). Computer-based instruction for military training. *Defense Management Journal, 2nd Quarter,* 46-54.

Ornstein, A.C. (1980). Teacher salaries: Past, present, and future. *Phi Delta Kappan, 61,* 677-679.

Ornstein, A.C., & Miller, H.L. (1980). Looking into education: *An introduction to American education.* Chicago: Rand McNally.

Osborn, A.F. (1963). *Applied imagination (3rd ed.).* New York: Scribner's.

O'Sullivan, J.T., & Pressley, M. (1984). Completeness of instruction and strategy transfer. *Journal of Experimental Child Psychology, 38,* 275-288.

Owen, L. (1985). *None of the above: Behind the myth of scholastic aptitude.* Boston: Houghton Mifflin.

Page, E.B. (1958). Teacher comments and student performances: A 74-classroom experiment in school motivation. *Journal of Educational Psychology, 49,* 173-181.

Palincsar, A.S. (1986). The role of dialogue in providing scaffolded instruction. In J. Levin & M. Pressley (Eds.), *Educational Psychologist, 21 (Special issue on learning strategies),* 73-98.

Palincsar, A.S., & Brown, A.L. (1984). Reciprocal teaching of comprehension-fostering and monitoring activities. *Cognition and Instruction, 1,* 117-175.

Pallas, A.M., & Alexander, K. (1983). Sex differences in quantitative SAT performance: New evidence on the differential coursework hypothesis. *American Educational Research Jouranl, 20,* 165-182.

Papert, S. (1980). *Mindstorms.* New York: Basic Books.

Park, O., & Tennyson, JR.D. (1980). Adaptive design strategies for selecting number and presentation order of examples in coordinate concept acquisition. *Journal of Educational Psychology, 72,* 362-370.

Pattison, P., & Grieve, N. (1984). Do spatial skills contribute to sex differences in different types of mathematical problems? *Journal of Educational Psychology, 76,* 678-689.

Pauk, W. (1984). *How to study in college (3rd ed.).* Boston: Houghton Mifflin.

Paulman, R.G., & Kennelly, K.J. (1984). Test anxiety and ineffective test taking: Different names, same construct? *Journal of Educational Psychology, 76,* 279-288.

Pavio, A. (1971). *Imagery and verbal processes.* New York: Holt, Rinehart & Winston.

Pearl, D., Routhlet, L., & Lazar, J. (Eds.). (1982). *Television and behavior: Ten years of scientific progress and implications for the eighties (Vols. 1 & 2).* Washington, DC: U.S. Government Printing Office.

Peeck, J., van den Bosch, A.B., & Kreupeling, W.J. (1982). Effect of mobilizing prior knowlege on learning from text. *Journal of Educational Psychology, 74,* 771-777.

Pelham, W.E., & Murphy, H.A. (1986). Attention deficit and conduct disorders. In M. Hersen (Ed.), *Pharmacological and behavioral treatment: An integrative approach* (pp. 108-148). New York: Wiley.

Peper, R.J., & Mayer, R.E. (1986). Generative effects of note taking during science lectures. *Journal of Educational Psychology, 78,* 34-38.

Perkins, D.N. (1986). Thinking frames. *Educational Leadership, 43,* 4-11.

Peterson, P. (1979). Direct instruction reconsidered. In P. Peterson & H. Walberg (Eds.), *Research on teaching: Concepts, findings, and implications.* Berkeley, CA: McCutchan.

Peterson, P.L., & Comeaux, M.A. (1989). Assessing the teacher as a reflective professional: New perspectives on teacher evaluation. In A. Woolfolk (Ed.), *Research perspectives on the graduate preparation of teachers* (pp. 132-152). Englewood Cliffs, NJ: Prentice Hall.

Peterson, P., Janicki, T.C., & Swing, S.R. (1980). Aptitude-treatment interaction effects of three social studies teaching approaches. *American Educational Research Journal, 17,* 339-360.

Peterson, S.E., Degracie, J.S., & Ayabe, C.R. (1987). A longitudinal study of the effects of retention/promotion on academic achievement. *American Educational Research Journal, 24,* 107-118.

Petkovich, M.D., & Tennyson, R.D. (1984). Clark's "learning from media": A critique. *Educational Communication Technology Journal, 32,* 233-241.

Pettegrew, L.S., & Wolf, G.E. (1982). Validating measures of teacher stress. *American Educational Research Jouranl, 19,* 373-396.

Pfeiffner, L.J., Rosen, L.A., & O'Leary, S.G. (1985). The efficacy of an all-positive approach to classroom management. *Journal of Applied Behavior Analysis, 18,* 257-261.

Piaget, J. (1974). *Understanding causality* (D. Miles and M. Miles, Trans.). New York: Norton.

Platt, W., & Baker, B.A. (1931). The relation of the scientific "hunch" to research. *Journal of Chemical Evaluation, 8,* 1969-2002.

Pogrow, S. (1988). The computer movement cover-up. *Electronic Learning, 7(7),* 6-7.

Popham, W.J. (1969). Objectives and instruction. In W. J. Popham, E. W. Eisner, H. J. Sullivan, & L. I. Tyler (Eds.), *Instructional objectives (Monograph Series on Curriculum Evaluation, No. 3).* Chicago: Rand McNally.

Posner, M.I. (1973). *Cognition: An introduction.* Glenview, IL: Scott, Foresman.

Premack, D. (1965). Reinforcement theory. In D. Levine (Ed.), *Nebraska symposium on motivation (Vol. 13).* Lincoln, NE: University of Nebraska Press.

Pressley, M. (1986). The relevance of the good strategy user model to the teaching of mathematics. In J. Levin & M. Pressley (Eds.), *Educational Psychologist, 21 (Special issue on learning strategies),* 139-161.

Pressley, M., Levin, J., & Delaney, H.D. (1982). The mnemonic keyword method. *Review of Research in Education, 52,* 61-91.

Pring, R. (1971). Bloom's taxonomy: A philosophical critique. *Cambridge Journal of Education, 1,* 83-91.

Purkey, W.W. (1970). *Self-concept and school achievement.* Englewood Cliffs, NJ: Prentice Hall.

Quality Education Data (1988). *Microcomputer and VCR usage in schools, 1987-1988.* Denver: Quality Education Data.

Raudsepp, E., & Haugh, G.P. (1977). *Creative growth games.* New York: Harcourt Brace Jovanovich.

Ravitch, D. (1985). Scapegoating the teachers. In F. Schultz (Ed.), *Annual editions: Education, 1985/1986* (pp. 212-221). Guilford, CT: Duskin.

Redfield, D.L., & Rousseau, E.W. (1981). A meta-analysis of experimental research on teacher questioning behavior. *Review of Educational Research, 51,* 181-193.

Reed, S.K. (1982). *Cognition: Theory and applications.* Monterey, CA: Brooks/Cole.

Reid, D.K., & Hresko, W.P. (1981). *A cognitive approach to learning disabilities.* New York: McGraw-Hill.

Reimer, R.H., Paolitto, D.P., & Hersh, R.H. (1983). *Promoting moral growth: From Piaget to Kohlberg (2nd ed.).* New York: Longman.

Reis, S.M. (1981). *An analysis of the productivity of gifted students participating in programs using the revolving door identification model.* Storrs, CT: University of Connecticut, Bureau of Educational Research.

Renzulli, J.S., & Smith, L.H. (1978). *The Learning Styles Inventory: A measure of student preferences for instructional techniques.* Mansfield Center, CT: Creative Learning Press.

Resnick, L.B. (1981). Instructional psychology. *Annual Review of Psychology, 32,* 659-704.

Rhode, G., Morgan, D.P., & Young, K.R. (1983). Generalization and maintenance of treatment gains of behaviorally handicapped students from resource rooms to regular classrooms using self-evaluation procedures. *Journal of Applied Behavior Analysis, 16,* 171-188.

Rice, M.I. (1984). Cognitive aspects of communicative development. In R.Schiefelbusch & J. Pickar (Eds.), *The Acquisition of communicative competence.* Baltimore: University Park Press.

Rickards, J., & August, G.J. (1975). Generative underlining strategies in prose recall. *Journal of Educational Psychology, 67,* 860-865.

Rist, R. (1970). Student social class and teacher expectations: The self-fulfilling prophecy in ghetto education. *Harvard Educational Review, 40,* 411-451.

Robinson, C.S., & Hayes, J.R. (1978). Making inferences about relevance in understanding problems. In R. Revlin & R. E. Mayer (Eds.), *Human reasoning.* Washington, DC: Winston.

Robinson, D.W. (1978). Beauty, monster, or something in between? 22 views of public schooling. *The Review of Education, 4,* 263-274.

Robinson, F.P. (1961). *Effective study.* New York: Harper and Row.

Roemer, R.E. (1978). The social conditions for schoolings. In A. B. Calvin (Ed.), *Perspectives on education.* Reading, MA: Addison-Wesley.

Roethlisberger, F.J., & Dickson, W.J. (1939). *Management and the worker.* Cambridge, MA: Harvard University Press.

Rosch, E.H. (1973). On the internal structure of perceptual and semantic categories. In T. Moore (Ed.), *Cognitive development and the acquisition of language.* New York: Academic Press.

Rosch, E.H. (1975). Cognitive representations of semantic categories. *Journal of Experimental Psychology, 104,* 192-233.

Rosenshine, B. (1979). Content, time, and direct instruction. In P. Peterson & H. Walberg (Eds.), *Research on teaching: Concepts, findings, and implications.* Berkeley, CA: McCutchan.

Rosenshine, B. (1986). Synthesis of research on explicit teaching. *Educational Leadership, 43(7),* 60-69.

Rosenshine, B. (1988). Explicit teaching. In D. Berliner & B. Rosenshine (eds.), *Talks to teachers* (pp. 75-92). New York: Random House.

Rosenshine, B., & Furst, N. (1973). The use of direct observation to study teaching. In R. Travers (Ed.), *Second handbook of research on teaching.* Chicago: Rand McNally.

Rosenshine, B., & Stevens, R. (1986). Teaching functions. In M. Wittrock (Ed.), *Handbook of research on teaching* (3rd ed., pp. 376-391). New York: Macmillan.

Rosenthal, R. (1973). The Pygmalion effect lives. *Psychology Today,* pp. 56-63.

Rosenthal, R. (1976). *Experimenter effects in behavioral research (enlarged ed.).* New York: Halsted Press.

Ross, S.M. (1984). Matching the lesson to the student: Alternative adaptive designs for individualized learning systems. *Journal of Computer-Based Instruction, 11,* 42-47.

Ross, S.M. (1986). *BASIC programming for educators.* Englewood Cliffs, NJ: Prentice Hall.

Ross, S.M., McCormick, D., Krisak, N., & Anand, P. (1985). Personalizing context in teaching mathematical concepts: Teacher-managed and computer-managed models. *Educational Communication Technology Journal, 33,* 169-178.

Rothman, R. (1988, April 1). "Computer competence" still rare among students, assessment finds. *Education Week*, p. 20.

Rothrock, D. (1982). The rise and decline of individualized instruction. *Educational Leadership, 39,* 528-531.

Rotter, J. (1954). *Social learning and clinical psychology.* Englewood Cliffs, NJ: Prentice Hall.

Rowe, M.B. (1974). Wait-time and rewards as instructional variables: Their influence on language, logic, and fate control. Part 1: Wait-time. *Journal of Research in Science Teaching, 11,* 81-94.

Rumelhart, D. (1977). Understanding and summarizing brief stories. In D. LaBerge & S. J. Samuels (Eds.), *Basic processes in reading.* Hillsdale, NJ: Erlbaum.

Rumelhart, D., & Ortony, A. (1977). The representation of knowledge in memory. In R. Anderson, R. Spiro, & W. Montague (Eds.), *Schooling and the acquisition of knowledge.* Hillsdale, NJ: Erlbaum.

Rust, L.W. (1977). Interests. In S. Ball (Ed.), *Motivation in education.* New York: Academic Press.

Ryans, D.G. (1960). *Characteristics of effective teachers, their descriptions, comparisons and appraisal: A research study.* Washington, DC: American Council on Education.

Sadker, M., & Sadker, D. (1985, March). Sexism in the schoolroom of the '80s. *Psychology Today,* pp. 54-57.

Sadker, M., & Sadker, D. (1986). Questioning skills. In J. Cooper (Ed.), *Classroom teaching skills* (3rd ed., pp. 143-180). Lexington, MA: D. C. Heath.

Salili, F., Maehr, M.L., Sorensen, R.L., & Fyans, L.J. (1976). A further consideration of the effect of evaluation on motivation. *American Educational Research Journal, 13(2),* 85-102.

Sandefur, J.T. (1985). Competency assessment of teachers. *Action in Teacher Education, 7,* (1-2), 1-6.

Sarnacki, R.E. (1979). An examination of test-wiseness in the cognitive test domain. *Review of Research in Education, 49,* 252-270.

Savage, T.V. (1983). The academic qualifications of women choosing education as a major, *Journal of Teacher Education, 34,* 14-19.

Scarr, S., & Carter-Saltzman, L. (1982). Genetics and intelligence. In R. Sternberg (Ed.), *Handbook of human intelligence.* New York: Cambridge University Press.

Scarr, S., Weinberg, R.A., & Levine, A. (1986). *Understanding development.* New York: Harcourt Brace Jovanovich.

Schiedel, D., & Marcia, J. (1985). Ego integrity, intimacy, sex role orientation, and gender. *Developmental Psychology, 21*, 149-160.

Schoenfeld, A.H. (1979). Explicit heuristic training as a variable in problem solving performance. *Journal for Research in Mathematics Education, 10*, 173-187.

Schon, D. (1983). *The reflective practioner.* New York: Basic Books

School Sales Surge (1985, November/December). *Electronic Learning*, p. 12.

Schug, M. (1985). Teacher burnout and professionalism. In F. Schultz (Ed.), *Annual Editions: Education, 1985/1986* (pp. 212-221). Guilford, CT: Duskin.

Seiber, J.E., O'Neil, H.F., & Tobias, S. (1977). *Anxiety, learning, and instruction.* Hillsdale, NJ: Erlbaum.

Self, J.A. (1974). Student models in computer-aided instruction. *International Journal of Man-Machine Studies, 6*, 261-276.

Seligman, C., Tucker, G., & Lambert, W. (1972). The effects of speech style and other attributes on teachers' attitudes toward pupils. *Language in Society, 1*, 131-142.

Serralde de Scholz, H.C., & McDougall, R. (1978). Comparison of potential reinforcer ratings between slow learners and regular students. *Behavior Therapy, 9*, 60-64.

Shane, H.G. (1982). The silicon age and education. *Phi Delta Kappan, 63*, 303-308.

Shavelson, R.J., & Bolus, R. (1982). Self-concept: The interplay of theory and methods. *Psychology, 74*, 3-17.

Shavelson, R.J., Hubner, J.J., & Stanton, G.C. (1976). Self-concept: Validation of construct interpretations. *Review of Educational Research, 46*, 407-442.

Shavelson, R.S., & Dempsey, N. (1975). *Generalizability of measures of teacher effectiveness and teaching process* (Beginning Teacher Evaluation Study, Tech. Rep. No. 3). San Francisco: Far West Laboratory for Educational Research and Development.

Sherman, J.G., Ruskin, R.S., & Semb, G.B. (Eds.) (1982). *The Personalized System of Instruction: 48 seminal papers.* Lawrence, KS: TRI Publications.

Shields, P., Gordon, J., & Dupree, D. (1983). Influence of parent practices upon the reading achievement of good and poor readers. *Journal of Negro Education, 52*, 436-445.

Shostak, R. (1986). Lesson presentation skills. In J. Cooper (Ed.), *Classroom teaching skills* (3rd ed., pp. 114-138). Lexington, MA: D. C. Heath.

Shuell, T.J. (1981). Dimensions of individual differences. In F. H. Farley & N. J. Gordon (Eds.), *Psychology and education: The state of the union.* Berkeley, CA: McCutchan. (a)

Shuell, T.J. (1986). Cognitive conceptions of learning. *Review of Educational Research, 56,* 411-436.

Shulman, L.S. (1987). Knowledge and teaching: Foundations of the new reform. *Harvard Educational Review, 19(2),* 4-14.

Siegal, M.A., & Davis, D.M. (1986). *Understanding computer-based education.* New York: Random House.

Simon, D.P., & Chase, W.G. (1973). Skill in chess. *American Scientist, 61,* 394-403.

Simon, W. (1969). Expectancy effect in the scoring of vocabulary items: A study of scorer bias. *Journal of Educational Measurement, 6,* 159-164.

Skinner, B.F. (1953). *Science and human behavior.* New York: Macmillan.

Skinner, B.F. (1954). The science of learning and the art of teaching. *Harvard Educational Review, 24,* 86-97.

Skinner, B.F. (1984). The shame of American education. *American Psychologist, 39,* 947-954.

Slavin, R. (1978). Student teams and achievement divisions. *Journal of Research and Development in Education, 12,* 38-48.

Slavin, R. (1980). Effects of individual learning expectations on student achievement. *Journal of Educational Psychology, 72,* 520-524.

Slavin, R. (1980). *Using student team learning (rev. ed.).* Baltimore: The Johns Hopkins University, Center for Social Organization of Schools. (b)

Slavin, R. (1983). *Cooperative learning.* New York: Longman.

Slavin, R. (1986). *Educational psychology: Theory into practice.* Englewood Cliffs, NJ: Prentice Hall.

Slavin, R., & Karweit, N. (1984). *Mathematics achievement effects of three levels of individualization: Whole class, ability grouped, and individualized (Report No. 349).* Baltimore: The Johns Hopkins University, Center for Social Organization in Schools.

Sleeter, C.E., & Grant, C.A. (1987). An analysis of multicultural education in the United States. *Harvard Educational Review, 57,* 421-444.

Smith, F. (1975). *Comprehension and learning: A conceptual framework for teachers.* New York: Holt, Rinehart & Winston.

Smith, S.M., Glenberg, A., & Bjork, R.A. (1978). Environmental context and human memory. *Memory and Cognition, 6,* 342-353.

Snow, R.E. (1969). Unfinished Pygmalion. *Contemporary Psychology, 14,* 197-199.

Snow, R.E. (1977). Research on aptitude for learning: A progress report. In L. Shulman (Ed.), *Review of research in education.* Itasca, IL: F. E. Peacock.

Snowman, J. (1984). Learning tactics and strategies. In G. Phye & T. Andre (Eds.), *Cognitive instructional psychology.* Orlando, FL: Academic Press.

Snyderman, M., & Rothman, S. (1987). Survey of expert opinion of intelligence and aptitude testing. *American Psychologist, 42,* 137-144.

Soar, R.S., & Soar, R.M. (1979). Emotional climate and management. In P. Peterson & H. Walberg (Eds.), *Research on teaching: Concepts, findings, and implications.* Berkeley, CA: McCutchan.

Solomon, G. (1986, March). Electronic research. *Electronic Learning,* pp. 37-40.

Soloway, E., Lockhead, J., & Clement, J. (1982). Does computer programming enhance problem solving ability? Some positive evidence on algebra word problems. In R. J. Seidel, R. E. Anderson, & S. B. Hunter (Eds.), *Computer literacy.* New York: Academic Press.

Spearman, C. (1927). *The abilities of man: Their nature and measurement.* New York: Macmillan.

Stallings, J. (1980). Allocated academic learning time revisited, or beyond time on task. *Educational Researcher, 9,* 11-16.

Starch, D., & Elliot, E.C. (1913). Reliability of grading work in history. *Scholastic Review, 21,* 676-681. (a)

Starch, D., & Elliot, E.C. (1913). Reliability of grading work in mathematics. *Scholastic Review, 21,* 254-259. (b)

Stein, B.S., Littlefield, J., Bransford, J.D., & Persampieri, M. (1984). Elaboration and knowledge acquisition. *Memory and Cognition, 12,* 522-529.

Sternberg, R. (1985). Beyond IQ: *A triarchic theory of human intelligence.* New York: Cambridge University Press.

Sternberg, R. (1986). *Intelligence applied: Understanding and increasing your own intellectual skills.* New York: Harcourt Brace Jovanovich.

Sternberg, R., & Davidson, J. (1982, June). The mind of the puzzler. *Psychology Today,* pp. 37-44.

Stewart, J.R. (1980). Teachers who stimulate curiosity. *Education, 101*, 158-165.

Stipek, D.J. (1988). *Motivation to learn*. Englewood Cliffs, NJ: Prentice Hall.

Straus, M.A., Gelles, R.J., & Steinmetz, S.K. (:1980). Behind closed doors: *Violence in the American family*. New York: Doubleday.

Sulzer-Azaroff, B., & Mayer, G.R. (1986). *Achieving educational excellence using behavioral strategies*. New York: Holt, Rinehart & Winston.

Suppes, P. (1966). The uses of computers in education. *Scientific American, 215(3)*, 207-220.

Suppes, P. (1984). Observations about the application of artificial intelligence research to education. In D. F. Walker & R. D. Hess (Eds.), *Instructional software: Principles and perspectives for design and use* (pp. 298-306). Belmont, CA: Wadsworth.

Suppes, P., Jerman, M., & Brian, D. (1968). *Computer-assisted instruction: The 1965-66 Stanford arithmetic program*. New York: Academic Press.

Suppes, P., & Macken, E. (1978). The historical path from research and development to operational use of CAI. *Educational Technology, 18*, 9-12.

Suppes, P., & Morningstar, M. (1972). *Computer-assisted instruction at Stanford, 1966-1968: Data, models, and evaluation of the arithmetic programs*. New York: Academic Press.

Swift, J., & Gooding, C. (1983). Interaction of wait-time, feedback, and questioning instruction in middle school science teaching. *Journal of Research in Science Teaching, 20*, 721-730.

Taylor, J.B. (1983). Influence of speech variety on teachers' evalutions of reading comprehension. *Journal of Educational Psychology, 75*, 662-667.

Taylor, R.P. (Ed.). (1980). *The computer in the school: Tutor, tool, tutee*. New York: Teachers College Press.

Tenbrink, T.D. (1986). Writing instructional objectives. In J. Cooper (Ed.), *Classroom teaching skills* (3rd ed., pp. 71-110). Lexington, MA: D. C. Heath.

Tennyson, R.D., & Cocchiarella, M.J. (1986). An empirically based instructional design theory for teaching concepts. *Review of Educational Research, 56*, 40-71.

Tennyson, R.D., & Rothen, W. (1977). Pre-task and on-task adaptive design strategies for selecting number of instances in concept acquisition. *Journal of Educational Psychology, 69*, 586-592.

Terman, L.M., & Oden, M.H. (1959). The gifted group in mid-life. In L. M. Terman (Ed.), *Genetic studies of genius (Vol. 5)*. Stanford, CA: Stanford University Press.

Terwilliger, J.S. (1971). *Assigning grades to students*. Glenview, IL: Scott, Foresman.

Thomas, E.L., & Robinson, H.A. (1972). *Improving reading in every class: A sourcebook for teachers*. Boston: Allyn & Bacon.

Thompson, T.J. (1979). An overview of microprocessor central processing units (CPUs). *Educational Technology, 10*, 41-44.

Thorndike, E.L. (1913). Educational psychology. *In The psychology of learning (Vol. 2)*. New York: Teachers College, Columbia University.

Thorndike, R., Hagen, E., & Sattler, J. (1986). *The Stanford-Binet Intelligence Scale (4th ed.)*. Chicago: Riverside.

Thurstone, L.L. (1938). Primary mental abilities. *Psychometric Monographs, No. 1*.

Tiedt, P.L., & Tiedt, I.M. (1979). *Multicultural education: A handbook of activities, information, and resources*. Boston: Allyn & Bacon.

Timmer, S.G., Eccles, J., & O'Brien, K. (1988). How children use time. In F. Juster & F. Stafford (Eds.), *Time, goods, and well-being*. Ann Arbor, MI: Institute for Social Research, University of Michigan.

Tobias, S. (1979). Anxiety research in educational psychology. *Journal of Educational Psychology, 71*, 573-582.

Tobias, S. (1981). Adaptation to individual differences. In F. Farley & N. Gordon (Eds.). *Psychology and education: The state of the union*. Berkeley, CA: McCutchan.

Tobias, S. (1982, January). Sexist equations. *Psychology Today,* pp. 14-17. (a)

Tobias, S. (1982). When do instructional methods make a difference? *Educational Researcher, 11(4)*, 4-10. (b)

Tobias, S., & Duchastel, P. (1974). Behavioral objectives, sequence, and anxiety in CAI. *Instructional Science, 3*, 232-242.

Tobin, K. (:1987). The role of wait time in higher cognitive learning. *Review of Educational Research, 56*, 69-95.

Torrance, E.P. (1972). Predictive validity of the Torrance tests of creative thinking. *Journal of Creative Behavior, 6*, 236-262.

Torrance, E.P. (1986). Teaching creative and gifted learners. In M. Wittrock (Ed.), *Handbook of Researach on Teaching (3rd ed.)*. New York: Macmillan.

Torrance, E.P., & Hall, L.K. (1980). Assessing the future reaches of creative potential. *Journal of Creative Behavior, 14,* 1-19.

Travers, R.m.W. (1977). *Essentials of learning (4th ed.)*. New York: Macmillan.

Travers, R.M.W. (1982). *Essentials of learning: The new cognitive learning for students of education (5th ed.)*. New York: Macmillan.

Tyler, L.E. (1974). *Individual differences: Abilities and motivational directions*. New York: Appleton-Century-Crofts.

Ure, A. (1861). *The philosophy of manufactures: Or an exposition of the scientific, moral, and commercial economy of the factory system of Great Britain (3rd ed.)*. London, H. G. Bohn.

Vaillant, G.E., & Vaillant, C.O. (1981). Natural history of male psychological health, X: Work as a predictor of positive mental health. The *American Journal of Psychiatry, 138,* 1433-1440.

Van Houten, R., & Doleys, D.M. (1983). Are social reprimands effective? In S. Axelrod & J. Apsche (Eds.), *The effects of punishment on human behavior*. San Diego: Academic Press.

Van Mondrans, A.P., Black, H.G., Keysor, R.E., Olsen, J.B., Shelley, M.F., & Williams, D.D. (1977). Methods of inquiry in educational psychology. In D. Treffinger, J. Davis, & R. R. Ripple (Eds.), *Handbook on teaching educational psychology*. New York: Academic Press.

Veenman, S. (1984). Perceived problems of beginning teachers. *Review of Educational Research, 54,* 143-178.

Vernon, P.E. (1979). *Intelligence: Heredity and environment*. San Francisco: W. H. Freeman.

Vidler, D.C. (1977). Curiosity. In S. Ball (Ed.), *Motivation in education*. New York: Academic Press.

Vygotsky, L.S. (1986). *Thought and language*. Cambridge, MA: MIT Press.

Vygotsky, L.S. (1978). *Mind in society: The development of higher mental processes*. Cambridge, MA: Harvard University Press.

Wadsworth, B.J. (1984). *Piaget's theory of cognitive development: An introduction for students of psychology and education (3rd ed.)*. New York: Longman.

Walberg, H.J., Pascal, R.A., & Weinstein, T. ((1985). Homework's powerful effects on learning. *Educational Leadership, 42(7),* 76-79.

Walker, D.F., & Hess, R.D. (:1984). *Instructional software: Principles and perspectives for design and use.* Belmont, CA: Wadsworth.

Ward, B., & Tikunoff, W. (1976). The effective teacher education problem: Application of selected research results and methodology to teaching. *Journal of Teacher Education, 27,* 48-52.

Waxman, H.C., & Walberg, H.J. (:1982). The relation of teaching and learning: A review of reviews of process-product research. *Contemporary Educational Review, 1,* 103-120.

Weaver, W.T. (1979). The need for new talent in teaching. *Phi Delta Kappan, 61,* 29-46.

Webb, N. (1980). A process-outcome analysis of learners in group and individual settings. *Educational Psychology, 15,* 69-83.

Webb, N. (1982). Student interaction and learning in small groups. *Review of Educational Research, 52,* 421-445.

Webb, N. (1985). Verbal interaction and learning in peer-directed groups. *Theory into Practice, 24,* 32-39.

Wechsler, D. (1958). *The measurement and appraisal of adult intelligence (4th ed.).* Baltimore: Williams & Wilkins.

Weiner, B. (1979). A theory of motivation for some classroom experiences. *Journal of Educational Psychology, 71,* 3-25.

Weiner, B. (1980). The role of affect in rational (attributional) approaches to human motivation. *Educational Researcher, 9,* 4-11.

Weiner, B. (1984). Principles for a theory of student motivation and their application within an attributional framework. In R. Ames & C. Ames (Eds.), *Research on motivation in education (Vol. 1).* Orlando, FL: Academic Press.

Weiner, B., Russell, D., & Lerman, D. (1978). Affective consequences of causal ascriptions. In J. H. Harvey, W. J. Ickes, & R. F. Kidd (Eds.). *New directions in attribution research (Vol. 2).* Hillsdale, NJ: Erlbaum.

Weinstein, C.S. (1977). Modifying student behavior in an open classroom through changes in the physical design. *American Educational Research Journal, 14,* 249-262.

Weinstein, C.E., & Mayer, R.E. (1985). The teaching of learning strategies. In M. C. Wittrock (Ed.), *Handbook of research on teaching (3rd ed.).* New York: Macmillan.

Wessells, M.G. (1982). *Cognitive psychology.* New York: Harper and Row.

West, C.K., Fish, J.A., & Stevens, R.J. (1980). General self-concept, self-concept of academic ability and school achievement: Implication for causes of self-concept. *Australian Journal of Education, 24.*

White, E.M. (1984). Holisticism. *College Composition and Communication, 35,* 400-409.

White, K.R. (1982). The relation between socioeconomic status and academic achievement. *Psychological Bulltein, 91(3),* 461-481.

White, R.W. (1959). Motivation reconsidered: The concept of competence. *Psychological Review, 66,* 297-333.

Why Teachers Fail. (1984, September 24). *Newsweek,* pp. 64-70.

Wilkins, W.E., & Glock, IM.D. (1973). *Teacher expectations and student achievement: A replication and extension.* Ithaca, NY: Cornell University Press.

Willerman, L. (1979). *The psychology of individual and group differences.* San Francisco: W. H. Freeman.

Wilson, S.M., Shulman, L.S., & Richert, A.R. (1987). 150 different ways of knowing: Representations of knowledge in teaching. In J. Calderhead (Ed.), *Exploring teacher thinking* (pp. 104-124). London: Cassell.

Winett, R.A., & Winkler, R.C. (1972). Current behavior modification in the classroom: Be still, be quiet, be docile. *Journal of Applied Behavior Analysis, 15,* 499-504.

Winograd, P., & Johnston, P. (1982). Comprehension monitoring and the error-detection paradigm. *Journal of Reading Behavior, 14,* 61-76.

Witkin, H.A., Moore, C.A., Goodenough, D.R., & Cos, R.W. (1977). Field-dependent and field-independent cognitive styles and their educational implications. *Review of Educational Research, 47,* 1-64.

Wittrock, M.C. (1978). The cognitive movement in instruction. *Educational Psychologist, 13,* 15-30.

Wlodkowski, R.J. (1981). Making sense out of motivation: A systematic model to consolidate motivational constructs across theories. *Educational Psychologist, 16,* 101-110.

Woolfolk, A.E., & Brooks, D. (1983). Nonverbal communication in teaching. In E. Gordon (Ed.), *Review of research in education (Vol. 10).* Washington, DC: American Educational Research Association.

Woolfolk, A.E., & Woolfolk, R.L. (1974). A contingency management technique for increasing student attention in a small group. *Journal of School Psychology, 12,* 204-212.

Yerkes, R.M., & Dodson, J.D. (1908). The relation of strength of stimulus to rapidity of habit formation. *Journal of Comparative Neurology, 18,* 459-482.

Young, T. (1980). Teacher stress: One school district's approach. *Action in Teacher Education, 2,* 37-40.

Zimmerman, D.W. (1981). On the perennial argument about grading "on the curve" in college courses. *Educational Psychologist, 16,* 175-178.